THE EARLY
ROUSSEAU

CORNELL UNIVERSITY PRESS

First published 1967

Library of Congress Catalog Card Number: 67-15958

PRINTED IN THE UNITED STATES OF AMERICA
BY KINGSPORT PRESS, INC.

JEAN-JACQUES ROUSSEAU

Portrait by Allan Ramsay, painted in England in March 1766 while Rousseau was a guest of David Hume. (Reproduced by permission of the National Gallery of Scotland.)

THE EARLY ROUSSEAU

Mario Einaudi

CORNELL UNIVERSITY PRESS

Ithaca, New York

Preface

TODAY Rousseau is increasingly seen as the most influential thinker of the eighteenth century. His views, on men and society, on private and public life, on economics and government, seem astonishingly relevant to twentieth-century problems. He is, therefore, being read now with a care and a thoroughness he did not always get in his own time and for many years afterward. Perhaps only in the last two generations has Rousseau's thought, in all its extraordinary complexity, begun to be fully understood.

As all of his writings are taken into account, one realizes how much has been missed before, and how simple and inadequate have been some of the earlier criticisms. One begins also to be more aware of the importance and variety of what Rousseau wrote before 1756, and a renewed inquiry into the politics and economics of the early Rousseau seems necessary to a better comprehension of the later work.

The early Rousseau is, of course, well known as the author of the two *Discourses,* one on arts and sciences, the other on inequality. He is known also for his *Political Economy* and, by the specialists, for the essay *State of War* and the *Letter to Voltaire* on the Lisbon earthquake. But too few readers have paid serious attention to the Dedication and the long footnotes of the *Dis-*

[v]

course on Inequality. And even fewer have seen the earlier fragments on history and education; the poems and long letters to
his friends Bordes, Parisot, and Conzié; all the replies to his
critics, in particular the *Observations* and the *Last Reply;* the
Preface to *Narcisse* and the letter to Philopolis; all the writings
on Saint Pierre, the *Discourse on Wealth,* and the many early
autobiographical and other fragments.

A reading of what Rousseau wrote in the twenty years from
1737 to 1756 brings forth the importance and singular coherence
of this period of his life, and illuminates much of what was to
come afterward.[1] These years have a special attractiveness for the
modern reader, who not only sees Rousseau with fresh eyes but
also discovers new evidence which, placed in its proper context,
adds a great deal to the picture of Rousseau's mind. For it is
within this span of time that many of the misunderstandings,
many of the difficulties of interpretation, find their origin. It is
during this period that Rousseau begins to express himself in
what his contemporaries believed to be the paradoxes of a madman, and what many of his later critics felt were views which
could not be reconciled with the thought of his major works.

The modern reader who in a systematic way tries to look at
everything Rousseau said in those twenty years discovers a wealth
of themes not smaller than that of the later years. The analysis
of man, of the different stages of social development, and of the
successive transformations of man as he goes through them; the
tensions of civil life and the anxious look at the future; the dis-
section of government and economic issues and classes; the
building of the ideal state—all are there. In the end the reader
gathers an unexpectedly rich harvest.

[1] See the Index for an inventory of the writings of Rousseau used in
this book.

For Rousseau had written on history and about his own readings, and dealt with the problems of educating a young man. He had developed his views on nature, man, and civilization in half a dozen vigorous and detailed statements. He had written on war and peace and the conditions for a united Europe, on providence and on civil religion. He had dealt with property as the root of inequality and outlined the premises and institutions of the ideal republic. He had faced the issues of justice, of the rich and the poor, and of the economic tasks of the state. When all this is added up the sum total is very impressive. Rousseau remains a difficult writer. But the difficulties are not those of incoherence.

The year 1756 appears as a logical cutoff point. In that year (just before Rousseau's break with some of his closest friends) the curtain falls on the first act of Rousseau's life. He has published enough to show where the core of the present unhappiness of man is to be found. He has tried to return to Geneva in a final demonstration of the seriousness of his views on man and the state, and has failed. He has now retired to the quiet of Montmorency, where the writing—in feverish haste in the space of a few years—of the *Nouvelle Héloïse,* the *Social Contract,* and *Emile* will begin.

This book attempts first to give an explanation of the Rousseau revival and its meaning; then follows a series of brief sketches placing Rousseau in his contemporary setting. Chapters III–VIII analyze, in rough chronological order, the unfolding of Rousseau's thought and the growth of its major themes.

Throughout, let it be said at once, there is no undue restraint in quoting Rousseau at length, from both his famous and his less famous pieces. Apart from the fact that many of the lines taken from his less famous pieces prove to be as quotable as the familiar ones, it was felt that the beauty and the tenderness, the strength, the anger and the irony, of what Rousseau wrote are too great to hide.

The concluding chapter deals with the subsequent history of some of the main strands of ideas caught up in the course of the discussion: it is more a series of reminders than a systematic review.

MARIO EINAUDI

Paris, 1966

Contents

THE EARLY
ROUSSEAU

I

Rousseau Today

The New Understanding of Rousseau

ONLY a few of the thinkers who make up our cultural heritage are subjected in successive centuries to the kind of reappraisal which, in its intensity, expresses an urgent need to seek fresh guidance in their thought. And even more rarely does the reappraisal, when it comes, sharply alter the outlines of the accepted tradition.

Among those affected by our constant rewriting of the past, Rousseau stands out for the depth of the scrutiny to which he has been subjected, and for the significance of the changes in the way we look at him. That this should have happened to Rousseau more than to any other writer of the last three hundred years is proof enough of the central position he occupies today and also of his greatness. Not only do we know more about him but we read him in a manner that seems for the first time to do justice to what he was trying to say. As a result, we feel that Rousseau is very close to our thinking and to the problems of our age. The publication at this point of the first worthy edition of his works [1]

[1] Jean-Jacques Rousseau, *Oeuvres complètes*, gen. eds. Bernard Gagnebin and Marcel Raymond (Paris, la Pléiade): Vol. I, *Les Confessions,*

is symbolic of this re-evaluation of Rousseau's thought, which for the first time is seen as wholly relevant to the political and moral issues confronting modern man.

Nearly two hundred years after his death, Rousseau has come of age, as the times and the problems of organized societies have changed and have in effect developed in ways that Rousseau often anticipated. In the last fifty years in particular we have experienced, or have come very close to experiencing—in 1914, in 1929, in 1939, in 1945—many of the ultimate consequences of the phenomena of disintegration, loneliness, chaos, and selfishness, which are at the center of Rousseau's preoccupations. It is in a way reassuring, therefore, to witness the extraordinary and fruitful efforts of recent years to grapple with what for so long had appeared to be the unfathomable mysteries and contradictions of Jean-Jacques. Sometimes it was said that the unity of his thought was being sought out. Indeed, this was a most valuable undertaking, as unity there is, and to have shown it meant the rescue of Rousseau from simpleminded critics who had written him off by adding up literal proofs that on one day he said white and on another black.

But more important than the unity, the modern critics and readers have found the torment and the tensions of Rousseau: for they have seen in them the root of his meaning, a meaning which goes well beyond any attempt at system and completeness. It required the sensitive nature of a poet such as Amiel, already nearly a century ago, to discover the miracle of a man alone

---

Autres Textes autobiographiques (1959), eds. B. Gagnebin, R. Osmont, and M. Raymond; Vol. II, *La Nouvelle Héloïse, Théâtre-poésies, Essais littéraires* (1961), ed. B. Guyon, J. Scherer, and C. Guyot; Vol. III, *Du Contrat social, Ecrits politiques* (1964), ed. R. Derathé, F. Bouchardy, J. Starobinski, S. Stelling-Michaud, J.-D. Candaux, and J. Fabre. Two more volumes are to come. This edition is notable for its textual care, its completeness, the interest of its introductions, and the extraordinary wealth of its annotations. Whenever possible, it will be the one referred to (cited throughout as O.C.).

against the wealthy and the powerful and the vain world of letters and philosophy, and to suggest that the key thought of Rousseau could be brought back to what he had said in the *Emile:* "All is well as it comes from the hands of the Author of things, everything degenerates in the hands of man." [2]

Throughout the eighteenth and nineteenth centuries the venomous portrait of Madame d'Epinay, the sad witticisms of Voltaire, the ill-informed judgment of Burke, mattered more than Kant's reading of Rousseau. Often this was due to an implicit rejection of Rousseau or to an incapacity to read him; sometimes it was due to the difficulties of placing Rousseau in the attractive simplicities of eighteenth-century rationalism, and to a stubborn wish to resolve all doubts and to see the development of a clear system where everything would find its place.

Hence the vagaries, the misinterpretations, the unresolvable conflicts between extreme individualism and collectivism. Rousseau appears one time as the ideologue of the French Revolution; another time as the father of modern totalitarianism. Rousseau, the sick man obsessed by the fears of conspiracies that never existed. Rousseau the primitivist, the enemy of society, and the propounder of a return to nature. Rousseau the incurable dreamer and utopian.

We appear today to have entered a new phase, one in which respect for the writer, seen at last in the complexity of all his work, and the growing awareness of what Rousseau stood for and of its value for us, are the chief aspects. As a result, a new Rousseau is slowly emerging from the fogs of yesterday.[3]

[2] H.-F. Amiel, "Caractéristique générale de Rousseau," in *Jean-Jacques Rousseau jugé par les genevois d'aujourd'hui* (Genève, published on the occasion of the 100th anniversary of Rousseau's death, July 2, 1878), 23–64.

[3] Many of the new trends are to be found in Peter Gay, *The Party of Humanity* (New York, 1964), ch. 8, "Reading about Rousseau," 211–38. Gay pays a deserved tribute to the work of Lanson, Vaughan, Wright, Cassirer, Derathé, and Starobinski.

Rousseau is no longer the confirmed liar he was thought to be. Serious efforts to check the narrative of his life have generally led to cumulative proof of its reliability. Key episodes which until very recently were believed to be prime evidence of Rousseau's inability to tell the truth, seem to have occurred exactly as Rousseau said they did: the stories of his conversion, his life in Savoy, his role in Venice, his life in Paris, are today seen as accurate renderings of the facts.[4] What now strikes the scholars interested in this aspect of Rousseau's personality is his recall of the past and his painstaking care in putting the facts down on paper.

Far more important is that Rousseau has become more comprehensible today than at any other time. His ideas are no longer seen as paradoxes, flights of the fancy, or perverse attempts to say the contrary of what was the common opinion of his times. Rather, they appear for what they were intended to be, with a relevance and a complexity of structure which make them all the more meaningful to us.

The state of nature, for example, is seen for what it certainly was in Rousseau's mind: a model, a standard of measurement, a point of reference as we try to decide what has to be done. The natural man of Rousseau's state of nature is not necessarily related to any particular man who has existed or with whom we are acquainted. He is a starting point from which we may proceed to solve our problems. Rousseau openly tells us that the state of nature he is talking about may never have existed, but that its perception is no less vital to us if we want to make comparisons and if we want to be in a position to evaluate our own state of affairs. Modern anthropologists have been taken by

---

[4] Cf. Bernard Gagnebin, "Vérité et véracité dans les *Confessions*," in a volume published under the auspices or the Comité National pour la Commémoration de J.-J. Rousseau, *Jean-Jacques Rousseau et son oeuvre* (Paris, 1964), 7–20. Gagnebin adds that, by saying that he possessed the truth, "Rousseau was led to justify all his acts, even when they could be criticized."

this approach, and in this image of a natural man not to be confused with presocial man they find a wonderfully fruitful tool for the comparative study of societies.[5]

If we begin to see the state of nature and the state of man under this ideal light, then a number of related issues become clear and acquire their proper place in the general context of Rousseau's thought. Savage man is obviously not natural man. As a matter of fact, the savage is far advanced on the ladder of human evolution. He is a fairly recent type and Rousseau may like him simply because he is less corrupt than contemporary man, but he is certainly no model and he may be separated by an immeasurable passage of time and by great qualitative differences from natural man. We have to study him, of course, because everything that can help to illuminate our plight is vital; but there can be for modern man no return to the condition of the good savage. Such a return might not even be possible if we set our minds to it, but Rousseau wants something far more difficult— namely, a shift toward the ideals of natural man. He is but a shadow, and is hard to describe, while savages still abound. Savages are useful, because by their behavior they can tell us what is wrong with ourselves and can give us clues as to the essence of natural man. But just as savages do not come to live in Europe, so Europeans should not become savages or go and live with them. There is no possibility for civilized man of going back to primitive life; the only issue is whether it is possible for him to improve himself, and this can be done only by moving forward, carrying with him the vision of natural man.[6]

[5] Claude Lévi-Strauss finds in Rousseau's *Discourse on Inequality* a chief source of inspiration. See *Tristes Tropiques* (Paris, 1955), 284, 353.

[6] Arthur Lovejoy's crucial role in dispelling the myth cultivated with such care by many eighteenth-century *philosophes* should be recalled here. See "The Supposed Primitivism of Rousseau's *Discourse on Inequality*" (1923), in *Essays in the History of Ideas* (Baltimore, 1948), 14–37.

Similarly, the idea of the general will can be grasped as an attempt to separate the selfish from the unselfish, as a definition of civic duty found in the capacity to distinguish "among our interests those coming from a fallacious self-love founded on ambition and property, and those coming from nature in its present condition, and to accept the appropriation of common interests and their superior value as attested by conscience, in spite of the apparent and strong prestige of our particular interests." [7]

Again, just as it was not necessary that the state of nature be identified with any given time and place, it is not necessary that the general will be an immediately realizable goal. We can begin to see both concepts as ideal poles in the life of man, the first having to do with his past, the second with his future. For Rousseau, then, the questions are: How far have we traveled away from the state of nature? and What are the difficulties we must overcome to get close to the general will? As Jean Fabre points out, the two concepts are norms on which thought must regulate itself, instruments of measurement to determine the concordance or the discordance between the real and the possible, between fact and right. [8]

As we look today, and read properly for the first time, at those autobiographical writings to which Rousseau dedicated the last fifteen or twenty years of his life in an immense effort to justify and clarify what he had said and done (and not out of personal exhibitionism as so many have so firmly believed), as we go through the endless pages of the *Confessions*, of the *Dialogues*, and finally of the *Dreams of a Solitary Walker*, it

[7] Pierre Burgelin, *La Philosophie de l'existence de J.-J. Rousseau* (Paris, 1952), 543.

[8] "Réalité et Utopie dans la pensée politique de J.-J. Rousseau," *Annales de la Société J.-J. Rousseau*, XXXV (Geneva, 1959–1962), 192–4. (Hereafter referred to as *Annales*.)

becomes clear that the earlier political concerns of his life are not forgotten. If it is true that Rousseau's motto, *vitam impendere vero*, becomes *vitam impendere sibi*,[9] it is quite impossible today to deny the social and political content of even the most personal pages in which Rousseau tells us he has cut himself off from the world. Over and over again in his last work, the *Dreams of a Solitary Walker*, Rousseau sings the praise of the active life, assuring us that he is not anxious to have others join him in his solitude and that he is still thinking about the problem of freedom.[10]

Rousseau's madness becomes a responsible madness in which the world is not forgotten. Out of the strains and absurdities of his life emerges a pattern of action and belief which modern man finds understandable and valuable in sorting out the issues he faces.

Thus, Rousseau's position in the history of ideas is now becoming much more clearly etched. While many of the figures of prerevolutionary times, from Hobbes to Montesquieu, retain either the key position in past developments or the frozen dignity that will forever belong to them, Rousseau has come to life and addresses himself to us as someone who, in the midst of a society of letters which was singularly blind, had the most astonishing insights and anticipations of the future.

Rousseau's work, and especially the *Discourse on Inequality*, is now seen as a major study of the evolution of mankind. Bertrand de Jouvenel gives Rousseau the place he deserves:

Rousseau is the first great exponent of social evolution. His was the first attempt to depict systematically the historic progress of human

[9] Jean Starobinski, *Jean-Jacques Rousseau, la transparence et l'obstacle* (Paris, 1958), 249.

[10] See the essay by Jacques Proust, "Le Premier des pauvres, essai sur *Les Rêveries du promeneur solitaire*," *Europe* (November–December 1961), 13–21.

society. Here he comes a full century before Engels and all the others who were to make the evolution of human society a popular theme. His concern to mark out stages of social development and to bring out the factors which he deemed effective in the process, is impressive against the background of contemporary writings. Everybody was then talking about progress, but in a very loose manner, and Rousseau was the only one who thought of it as a process to be understood.[11]

For these reasons, Claude Lévi-Strauss has recognized Rousseau as an anthropologist among philosophers: "Rousseau our master, Rousseau our brother, toward whom we have shown so much ingratitude, but to whom each page of this book ought to be dedicated." For Lévi-Strauss, Rousseau, unlike Voltaire, has shown for the many societies he was examining a curiosity filled with sympathy for peasant customs and popular thoughts. Unlike Diderot, he never glorified the state of nature, but was the only one to use it as a tool "to show us how to get out of the contradictions where we are still lost in the wake of his enemies." In describing what we today call the neolithic age, he had come close to identifying the "unshakable bases of human society." [12]

Rousseau, the student of evolution, the anthropologist, can also give a new accent to the age-old polemics about wealth and poverty, the rich and the poor, property, luxury and conspicuous consumption.[13] He appears as a pathbreaker for later socialist thought, with this difference however, that his conclusion is not that everything hangs from economics, but that everything hangs from politics.

[11] Bertrand de Jouvenel, "Rousseau the Pessimistic Evolutionist," *Yale French Studies* (1961–1962), 83.

[12] *Tristes Tropiques,* 351–2.

[13] For two recent examples of the importance given to the economic aspects of Rousseau's thought, see Iring Fetscher, *Rousseaus Politische Philosophie* (Neuwied, 1960), esp. 213–59, and Otto Vossler, *Rousseaus Freiheitslehre* (Göttingen, 1963), 100–38, 366–89.

The reader of today, then, finds himself attracted by the originality, the rigor, the relevance, of Rousseau's thought. Even the younger scholars, who have often been tempted to consider the history of past ideas as a dreary form of intellectual activity, are driven to write such passages as this: "Not all the realism in the world can make it easier to forgive the world its inability to accommodate Rousseau's principles. For his principles are those which most forcibly demonstrate the connection between politics and moral life, which more clearly associate autonomous manhood and political activity. When we have understood Rousseau's principles, it is not too much to say, we have understood the distinction between a fully acceptable political order and one that is not." [14]

Two Fresh Lines of Interpretation

One may suggest two reasons for the new understanding of Rousseau. To use two concepts currently in vogue, one reason places itself at the existential level, the other at the level of dialectics. The first has to do with the discovery of the autobiographical writings of Rousseau. The second has to do with the perception of the meaning of the many hidden or open tensions inherent in Rousseau's work.

There is no question that what Rousseau has written about himself or about man—any man who could identify himself with Rousseau's tragic life, his self-analysis, and his perpetual quest for himself—has accounted for Rousseau's almost universal appeal. Today everywhere men see themselves reflected in the *Nouvelle Héloïse* and in the *Confessions*. There is the story of the fisherman meeting the Swiss scholar on the banks of the Senegal: " 'You come from Paris?' 'No, from Geneva.' Then, slowly, the fisherman pulls from his pocket an old

[14] George Kateb, *Utopia and its Enemies* (New York, 1963), 94.

copy of the *Nouvelle Héloïse:* 'Thus, you can go to Meillerie whenever you want.' " [15] And Lionel Gossman finds it "natural that in our own troubled and uncertain times, readers should be primarily interested in the subjective aspects of Rousseau and that they should turn most happily to those parts of his work in which they find an echo of their own concerns." [16] "Indeed it is in the intimate writings that we best find our man in Rousseau today." [17]

There is also no doubt that what we call Rousseau's dialectical tensions, by which we mean at times his pessimism, his skill in describing progress in terms of the difficulties it creates, the view of men's freedom to be gained only at a heavy price of suffering and of discipline, have become today familiar and accepted notions, so much do our ideas of progress differ from the linear simplicities of the Enlightenment, and so much have we learned to discount an ideal of freedom to be secured by restraints imposed upon a distant enemy called the state. Today we find Rousseau's tensions and "contradictions" most fruitful and illuminating.

Starobinski suggests that Rousseau's withdrawal upon himself has helped rather than weakened his historical influence.[18] This

[15] The story is told by Marcel Raymond in an opening address to *Rousseau et son oeuvre,* xxiii.

[16] Lionel Gossman, "Time and History in Rousseau," in *Studies on Voltaire and the Eighteenth Century,* ed. Theodore Besterman, Vol. XXX (Geneva, 1964), 311. Gossman's essay is, however, concerned, and quite rightly, with showing the historicity of Rousseau.

[17] A comment, quoted in part by Gossman, of Raymond Giraud, "Rousseau's Happiness—Triumph or Tragedy," *Yale French Studies,* (1961–1962), 75.

[18] "We have seen that his essential preoccupation shifted from history and social philosophy, to focus almost entirely upon the exigencies of his personal sensibility. But we must admit that this retreat toward singularity, far from weakening Rousseau's historical influence, has on the contrary reinforced it. If Rousseau has changed history (and not only literature), this is not the result only of his political theories and of his

has been so for many different reasons. It is in the nonpolitical writings, which go from the *Emile* to the *Dialogues,* that Rousseau reveals to his reader for the first time the whole life of man. It is here that we find what has been called Rousseau's "great discovery" of the child and of childhood, a period in the life of man with its own laws of development and its own wonders, reaching a state of maturity and perfection. This is indeed a time in the life of each man when the mythical golden age is lived and renewed, one in which "nature succeeds in achieving a balance of faculties and desires. This is a condition which is not troubled by memory, anticipation, imagination; it is the pure age of conservation of oneself and of one's well being." [19]

To this liberating concept Rousseau adds a description of man's internal life which surprises those who have been looking only at the hard outer appearance of man, who, moving about in his social relationships but bounded on all sides by the multiplicity of mediating factors modern civilization has created, can no longer maintain a link with the real world of his own being.[20]

---

views on history: it is the result, perhaps even more, of the myth developed around his exceptional existence" (*op. cit.,* 55). Starobinski emphasizes rather too much the view that this retreat has been accomplished at the expense of a concern for social philosophy.

[19] Burgelin, *op. cit.,* 485–6. Also see Burgelin's whole chapter on *Emile,* and cf. Gossman, *op. cit.,* 315: "The marvelous description of childhood and adolescence is, of course, one of the glories of the *Confessions.* . . . Rousseau's discovery of the child, the concreteness with which he portrayed him, the intense and unique life he revealed in him, these things were possible only in the context of his historical outlook."

[20] Gossman, *op. cit.,* 314. Gossman also recalls a passage in a draft of the introduction to the *Confessions* (O.C. I, 1149–50) in which Rousseau rejects the "false sincerity" of Montaigne: "The most sincere are truthful at most in what they say, but they lie because of their reticences, and what they are silent about changes so much what they appear to confess, that by telling only part of the truth they don't say anything. I place Montaigne at the head of these false truthtellers who want to deceive as they relate the truth. He shows himself with some faults, but

How splendidly, on the other hand, has Rousseau described the whole of man's inner life, the beauty of dreams, the happiness which comes from a direct contact with nature capable of eliminating all the mediating barriers stifling the life of man. In the happiness of contemplation and in the search for solitude, man seeks relief from the anguish of his daily life.[21]

The fundamental purpose of this introspection is to end mediation. To achieve that "transparence" which will reveal the true essence of man against the obstacles and the opacity of social relations in a world which has established itself upon injustice, Rousseau creates the transparence of the self which will free man.[22]

By eliminating mediation and establishing the immediacy of personal transparence, Rousseau believes he is setting up the necessary conditions for the existence of nonalienated man. Man

---

he gives himself only agreeable ones; no man has a hateful one. Montaigne's self-portrait resembles him, but it is a profile. Who knows whether a scar on his cheek or an empty eye on the side hidden from us might not have entirely changed his physiognomy."

[21] Marcel Raymond, "La Rêverie selon Rousseau et son conditionnement historique," in *Rousseau et son oeuvre*, 77–94; Giraud, *op. cit.*, 80–2.

[22] Jean Starobinski's work, *Jean-Jacques Rousseau, la transparence et l'obstacle*, already quoted, is a fundamental piece in the new dossier of Rousseau studies. As the author tells us in the Foreword, its purpose is more than an "internal analysis": "For it is obvious that one cannot interpret Rousseau's work without taking into account the world to which it is opposed. It is through the conflict with an unacceptable society that the inner experience acquires its privileged function. . . . Rousseau longs for the communication and the *transparence* of hearts; but he is frustrated in his expectation, and, choosing the contrary path, he accepts and provokes the *obstacle*, which allows him to withdraw into passive resignation and the certitude of his innocence." In his annotations of the *Discourse on Inequality*, Starobinski points to a number of examples of the role of transparence and obstacle in Rousseau's political writings, as in the formation of society, and in civic festivals (O.C. III, 1340, 1344–5).

is alienated—that is, cut off from real life and from communion with his fellows—by social reality and by the consequences of public opinion, of money, and of all the institutions that have been born since the decisive turning point in the history of man around which the *Discourse on Inequality* is built.[23] In Rousseau's "study of the human heart" we find "the chief reason for his enduring relevance."[24]

Down to Rousseau's last desperate pages, in which he describes himself as abandoned by all and alone on the face of the earth, the identification with the political fate of man is never lost. The *Discourse on Inequality* and the *Dialogues* develop along parallel lines. "The historical drama and the biographical drama have the same design."[25] In Rousseau's autobiographical writing, we see retraced the unfolding of our civilization.

It is therefore possible to say that all of Rousseau's work centers on the tensions between man and society and between the different stages of man's growth, on the dialectics of the historical process, on the contrast between being and appearing. We have, on the one hand, solitary man, who may find in himself perfection and happiness; on the other hand, social man, an integral part of a community in which he may find morality and freedom. The two stand apart and sometimes Rousseau tells us we must choose between the freedom of man and the freedom of the citizen. But are the two goals unreconcilable?[26]

[23] Cf. Bronislaw Baczko, "Rousseau et l'aliénation sociale," *Annales*, XXXV (1959–1962), 223–37.

[24] Judith N. Shklar, "Rousseau's Images of Authority," *American Political Science Review*, LVIII (1964), 932.

[25] Bertrand de Jouvenel, "Essai sur la politique de Rousseau," in de Jouvenel's edition of the *Contrat Social* (Geneva, 1947), 58.

[26] Robert Derathé seems to think they are: "No middle ground, no compromise between the two lives proposed by Rousseau as ideal or exemplary" ("L'Homme selon Rousseau," in *Etudes sur le Contrat Social* [Dijon, 1964], 215). But since Derathé feels that they are but two different moments of a common opposition to "the corrupt society of his

Certain it is that the contrast between nature and society is at the basis of Rousseau's work. They are two opposites of a dialectical development which has created all the problems man has to face.[27] Nothing is solved in the transition from nature to society. Man is changed by it and carries new difficulties with him. The entire historical process is a witness to its ambiguity and tension. Perhaps necessity, perhaps accident, have pushed man forward, but man himself is "the author of the evil which makes him bad and the slave of political institutions, prejudices, and factitious needs. He has created an opaque and divided world, which at the same time belongs and is foreign to him."[28]

It is true that only in this way does man succeed in acquiring the moral qualities which, as a member of a society, he possesses for the first time. But he is also, as a result of the events which are taking place in the course of history, multiplying the contradictions which beset him. Up to a certain point chance dominates, but later developments follow of necessity from the premises and the institutions accepted by man. The contrast between being and appearing gets worse. In the Preface to *Narcisse* Rousseau tells us that it has by now become impossible to let us ever see ourselves as we really are. And in the *Discourse on Inequality* he traces back to this fact the treachery and the vices which beset us.

Hence, Rousseau cannot avoid giving the impression of unhappiness in the century in which the achievement of happiness was considered not only possible but a right, of pessimism in the century in which confidence in progress was the rule. Living within the historical drama he had conceived, he saw progress leading to the disintegration of the community and alienation of man inevitable in the absence of any significant social ties man

times, and they both aim, though in divergent ways, at the realization of the same ideal of liberty and equality" (217), there would seem to be a relationship between them.

[27] Burgelin, *op. cit.*, 236 ff.   [28] Baczko, *op. cit.*, 232.

could understand. Rousseau's pessimism and sense of frustration come from his awareness that man is furiously seeking his own destruction through what he calls progress. The model Rousseau had built of an ideal state of nature and of an ideal social contract made it unavoidable that he would view with dismay the "golden century" in which he lived.

He had built two models for the two ideals of man: *Emile* on the one hand, and the citizen who had accepted the *Social Contract* on the other. His thought kept moving from one to the other in a perpetual *navette*. And yet there was no escape from time and history, and life must be lived within the boundaries of a concrete, earthbound experience. But the models were there, and Rousseau carried on to the end the dialogue between the happy and self-sufficient man who can view from afar a bloody world rent by civil war, and the disciplined citizen who finds in the acceptance of the contract both freedom and equality in an integrated community.[29]

In the end, certain choices are made which appear to eliminate in part the deep gloom that characterizes Rousseau. Very few can aspire to a self-sufficient solitary life. The duty of most of us is to stay where we are and fight it out. The point is not to consider progress the inevitable reward that man will reap with time; it should be to identify the problems which have to be solved if progress is to be achieved. There is nothing inherent in the mere condition of social life to bring about happiness. It must be a special kind of social life. What has been done pales

[29] Gossman, *op. cit.,* 343–4. Gossman writes: "Modern sensibility, which Rousseau did so much to cultivate and to explore, develops in growing opposition to society. . . . Thus it brings with it not joy and fulfillment, but misery and alienation, for it cuts the individual off from others without rebuilding the bridges that lead to them. . . . Awakened sensibility demands a new society constructed on its own principles of love and sympathy, but this society remains an ideal to which the reality of French society in the eighteenth century stands in absolute and apparently unresolvable opposition" (329–30).

into insignificance in comparison with what still has to be done.

As the reader is constantly buffeted among the dichotomies, the contrasts, the alternatives, the barriers, the different ideal standards, he may be baffled and he may incline to speak of the insuperable "contradictions" in Rousseau's thought. But today he rather tends to speak of them as truth-giving tensions which reveal deeper truths about human nature than he had suspected. These "contradictions" are the traps into which fall the excessively cartesian commentators. As Marcel Raymond says: "His truth, his unity, is not to be looked for always at the level of clear and distinct ideas, but at an underlying, deeper level. His thought, envisaged in its entirety, is less that of a discourse than that of dialectics. And his truth is not reducible to portable formulae." [30]

Or, as pointed out by Muntéano, it is idle to talk of Rousseau's "contradictions," because he himself is aware of them and studies them. In the *Dialogues* Rousseau is not showing himself off. He is in search of himself, quite a different thing. From beginning to end he knows he is moving from one extreme to the other with what he calls incredible speed, and he despises the geometers of the straight line,[31] the simplifiers who fail to understand human nature for what it is and to realize what it could do if the circumstances were right. For all his "contradictions" and obscurities, Rousseau is desperately trying to move ahead in an impossibly difficult and corrupt world.

What We See in Rousseau Today

Because Rousseau has made us ready to deal with both public and private man and with both liberty and discipline, his words

---

[30] *Rousseau et son oeuvre*, xxv.

[31] Basil Muntéano, "Les 'Contradictions' de J.-J. Rousseau," *ibid.*, 95–112.

throw a sharp shaft of light on our problems, many of which are the consequence of an industrial revolution Rousseau did not witness.

Given his "anthropocentric" view of the world,[32] Rousseau could only deplore the misuse of man viewed as a tool of production and in effect as no better than a machine. We have become keenly aware today of what Rousseau had to say about it. Better to misuse the land than to misuse man,[33] better a loss of efficiency and of output than a loss in the dignity and the hopes of man. What a dreadful future for any society reduced to the exploitation of man for the sake of so-called economic progress.

The unique and, if lost, irrecuperable qualities of man must be defended within a manageable community in which the emphasis is shifted from the *I* of the egoist and the reckless exploiter of man, to the *we* of responsible collective action.[34] Within such a community, the idea of freedom is bound to change and to lose the attractive simplicity of a mere right to be left alone. This right is not challenged and Rousseau defends stoutly the right of a man to walk in a forest to seek solitude, or the right of a man to be left alone with his conscience and his beliefs. But the other side of the coin of solitary man is integrated man, and man is integrated man most of the time, because what Rousseau is analyzing is organized society, where man is at every point brought into multiple relationships with his fellow men and with institutions, and the decisive component of free-

[32] "Man and his life . . . are in the forefront. . . . His thought is more psychological than metaphysical. It is anthropocentric. His conception of the world comes after that of man. . . . It is personal experience which leads to cosmic aspirations" (B. Groethuysen, *J.-J. Rousseau* [Paris, 1949], p. 238).

[33] Cf. Vossler, *op. cit.*, especially 385–6.

[34] De Jouvenel, "Rousseau the Pessimistic Evolutionist," 95, in giving this formula, suggests that the shift is feasible only in a "small and immutable" community. But even in the small community Rousseau foresaw the possibility of deep change.

dom becomes that of *not* being forced to do what one does not want to do.[35] Man is free when he can manage to salvage something from the maze and weight of fixed commitments, to be himself and to do what he must do in a way that will not do violence to his personality. As this notion of freedom seems to fit rather well the needs of the twentieth century, Rousseau's skill in shocking us is welcomed rather than resented.

Rousseau's complex notion of freedom is matched by his complex notion of nation. His name has long been attached to the idea of nationalism. But his views on the subject go beyond the traditional formal institutional notions with which we have bedecked this appealing monster. A nation is not made up merely of independence, sovereignty, boundaries, codified laws, armies, and central government. It is essentially a community of beliefs, and of laws that embody certain ideas of justice; it is a will to keep together even in the midst of diversity; it is an attachment to the beauties of the land. This is why Rousseau seems to be full of optimism when in spite of the smashing up and gradual disappearance of all the traditional outer trappings of a national state, he predicts the survival of the Polish nation and gives advice which, in the light of history, cannot be described as utopian. Poland's anarchical traditions, class divisions, land system, customs, and civic spirit will keep alive the idea and the ultimate realization of a Polish nation.[36]

In raising the question how nations communicate with one

[35] On this, cf. Shklar, *op. cit.*, 931; on liberty in *Emile,* see Burgelin, *op. cit.*, 495 ff.

[36] See the good discussion of this issue, and the contrast between Mably's "utopia" and Rousseau's "realism" on Polish affairs, in Fabre, "Réalité et Utopie," 205–13. To defend Polish traditions meant to reject the "French way of life," and "in those days the suggestions of the French way of life had perhaps an even stronger 'demonstration effect' than in our day the American way of life" (de Jouvenel, "Rousseau the Pessimistic Evolutionist," 91).

ould be in the end total isolation, with each man living in
l of strangers or enemies where all human contact would
44

off from his fellow man and from nature, man would
e wedded to those monstrous urban agglomerations which
au felt were the ultimate tragedy in the disintegration of
man being.[45] But if the recovery of natural man was
ible, perhaps the rescue of civilized man from the awful
e had built for himself was still possible. It certainly was
ing to be an easy task to make a citizen out of civilized
But the attempt had to be made, and certain standards and
les held in mind. One of the standards was what Rousseau
the "mediocre" state, or the happy middle ground, or the
ion in which no one would be very much above or below a
mean.[46] The standard to be imposed is one in which a
average (that is "mediocre") way of life is within the
of a community in which every citizen is a hard-working
pant. A society in which, through a variety of public
entions, order, continuity, and stability are achieved. This
not be a society made up only of independent farmers,
se the common tasks are many and exacting. But neither
it be an urban capitalistic machine-oriented one. It would,
, be a society in which politics had finally taken the upper
over economics. For there was nothing fatal about the laws

aczko, op. cit., 226–7.
f. the section on "Deterioration of Mores through Urbanization,"
Jouvenel, "Rousseau the Pessimistic Revolutionist," 87–90.
On Rousseau's état médiocre and juste milieu, cf. Fetscher, op. cit.,
.; Fetscher, "Rousseau's Concept of Freedom in the Light of his
sophy of History," Nomos IV, ed. Carl J. Friedrich (New York,
), 54–5 (and 56, where the restraining of "the dynamics of social
opment" is rightly seen as support for "a higher moral and political
om for the citizen"); Burgelin, op. cit., 501; Lévi-Strauss, op. cit.,

another, Rousseau poses one of the baffling issues in an age of
nationalism. He weakens one of the slogans of nineteenth-
century liberalism—that trade fosters peace—for his view is that
the competitiveness of international trade relations may foster
war. Rousseau leaves no room for illusions. Interdependence may
breed bitter rivalries.[37] But we also know that the autonomy of
the self-sufficient nation may lead to tensions within a stagnant
society ready in the end to do violence to its neighbors. The chief
value of Rousseau's warning is, then, that of dispelling the hope
that on an accelerated exchange of commodities or on other
economic policies one can build peace among nations.

But the preponderant weight of Rousseau's analysis seems
directed to what men do among themselves economically inside
the national community. His conclusions are the same. Given
the turn taken by human affairs, deepening injustice and chaos
are to be expected.

It is undoubtedly symbolic of this new way of looking at
Rousseau that one of the two distinguished editors-in-chief of the
new edition of Rousseau's complete works should in effect place
the third volume, which includes the political writings, under
the aegis of a *Discourse on Wealth* which has been practically
ignored until today.[38]

The fact is that Gagnebin is right, and that it is difficult to
overemphasize what Rousseau has to say about property, wealth,
money, and about the rich and the poor.

The famous battle cry of the *Discourse on Inequality* concerning property is seen now as a fundamental statement of Rousseau's views, never to be canceled by anything that he was to say
later, and not the result of mere literary whim in order to be
unpleasant and to shock his friends. Property becomes the pivot

[37] Stanley Hoffmann, "Rousseau on War and Peace," *American Political Science Review*, LVII (1963), 321.
[38] O.C. III, xxv–xxvi. Cf. infra, p. 224.

around which the evolution of mankind revolves. What he says is based upon a solid and detailed foundation of economic analysis,[39] and from it flow the train of consequences Rousseau never tires of developing.

What Rousseau envisaged was the outcome of a process of accumulation of property, of increasing reliance on money, of advancing technology, and arts, of more luxury, of a deepening gulf between the rich and the poor, and the final loneliness of social urbanized man. All this went against the "mediocre condition" he saw as the ideal. All this meant suffocation of moral and political values in an intricate network of selfish and greedy economic relationships.

Money he saw as the poison which destroyed direct and immediate human relationships. It was the mediator which did away with the immediacy and the transparence he so much wanted.[40] He pleads for a direct consumer's economy in which capital accumulation will not be possible. He deprecates the goals of a rising bourgeois society. With Burke he is seen as the enemy of modern capital.[41] He defends "obsolete" ideas which, as de Jouvenel points out,[42] Rousseau knows are obsolete, opposing as he does techniques and technocracy, economic progress, or policies of economic development which pay no attention to the human problems they create.[43]

[39] See Fabre, "Réalité et Utopie," 183; in general Vossler and Fetscher, cited above; Kateb, "Aspects of Rousseau's Political Thought," *Political Science Quarterly*, LXXVI (1961), 529 ("Every society necessitates restrictions and sacrifices; and Rousseau, with his matchless sense of the real, does not think that even the good society can be free of them").

[40] Starobinski, *op. cit.*, 129 ff.

[41] Eric Weil, "J. J. Rousseau et sa politique," *Critique* (Jan.–June 1952), 25.

[42] De Jouvenel, "Rousseau the Pessimistic Evolutionist," 93.

[43] Fabre, "Réalité et Utopie," 214–15: "In opposition to a blind civilization and to those it has chosen as its guides, Rousseau keeps saying that human problems cannot be defined and settled first of all in terms of

He was fighting a battle again
phetic vision which told him tha
the multiplication of ties due to th
rial requirements, meant a decreas
in the moral fiber of man. Unless
frenzy after wealth would unbala
among members of the communi
enter a period in which luxury
phenomenon and in which an i
classes would become a reality.

As many modern critics have re
to consider the age-old problem of
sion of a complex economic analy
and the technical and institutional
the widening gulf between rich and
being rich or of being poor, while
denied it—in some measure to ine
skills, was in greater measure due
And this was the point at which pol
to help steer a new course.

Modern civilization, in accepting a
not only between rich and poor but b
extreme poverty, was heading straigh
lives and qualities of *both* rich and
separate circles, the two classes tended
fashion the worst traits of each. No i
possible as long as this state of affairs

production and of consumption, that one m
equitably, but that the end of societies is n
man is essentially and not secondarily a mor
him as such and that therefore it is ne
blandishments of a materialistic economy th
'political economy.'"

of economic development. The community was free to decide on the future course of events. Often in the past man had lost his freedom and sharpened inequality because there were those who set out deliberately to seek those goals. Nothing prevented man from seeking with equal deliberation different ones.

On the way events would shape in the future, Rousseau was fairly consistent and clear. A gradual deterioration in human affairs and in the condition of man in society would continue. It would be a downward trend very difficult to stop. At times it even appears that the trend is developing into a spiral, with dramatic events taking place at an accelerated speed. Pessimism was justified by the evidence. It was true that no matter how bad things were, one was grateful for the little mercies of apparent order and the elimination of open banditry. But the world was touching bottom, almost, and found itself in a darkening valley far from the dazzling peaks the Enlightenment thought it had reached.

The question was whether anything could be done. It is quite probable that Rousseau thought that something could be done about small states, either because they were manageable owing to their size, or because the corruption of multiple-need societies had not yet reached them. Even here the best that might be hoped was a slowdown of the degenerative process.[47]

Such pessimism brings Rousseau to a consideration of the role of revolutions, or of the great upheavals which mark the crisis points in the history of civilization. At times, Rousseau speaks of the coming revolution as if it were a certainty or as if it were inevitable given the premises of its analysis. Since the foundations of contemporary society are based on injustice and on a principle, that of property, which is bound to deepen class antagonisms, a revolutionary explosion cannot be avoided.

[47] De Jouvenel, *Essai sur la politique de Rousseau*, 84.

Rousseau has no illusion as to the consequences of revolution in a great state: he begs us to imagine what would happen if the mass of French society started moving. Hence, it is clear that he would like to avoid a revolutionary showdown, if possible. He goes to great pains to show his conservatism and prudence and to deprecate violent commotions which can raise many more problems than they can solve.

Rousseau is facing the dilemma of the social critic who has offered the most damaging interpretation of the forces at work around him and has demonstrated the moral necessity of their doom, and who yet would like to stop short of what looks like the obvious conclusion. He manages to rise above the dilemma through his faith in the possibility that, adequately warned and educated and given the right circumstances, man, a moral being, can reassert himself over history and regain a mastery over his fate which hitherto history seems to have denied him.

The antagonism of nature and history, as Henri Gouhier has brilliantly shown,[48] can perhaps be eliminated on this high plane of moral man assuming his responsibilities as citizen. There is a remote and only half visible ideal of a state of nature, of a golden age, of a standard of perfection which we ought to bear in mind. On the other hand, there is all of history, with its hazards and unhappy chances, and with its mistakes. Things have happened

[48] Henri Gouhier, "Nature et histoire dans la pensée de Rousseau," *Annales*, XXXIII (1953–1955), 7–48. Starting from the opposition of nature and history, Gouhier argues that Rousseau's alternative is not state of nature or history: "An effective necessity condemns 'man of nature' to become 'man of man': but had man perforce to become what he has in fact become? Rousseau cannot dream of a 'return to the state of nature'; is he equally obliged to maintain the *status quo*? The question which is posed is therefore not: state of nature or history? but: this history or another one?" (20) And if property belongs to the historical order, "it does not belong to that effective necessity which makes history inevitable," for Rousseau speaks of calamitous chance. And if the right way was lost, the right way can be found (26).

which might not have happened. Is it impossible, then, to imagine that man will forever be unable to redress some of the mistakes he has made and try to achieve reconciliation between nature and history?

Rousseau says that it is not impossible. If it was absurd to express the satisfaction of so many eighteenth-century philosophers who thought the world to be on the eve of the greatest plenty, perfection, and pleasure it had ever seen, with man himself getting hints of immortality or at least of a possibility of life to which no finite term could be given, it was wrong to believe that nothing could be done to change a course Rousseau felt to be catastrophic for mankind. Therefore, Rousseau leaves us with the hope that the recovery of a worthy freedom for man in a well-ordered society is possible.

II

The Contemporary Setting

Places

THE Rousseau before us is the Rousseau of the twenty years from 1736 to 1756. The vicissitudes of those years are narrated in Books vi, vii, and viii of the *Confessions,* in the pages which start with the words "Here begins the short happiness of my life," and end with the retreat from Paris "under the jeerings of the Holbachian clan." [1]

Within this twenty-year span, three places are decisive in their influence on the intellectual development of Rousseau: Les Charmettes, Paris, and Geneva. The first is the symbol of the lost happiness of man as he moves from nature to society; the second represents the predicament of man trying, but failing, to get away from the civilization he has built. The third is the distant ideal of what the life of man might be. The years of Les Charmettes run from 1736 to 1742. Paris accounts for most of the years from 1742 to 1756. Geneva is but a memory and a point of reference, except for a few summer months in 1754.

Rousseau would like to remember the time at Les Charmettes as a haven of happiness, for it was undoubtedly spent close to

---

[1] *Confessions,* bk. vi, O.C. I, 225; bk. ix, O.C. I, 401.

nature and its beauties, a time of solitude, of manual work in the garden as well as of intensive work of the mind. It was, however, also a time filled with tensions and fears. There were serious illness and the premonition of death, the unhappiness at the crumbling of the foundations on which life with Madame de Warens rested, the first disquieting awareness of a large city, Lyon, where the opulence of civilization and commerce was displayed, and glimpses of the native city which might perhaps become the ideal city. Les Charmettes in the end became little more than the starting point of the road followed by man as he abandons the innocence of his original condition for life in society.

Paris is at first only a brief apparition. For Rousseau's introduction to political life takes place in one of the oldest political systems then in existence, that of Venice, and as a member of one of the oldest branches of public service, diplomacy.[2] What he finds out about both of them will leave in his mind the "germ of indignation against our stupid civil institutions in which real public good and real justice are always sacrificed to I do not know what apparent order, destructive in effect of all order and which only adds the sanction of public authority to the oppression of the weak and the iniquity of the strong."[3] And it is against the background of this major theme of the contrast between being and appearing that Rousseau will begin to think about his future work on political institutions.

In crossing the Alps, on his return from Venice to Paris, Rousseau gains some of the courage he needs to face the difficult years ahead of him and to tolerate the contrast between the

[2] Rousseau's dispatches of the years 1743 and 1744, written when he was secretary to the French ambassador, have been published in full for the first time as *Dépêches de Venise*, O.C. III, 1045–1234, with introduction and notes by Jean-Daniel Candaux.

[3] *Confessions*, bk. vii, O.C. I, 327.

appearance of order and the reality of disorder. Nature comes to his rescue, and convinces him of its superiority over art. He suddenly has a revelation of the beauty of the mountains and discovers their "amazing mixture of savage nature and of culti-vated nature," and he is struck by the gathering in one spot and at the same time of all the panoply of the earth—"on the East the flowers of spring, on the South the fruits of autumn, on the North the ice of winter"—in the midst of "pure and subtle" air where one feels a "greater lightness of body, a serenity of spirit." [4]

The years from 1744 to 1749 are indeed oppressive and hard. Rousseau feels the cruel pressures of deprivation and injustice in a way which he is to remember for the rest of his life, just as he is to remember the strength man can obtain from a direct contact with nature. He is struggling against poverty and is "disgusted with society and commerce with men." Paris is a "town where arrogance rules and where the virtuous poor are the object of contempt." [5] But even as he was driven to the humblest of work for the rich who could pay, he was also thinking furiously and reading the classics of political thought, from Bodin to Grotius, books of history both ancient and modern, and accounts of travels and of the ethnography of distant peoples. [6]

[4] See the famous description of the Valais in *La Nouvelle Héloïse*, i, 23, O.C. II, 76–84.

[5] Letter to Roguin, July 9, 1745, in *Correspondance générale* (here-after C.G.), ed. Th. Dufour (Paris, 1924–1934), I, 270; also in the new edition of Rousseau's correspondence now under way, *Correspon-dance complète de Jean-Jacques Rousseau* (hereafter C.C.), ed. R. A. Leigh (Geneva, 1965–), II, 83–6. Also see *Epître à M. de l'Etang*, O.C. II, 1150–3.

[6] The dispersion at auction between 1951 and 1958 of the archives of Madame Dupin, Rousseau's protector and employer, has revealed the intensity and range of Rousseau's work as shown by several thousands of pages of excerpts of readings and of essays written under Madame Dupin's dictation. Cf. the note of Gagnebin and Raymond, the editors of the *Confessions*, in O.C. I, 1413: "The inventory drawn up by M. A.

With the answer he gave in 1749 to the question posed by the Academy of Dijon, Rousseau tells us, there began a period of intense mental activity which lasted for several years, the years of fantastic, sudden success as well as of final crisis: "All my small passions were set aside by the enthusiasm for truth, for freedom, for virtue, and what is most amazing is that this effervescence maintained itself in my heart for more than four or five years in a measure perhaps as high as ever was found in the heart of any other man."[7] To find out what Rousseau thought and wrote in this decisive period of his life, to which he himself gives a singular unity of inspiration, is the main object of this book. He saw his task as that of setting forth his view of man's progress through time and of finding the causes of his downfall.

He has to do it, surrounded by adulation, in the city placed at the heart of the civilization he was condemning. When he is about to leave Paris for the Ermitage, he regrets it, not unmindful of what Paris had done for him. Happy is the man who can "live in the midst of friendship in the common fatherland of mankind, in this immense shelter open to all men, where both austere wisdom and foolish youth are equally happy; where humanity, hospitality, sweetness and all the charms of easy society rule . . . it is on this great theatre of fortune, of vice and sometimes of virtue, that one can profitably watch the spectacle of life; but it is in his own country that everyone should complete in peace his own."[8]

Yet he feels he has to go away. The year is 1755, and he finds unbearable the burdens placed on the successful writer by a

---

Sénéchal of the works consulted by Rousseau on behalf of Mme. Dupin shows that the writer has considerably increased his knowledge of political science (Bodin, Domat, Grotius), of history (not only the history of antiquity, but that of France, Spain, and England in modern times) and of ethnography."

[7] *Confessions*, bk. viii, O.C. I, 351.
[8] *Lettre à Philopolis*, O.C. III, 235.

commercial civilization. An author could be respectable only if his work did not become a trade. "It is too difficult to think nobly when one thinks only in order to live. In order to be able, in order to dare, to say great truths, one must not depend upon one's own success." [9] An escape from the city in spite of the "jeering" of his friends had become inevitable. The only question was whether the flight was to be again to the forest where the great thoughts of the *Discourse on Inequality* had come to him, or whether it was to be to an "ideal" city. Could Geneva be his salvation?

The issue of Geneva's influence on Rousseau is a perennial one, and learned and well-documented arguments have been developed to maintain it as well as to deny it. [10] But in any meaningful sense the answer must unquestionably be that Geneva's significance is both continuous and large.

This can be seen first of all in the flood of memories, recollections, and allusions, as well as of specific statements, to be found in Rousseau's work from the earliest words of longing in the *Confessions,* to the verses of *Le Verger* of 1737 and of the letters to Bordes of 1741 and to Parisot of 1742 [11]—to the statement that the winning of the prize for his first *Discourse* in 1750 "reawakened all the ideas which had caused me to write it, animated them with a new strength, and completed the fermentation in my heart of that first leaven of heroism and of virtue placed there in infancy by my father, my fatherland and Plutarch" [12]—to his declaration in the 1751 answer to the King of Poland that in order to carry out more fully the task he had set

[9] *Confessions,* bk. ix, O.C. I, 403.
[10] On the affirmative side of this question, see Gaspard Vallette, *J.-J. Rousseau, Genevois* (Paris, 1911); on the negative side, J. S. Spink, *J.-J. Rousseau et Genève* (Paris, 1934). On the entire problem of Rousseau and Switzerland, cf. the monumental work by François Jost, *J.-J. Rousseau, Suisse,* 2 vols. (Fribourg, 1961).
[11] Cf. infra, pp. 32, 69–70.   [12] *Confessions,* bk. viii, O.C. I, 356.

for himself, he would have to conduct his research in Geneva [13]—to his continuous relationship with Genevan exiles in Paris in the fifties and the political relevance of those relationships—everything points to a sum total of feelings, memories, and plans too strong to be set aside.

We also find that Rousseau's attitude toward Geneva is shaped by some of his fundamental views about man and nature. Like his father, many of the inhabitants of the city and of the surrounding villages on the lake and in the mountains were sturdy independent artisans—that is, men who in the midst of advanced society had maintained an autonomy of personality and of skills that made them better men. And the closing pages of part iv of the *Nouvelle Héloïse* confirm in moving terms the magic attraction that land had for Rousseau. That attraction was a combination of the irresistible charm of a wild and awesome nature and of political considerations. Rousseau contrasts the happiness and prosperity of the peasants of his fatherland, secure in the enjoyment of what their hard work has yielded, with the poverty of the neighboring Chablais, a land no less favored by nature, but ruled by distant princes. It was possible then "to distinguish the different effects of the two governments on the wealth, number, and happiness of man. It is thus . . . that the earth opens its fertile bosom and sheds its treasures to the happy peoples who cultivate it for themselves. It appears to smile and to come to life at the sweet appearance of liberty . . . On the other hand, the sad huts, the brush and thorny weeds covering a semi-desert land announce from afar that an absent master is ruling it." [14]

There is a great deal more: chiefly the hard and specific political meaning of Rousseau's attachment to Geneva. Rousseau considered himself a citizen of Geneva and always proudly pro-

[13] Cf. infra, pp. 88–9.
[14] *La Nouvelle Héloïse*, iv, 17, O.C. II, 515–6.

claimed himself one. There never was any fuzziness about the view Rousseau had of citizenship in Geneva. He was born a citizen, both his father and his mother belonging to the Geneva bourgeoisie. In 1762 he goes out of his way to praise someone who at that time is no longer his friend, d'Alembert, for the correct classification he had provided in his article on Geneva in Volume VII of the *Encyclopaedia*: "No other French author, as far as I know, has understood the true meaning of the word citizen." [15] D'Alembert had correctly distinguished between the four orders of persons who made up the population of Geneva in the eighteenth century: the citizen, the bourgeois, the habitants, and the natives. Rousseau, son of bourgeois parents and born in Geneva, was a citizen. As such he had those rights, including the one of belonging to the General Council, which he so proudly describes in his poem to Parisot. And if his views of what direct participation in the political system of Geneva actually meant were not quite in keeping with the realities of political life in Geneva after the crisis of 1738, they were far closer to the substance of things than has often been admitted.[16]

There was, above all, the attachment to a community which, at least in its history, and even then in its size, embodied many of the values Rousseau was developing in his political theory. In the happy phrase of Jean Fabre, Geneva "reappears every time Rousseau needs a middle term between the real and the true." [17] Geneva is the way station between a lost past and an unfathomable future.

Finally, the decision of Rousseau to return to Geneva in 1754

[15] *Contrat Social*, i, 6, O.C. III, 361–2.

[16] Cf. the precise comments of B. Gagnebin, in the discussion of the paper by O. Krafft, "Les Classes sociales à Genève et la notion de citoyen," in a volume published under the auspices of the Comité National Pour La Commémoration de J.-J. Rousseau, *Jean-Jacques Rousseau et son oeuvre* (Paris, 1964), 228–9.

[17] Jean Fabre, "Réalité et Utopie dans la pensée politique de Rousseau," *Annales*, XXXV (1959–1962), 198–9.

represents a turning point in his life and a fundamental moral and political commitment, if one assumes, as I think one must, that the intention to settle permanently in his native city was a real one.[18]

For a man dedicated by now to the thesis that to improve the condition of man it was necessary to improve the way he was governed, Geneva represented a good way out of the dilemma in which Rousseau was caught, on the one hand of the impossibility of a return to nature, on the other hand of the impossibility of life in the heart of a corrupt civilization. Rousseau tells us, with some exaggeration, that Voltaire, by deciding to settle in Geneva, spoiled everything. Having learned of that decision, Rousseau feels that Geneva is lost. "I might perhaps have gone and faced the storm, had I possessed the necessary talent. But what could I have done alone and shy and speaking very poorly, against an arrogant and opulent man supported by the credit of the Greats, brilliantly eloquent and already the idol of women and of young people?" [19]

Even if this were not true in any formal sense, it is true in a substantial sense, for Rousseau and Voltaire represented not only two different styles of life, but also two different philosophies. Rousseau knew furthermore that a cottage was ready for him in the silence of the forest of Montmorency. The shift to an "ideal" life would now have to take place not in the "ideal" city, but in the solitude of nature.

Men and Ideas

Rousseau's relationship with the men who together created what we call the century of lights was as complex as the strands

---

[18] Cf. infra, pp. 157–8, also for an appraisal of the Dedication of the *Discourse on Inequality* to the sovereign members of the republic, that is to the citizens who formed the General Council.

[19] *Confessions*, bk. viii, O.C. I, 396–7.

of the political thought of that century. No simplification is possible, but certain things are clear and should enable one to fix Rousseau's position within his times with some measure of precision.

The ties linking Rousseau to Montesquieu have often been thought to be difficult to identify and to evaluate. Perhaps Rousseau's attitude can best be described as one of distant awe for the great man who disappeared from the scene at the moment, in 1755, when the break between Rousseau and his closest friends began to appear probable. Montesquieu's authority could always be invoked in supporting Rousseau's views on such practical matters as the size of political communities, the operating devices of democracy, the issues which Rousseau's realism considered important and which on the other hand the cosmopolitanism of the Enlightenment viewed as trivialities not worthy of the attention of an era about to make discoveries of universal value that would guarantee permanently the happiness of men. Montesquieu was a pessimist and a relativist, and his mind was filled with a host of small problems which served to show how much prudence was needed in the handling of human affairs and he had therefore attracted the sarcastic scorn of Helvetius who thought the task of distinguishing between good and bad governments an infinitely easier one.

The *Esprit des Lois,* moreover, had so much to say in favor of so many of the principles close to his heart that Rousseau could not fail to find it to his liking. Thus: "political virtue is a renunciation of oneself . . . [which] may be defined as the love of laws and of fatherland." In an age where the drives of individuals to acquire and accumulate wealth were praised as contributing to the common welfare, Montesquieu writes that "the common sense and the happiness of individuals lies a great deal in the mediocrity of their talents and of their fortunes. A republic where laws will have formed many mediocre people . . . will govern itself wisely." And how could Rousseau, when writing the first *Discourse*, have forgotten that one year earlier he had read in the *Esprit des Lois* these words: "Greek politicians knew only one principle, that of virtue; those of today talk only about manufactures, commerce, finances, wealth, luxury." [20]

Hence, Rousseau is happy to acknowledge Montesquieu's greatness. He is among those to whom serious work on the peoples of the earth could be entrusted.[21] In the *Political Economy* his name is linked to that of Plato.[22] Indeed, a recent critic has been able to say that in appreciating the scope of the first *Discourse* "it might certainly be better to see in it less a declamation inspired by platonic chimeras, than the systematic development of certain affirmations of Montesquieu on the real values of politics." [23]

However well founded these words may be, and however frequent Rousseau's reliance on Montesquieu on "problems of convenience or adaptation," [24] we are aware of a certain reticence of Rousseau vis-à-vis Montesquieu. This is due to some contrasts of which Rousseau was keenly conscious. How much of Montesquieu's unhappiness about gross speculation, the rise of a new wealth and of a new class of enterprisers, was due to his feelings of distress, being himself one of the landowners who saw their power diminish in the midst of great economic turmoil and change? [25] If Rousseau was against urban wealth, it was not because he wanted to maintain the wealth of the provincial

---

[20] *Esprit des Lois*, IV, 5; V, 3.

[21] *Discours sur l'origine de l'inégalité*, O.C. III, 213.

[22] *Economie politique*, O.C. III, 273.

[23] A. Adam, "De Quelques Sources de Rousseau dans la littérature philosophique (1700–1750)," in *Rousseau et son oeuvre*, 128. Adam cites the last passage of Montesquieu quoted above.

[24] Fabre, "Réalité et Utopie," 191.

[25] This point is skillfully made by Jean Starobinski, *Montesquieu par lui-même* (Paris, 1953), 53.

nobility. Indeed, Montesquieu saw no harm in the "spirit of commerce" because it carried with it many other qualities of thrift, of work, of order. Luxury itself is necessary in monarchies, even though fatal in a democracy.[26]

But what really ultimately mattered was Rousseau's conviction that he was engaged in a different endeavor. Montesquieu had provided the most useful foundations for a study of politics. He might have been able to continue beyond that stage, but he did not. Rousseau feels he is continuing Montesquieu's work, but he is doing it not at the practical, but above all at the theoretical level, and the difference, he thinks, is very great. In the *Emile* Rousseau is quite explicit: "[Montesquieu] refrained from discussing the principles of political right; he was satisfied with treating of the positive law of established governments; and nothing in this world is more different than these two studies." [27] It is here that the historical approaches of the master and the disciple part way, as Rousseau seeks to fix his mind beyond the contingencies of time and place.

No such duality of judgment exists in the case of the other great literary figure dominating the mid-century, Voltaire. Even Rousseau's early and almost entirely formal praise, in the *Confessions* and in his first letter of 1745 to Voltaire [28] is already countered by his criticism in the *Verger*: he has no taste for frivolous authors whose goal is just to be witty. When he wants to consider human misery, he will read Montaigne and La Bruyère.[29]

Their relationship was altogether an unhappy and antagonis-

---

[26] *Esprit des Lois,* xxi, 14, 16; vii, 1, 4.   [27] *Emile,* bk. v.

[28] "Nothing of what Voltaire was writing escaped our attention. The pleasure I had in these readings inspired my desire to learn to write with elegance" (*Confessions,* bk. v, O.C. I, 214); "For the past fifteen years I have worked to make myself worthy of your attention" (letter to Voltaire, December 11, 1745, *C.G.* I, 275).

[29] *Verger,* O.C. II, 1129, 1124.

tic one. Rousseau felt he had tried to be respectful toward such a lofty personality, but Voltaire treated him with contempt and misunderstanding: "I don't like you at all, sir. . . . You have lost Geneva. . . . You have alienated from me my fellow-citizen. . . . It is you who will force me to die in a foreign land. . . . Of all the sentiments my heart nourished for you, there is only left the admiration one cannot refuse to your beautiful genius and a liking for your writings." [30]

It is difficult to see how it could have been otherwise, because more than any other leading "philosophe," Voltaire stood for what was opposed to the values Rousseau was defending. There were no common grounds on which a reconciliation could be brought about. Voltaire supported the doctrines and institutions of the civilization Rousseau had condemned. He was for property and wealth and luxury and for a suitably preponderant role in society and government for those who had acquired property and for those who knew how to enjoy the refinements of life which accumulated wealth provided. The new social role of writers, economists, and political philosophers was that of using for the advancement of culture and of human happiness the milieu in which they were operating. Thus in praising Melon's *Observations sur le commerce,* Voltaire had summed up with his usual fatal clarity the position of the Enlightenment: "Never before has literature been so tied up with finance. This is yet another of the claims to fame of our century." [31]

What Rousseau has to say about property fills Voltaire with indignation. He annotates angrily the *Discourse on Inequality*: "What if the man who has planted, sown and enclosed [his field]

---

[30] Letter to Voltaire, June 17, 1760, as given by Rousseau in the *Confessions,* bk. x, *O.C.* I, 541–2.

[31] *Oeuvres complètes,* Moland ed. (52 vols.; Paris, 1877–1885), XXII (1879), 364–5.

does not have the right to the fruit of his work?" He is shocked at the praise Rousseau bestows on the person who might have issued a warning against the private enclosure of land: "How is it possible to say that this unjust man, this thief, would have been the benefactor of mankind? This is the philosophy of a tramp who would like to see the wealthy robbed by the poor." The hope of Rousseau that sometime in the past or sometime in the future the ideal of a middleground with no extremes might have existed or might exist, Voltaire considers a "chimera," just as he views as utter fantasy Rousseau's image of the Hurons and of the Canadians, for he is convinced they are cannibals.[32]

Years later, in his *Idées républicaines*, Voltaire was to continue in a polemic against Rousseau which is far more than that, for this pamphlet is an uncompromising expression of an extreme utilitarian doctrine and of a rugged kind of liberalism which views the rights of rich and poor as equal, one to get fat, the other to starve: "The dress of the rich can no more be regulated than the rags of the poor. Citizens both, both must be equally free. Each will dress, eat, be housed if he can. If you stop the wealthy from eating wild cocks, you damage the poor who might support his family by selling them." There was no doubt in Voltaire's mind that laws against luxury can please only "the lazy . . . the jealous poor who do not want to work or to allow

[32] Cf. G. R. Havens, *Voltaire's Marginalia on the Pages of Rousseau* (Columbus, 1933), 15, 17, 145. Of course, Voltaire expresses the same shocked view of Rousseau's madness throughout his work: "Thus, according to this great philosopher, a thief, a destroyer, would have been the benefactor of mankind; and an honest man should have been punished for telling his children: let us imitate our neighbor, he has enclosed his field, animals will no longer prey on it, his land will become more fertile, let us till ours as he is tilling his, he will help us and we will help him; each family cultivating its enclosure, we will be better nourished, healthier, more tranquil, less unhappy" (*Oeuvres complètes*, XIX, 380; also, XXVII, 339–40).

those who do to enjoy life." [33] For Voltaire, as Morazé points out, fatherland equaled property. What is my country if not a good field which I cultivate and which belongs to me? [34]

When a friend of Rousseau, Romilly, raised some questions about Voltaire's presence in Geneva, this was the result: "I was one day with a wealthy merchant of Geneva, who often sees Voltaire, and the conversation fell on Voltaire's stay near Geneva. I tried to prove that his sojourn would only lead to a weakening of religion, to an increase in the taste for luxury and in dissipation, and would consequently be too contrary to good customs. What? he answered with heat, you do not know that since Voltaire's arrival in this country the city of Geneva alone has benefited by more than 200,000 livres?" [35] Also, it was easy for Voltaire to remain with an asylum from which he could thunder against tyrants. Indeed, "all the more cowardly as he was safe." [36]

This was a prudent liberalism ready to accept the practices of enlightened despotism, of a system which, with due and essential homage to freedom of thought and of dissent, would be able to

[33] *Oeuvres complètes*, XXIV, 413–32. Luxury was "a necessary consequence of property, without which no society can subsist, and of a great inequality of fortunes, which is the consequence not of the right of property but of bad law" (*ibid.*, XX, 18). But Voltaire found good a political system based on property qualifications, and in any case who was against luxury?—"The poor, in a fit of bad humour" (XXXIV, 200).

[34] Charles Morazé, *La France bourgeoise* (Paris, 1952), 74 Morazé also writes: "If we open the *Encyclopédie*, we find that it is the collection of all the good ways of producing wealth . . . while it offers the philosophical justification of this love for the goods of the earth" (69).

[35] Fragment of an unpublished letter of Romilly to Rousseau, 1763, published by Michel Launay, "La Société française d'après la correspondance de Rousseau (textes inédits)," *Annales historiques de la Révolution française* (1962), 418–9.

[36] Diderot, *Lettre apologétique*, March 25, 1781, in Herbert Dieckmann, *Inventaire du fonds Vandeul et inédits de Diderot* (Geneva, 1951), 243.

hold in check the vagaries of the mob and to regulate the disturbances which might hamper the leisure of the rich. Voltaire could not even understand, let alone like, what Rousseau wanted with his austere and democratic society, in which hard work was a universal duty. The abstractions of the general will seemed to him to be close to folly: he would certainly refuse to cross a bridge built by magistrates or priests. Or to trust a community in which money and property were not key standards. Should those without land or a house have a right to vote? "They have no more a right to it than a clerk paid by merchants would have to regulate their commerce." [37]

A properly organized community needed sharply defined and divided classes and a mass of penniless peasants to do their duty as wage laborers and soldiers. The latter would share in the happiness of others: "They will be free to sell their labor as best they can. This liberty will replace property. The certain hope of a just salary will sustain them. They will cheerfully raise their families in their painful and useful trades. It is above all this class of men so despised in the eyes of the powerful, which is the nursery of soldiers." [38] How brilliantly does Voltaire provide the bridge between the earlier, seventeenth-century, expressions of such views and their full-fledged practical realization a hundred years later. How happy the vision of a future built on such foundations. How convinced he was, with his optimistic determinism, that all would be well in the end, provided a climate of tolerance and freedom was allowed to flourish, one in which everyone would do as he pleased.

That Rousseau saw this as one of the overriding issues of the times is made clear by his letter to Voltaire on the Lisbon earthquake. It is necessary to be active participants and not passive spectators if one wanted that all should be well one day. If in

[37] *Idées républicaines, Oeuvres complètes*, XXIV, 417, 425.
[38] *Oeuvres complètes*, XX, 293.

the natural order all is necessary, in the moral order man becomes responsible and it is his duty to see that the practical arrangements that are not working well be set aside for better ones: "If Rousseau defends moral freedom, it is because he is moved by a will of revolutionary change." [39]

But Montesquieu and Voltaire were fairly remote figures. In the exchanges and troubles of daily life what mattered more was the tangled mass of encyclopedists, *philosophes,* scientists, men and women of letters, literary middlemen and peddlers, of which, during the period under consideration, Rousseau was part. With each of the protagonists of the play, Rousseau entertained different relationships: with many, of close and steady friendship, with others of friendship turning into bitter enmity. Only that part of the story which is related to ideas will be recounted here, for it is more profitable to consider Rousseau's place within the contemporary setting by focusing our attention on the substantive issues which by themselves are enough to establish a tolerably clear picture. Paraphrasing Voltaire, Rousseau refused to be a member of the team, but the reason was that he was playing a different game.

Very useful to clarify the issues is d'Alembert, the tireless worker, the scientist, the co-editor of the *Encyclopédie,* the friend of Rousseau in the forties. He was a member of the group that rallied around Rousseau during the noisy quarrel which divided Paris between supporters of French music and supporters of Italian music. [40] The former, Rousseau tells us, included

[39] Jacques Proust, *Diderot et l'Encyclopédie* (Paris, 1962), 324. As Proust says, Rousseau is not passive but wants to work actively for the dawn of that day in which all will be well (325). For the Lisbon earthquake letter of 1756, see infra, pp. 201–207.

[40] This was taking place in 1753 when the crisis between the Paris Parliament and the Monarchy was at its peak. But Grimm relates that "the quarrels of the Paris Parliament with the Court, its exile . . . all these events have been a topic of conversation in Paris for only 24 hours

"the great and the rich," the smaller band of the latter was made up of lively, enthusiastic, and fine musicians.[41]

D'Alembert had supported Rousseau's collaboration to the *Encyclopédie* and had referred in flattering terms, even though critically, to his friend in the *Preliminary Discourse* of 1751,[42] while Rousseau was to include him in the *Discourse on Inequality* among those capable of serious anthropological work.[43] And the ever-present Grimm could still say in 1754 that d'Alembert in his *Mélanges de littérature,* published early in 1753, had expressed views that were not too far from those of Rousseau.[44]

These friendly beginnings could not last, for underlining everything was a difference of views which explains the clash between Rousseau and the Enlightenment. What d'Alembert was to say about the *Nouvelle Héloïse* and *Emile* is relevant. D'Alembert charges Rousseau with having written until then works based upon an often false and always worthless metaphysics. He had depicted "a gigantic and imaginary nature," something of no value, d'Alembert must feel, while man would have been more receptive to a recognizable description of nature through which he might move. One merit of the *Nouvelle Héloïse,* however, appears to be that this distant nature, suitable only for giants, has shrunk, and we can take pleasure in "the episodes, the sidelights, the details on domestic economy, on the pleasure of

---

and no matter what this respectable body has done in the past year to fix upon itself the eyes of the public, it has never secured for itself one thirtieth of the attention given to the revolution in music." (*Correspondance littéraire,* Tourneux ed. [Paris, 1877], II, 258–9.)

[41] *Confessions,* bk. viii, O.C. I, 384, 1447.   [42] Cf. infra, pp. 87–88.

[43] O.C. III, 213.

[44] *Ibid.,* 319–20. The 1753 edition of the *Mélanges* was limited to two volumes. The *Eléments de philosophie* appeared only in the edition of 1759, expanded to 5 volumes.

life in the country." But this not enough to make one forget that this is the work of someone who has withdrawn from society and has lost touch with reality. According to d'Alembert, the *Emile* shows this withdrawal too, and proves that Rousseau's philosophy is not in his head but in his heart.

The major fault with Rousseau then lies in his wasting so much energy and intelligence in considering "man in a condition of abstraction, in those metaphsical conditions in which he never was and never will be." D'Alembert cannot approve of Rousseau's attempt to understand the present through the recovery of the image of an ideal natural man. Rousseau's insistence on telling us that social man is not natural man but a corrupted man, and that the loss of man's primitive and original perfection is not his fault but the result of intercourse with his fellow men, is useless: "You want, I will tell him, to educate a child who must live among monsters, and you want to make of him a giant. This is not feasible; the giant will shock the monsters, who will all rally against him and chase him away under a hail of stones. Make then of your child a monster like the others, but perhaps as little a monster as possible, enough of a monster not to be disliked by his fellow monsters, but not enough to be disliked by himself."

D'Alembert has understood the revolutionary character of what Rousseau stands for. He himself, in the *Eléments de philosophie,* had described the mid-century as an age of unparalleled transformation in the development of mankind:

If one examines carefully the mid-point of the century in which we live, the events which excite us or at any rate occupy our minds, our customs, our achievements, and even our diversions, it is difficult not to see that in some respects a very remarkable change in our ideas is taking place, a change whose rapidity seems to promise an even greater transformation to come. . . . Spreading through nature in all directions like a river which has burst its dams, this fermentation has swept with a force of violence everything along with it which stood in its way. . . . Thus from the principles of the secular sciences to the foundations of religious revelation, from metaphysics to matters of taste, from music to morals, from the scholastic disputes of theologians to matters of trade, from the laws of princes to those of peoples, from natural law to the arbitrary laws of nations . . . everything has been discussed and analyzed, or at least mentioned.[45]

Now, just a few years later, the fire seems gone and the lights are dimming. Victory against the "enemy," wherever he may be found, is unlikely: "The true purpose of the philosopher, when he really wants to be useful, is not that of unleashing himself against evil, it is rather to find remedies and, if he cannot do otherwise, palliatives. It is not a question of defeating the enemy, for he is too entrenched in the country to undertake to chase him away. We must engage in guerrilla warfare." [46] How often did the optimism and rationalism, the geometric perfection, the faith in unlimited progress, and the universal unifying concepts of the Enlightenment narrow themselves down to a *guerre de chicane?*

In spite of the lowered sights, any development from the present was still to be a forward one: whether in a straight line or in a zig-zag line, there would be progress toward a future of happiness and freedom, since man was at last succeeding through arts and sciences in creating the necessary foundations. This was precisely what Rousseau did not accept: a future based on what man was doing today would be dark indeed.

Grimm provides another illustration of the difficulties of rec-

[45] "Tableau de l'esprit humain au milieu du XVIII° siècle," *Eléments de philosophie,* in *Mélanges de littérature, d'histoire et de philosophie* (Amsterdam, 1759), IV, 2–6. Translated and quoted by Ernst Cassirer, *The Philosophy of the Enlightenment* (Princeton, 1951), 3–4.

[46] D'Alembert's comments on Rousseau are taken from his *Jugement sur la Nouvelle Héloïse* and *Jugement sur Emile,* probably written in 1762. *Oeuvres posthumes* (Paris, 1799), I, 121, 123, 125, 128, 133–4.

onciling the Enlightenment and Rousseau. As a brilliant and indefatigable transmitter of ideas, news, and gossip, his words are the faithful echo of the prevailing thoughts of his times and of the moral corruption before power and money which sometimes accompanied them. Grimm is fascinated by the style, the polemical power and wit of Rousseau. He is also impressed by the "very philosophical" discussion of the origins of languages and of love in the *Discourse on Inequality*. These unexpected glimpses into prehistory are wonderfully entertaining. Still dwelling on the remote past, Grimm likes Rousseau's analysis of the state of nature which avoids modern confusions, of which Hobbes and Pufendorf are particularly guilty: "The citizen of Geneva is right to reproach all philosophers who have thought about this important matter for their failure to have a clear idea of the state of nature, to have always confused it with the civil state and to have continuously transferred to the state of nature ideas which they had found in society." [47]

Grimm obviously does not realize the importance of what he has said and must still believe he is praising Rousseau on topics lost in the night of time and with no bearing whatever on the present. For when it comes to the present, according to Grimm, Rousseau is clearly wrong. His picture of the woes of modern society is no more than a "masterpiece of eloquence." His criticisms of arts and sciences are fallacious, for the progress of civilization cannot be stopped. Rousseau has confused the animal condition with the condition of man. In persisting in his attack on the modern world in the preface to *Narcisse*, he is simply worsening the bad impression already produced by a bad play. Rousseau is a misanthrope: "One is tempted to say that he has taken it upon himself to make men hate their existence and that

[47] Grimm, *Correspondance littéraire*, II, 105; III, 58, 54.

he never talks to them about reason and happiness, except to warn them that they are a thousand leagues away from them and that they will never get near them." [48]

The list could be lengthened. The names of d'Holbach [49] and Helvétius would appear on it. Rousseau's rejection of utilitarianism, atheism, determinism, would be seen as a primary reason of conflict. Often too the rupture could be brought back to the way in which the present was being used or interpreted. Conversely, it was surely not by accident that Rousseau found himself much closer to those writers who, beginning with inquiries into the origins of mankind, had either reached conclusions which Rousseau felt supported his own views, or had simply been more cautious or open-minded in drawing from them inferences applying to the present condition of man.

Condillac and Buffon belong to this group. Rousseau's friendship with Condillac, the brother of Mably, went back to Rousseau's early years in Paris. It was never disturbed and a third of a century later, in 1776, Rousseau, having failed in his attempt to leave his manuscript of the *Dialogues* on the altar of Notre Dame, turned for help to Condillac, who was, "it is true, philoso-

[48] *Ibid.*, III, 58; II, 320–2; IV, 395. For a somewhat different summary of Grimm's attitude toward Rousseau, by Gagnebin and Raymond, cf. O.C. I, 1499–1501.

[49] Rousseau sometimes describes his enemies as "Holbackiens" (*Confessions*, bk. ix, O.C. I, 438) and the "conspiracy" of his former friends as "Holbachique" (*ibid.*, 401). He had found d'Holbach's friendship, acquired through Diderot, a curious one: "All my friends became his friends, which was natural enough: but none of his became mine, which was less so" (*Confessions*, bk. viii, O.C. I, 369). At that time, his uneasiness derived from d'Holbach's great wealth. "You are too wealthy," he had once told him (*ibid.*, 371). D'Holbach's materialism was to find its expression in the *Système de la nature* of 1770. On d'Holbach and Rousseau, cf. Pierre Naville, *D'Holbach et la philosophie scientifique au XVIIIe siècle* (Paris, 1943), 72–83.

pher, author, academician," but who was also honest.[50] Rousseau had found Condillac's *Essai sur l'origine des connaissances humaines* of 1746 of great help in this study on the origins of languages. If Rousseau cannot just repeat what Condillac had said in his research, even though it confirms his views and has given him his initial ideas, it is because there are discrepancies in their analyses. The chief is that while Condillac presupposes "some kind of society already established among the inventors of language," for Rousseau this is the very question around which the issue revolves.[51]

Buffon was another contemporary who raised the questions and doubts Rousseau felt had to be raised. Hence, his gratitude for someone who had, more than Condillac, contributed to his understanding and his fund of ideas about early man. Buffon's *Histoire naturelle* had begun to appear in 1749, at the very moment when Rousseau was beginning to concern himself with the problem of original man. By 1753, when Rousseau was writing his *Discourse on Inequality*, the sixth volume of Buffon's work had been published, dealing with the natural history of man. In it one could perhaps find the beginning of a solution to a problem not unworthy of the Aristotle of the century: "What experiments might be necessary to obtain a knowledge of natural man; and how could we carry out these experiments within society?" [52] He had found in Buffon an analysis of the issue

---

[50] *Histoire du précédent écrit*, O.C. I, 981.

[51] *Discours sur l'origine de l'inégalité*, O.C. III, 146. On Condillac's influence and the whole problem of Rousseau's sources, cf. Jean Morel, "Recherches sur les Sources du *Discours de l'inégalité*," *Annales*, V (1909), 119–98. For a perceptive discussion of the importance of contemporary studies on language and the relationships and differences between Condillac, Diderot, and Rousseau on these matters, see Franco Venturi, *La Jeunesse de Diderot* (Paris, 1939), 239–40, 262 ff.

[52] O.C. III, 123–4.

astonishingly close to his own: "Savage man is . . . of all the animals the most singular, the least known, the most difficult of description, but we distinguish so little between what nature alone has given us and what has been communicated to us by education, art and example . . . that it would not be surprising if we failed to recognize ourselves entirely in the portrait of a savage, if he were presented to us with the true colors and with the natural traits alone which make up his character." If the philosopher could really look at a savage, "perhaps he could clearly see that virtue belongs to savage man more than to civilized man, and that vice was born only in society." [53] Just as clearly Rousseau valued the anthropologists of his time more than the philosophers. They were helping him more in the concrete tasks at hand.

But the dominant figure in this sketch must be that of Diderot. Rousseau and Diderot: the two "enemy brothers." There was their strong youthful friendship and their common work, the close early identity of views followed by a widening gap. The bleak and long silences. In the end, Diderot's recognition of the ambivalence of his own position. In sum, Diderot's relationship with Rousseau provides a most fascinating instance of the tribulations of literature and philosophy in the eighteenth century.

The two friends were tied by the closest links for more than a dozen years, and during all that time one looked to the other

[53] I owe this quotation to Starobinski, O.C. III, 1295–6; cf. also, 1316–7. Every student of Rousseau is indebted to him for his brilliant annotations of the *Discourse on Inequality*. Starobinski writes (1295) that "the idea of an experimental reconstruction of the origins," accepted in the eighteenth century, was derived chiefly from Locke and from the experiments he advocates to prove that man has no innate ideas. One could add that this is an instance of Locke's ambiguity. For in the fields of society and government the idea is certainly abandoned. And this is one of the reasons why Rousseau's ideas could find such meager support in the *Two Treatises*.

with the affection and interest that Rousseau makes very plain in the *Confessions*. Nothing could exceed the agonies of Rousseau when Diderot was jailed, and the usefulness of his friend's advice for the *Discourse on Inequality* was very great.[54] In those same years Diderot probably learned a great deal from Rousseau,[55] and until the early fifties the similarity of their views was striking. They were both moved to denounce the weaknesses of contemporary society, "a style of life . . . a morality which only recognizes . . . useful virtues and prudence." [56] They both accepted Montesquieu's views on the classical city. In his articles in the *Encyclopédie* on agriculture, man, and the legislator, it is Diderot who laments luxury, progress, property. If there is immediate agreement at Vincennes between Rousseau and Diderot on the proper answer to give to the academy of Dijon, it is also because Diderot as well would like to deal a blow to the "idolatry of intelligence." [57]

This community of views did not last. While Rousseau refused to modify his position, Diderot shifted his grounds. He may never have taken the "paradoxes" of the *First Discourse* with the deadly seriousness of Rousseau. His style of life changed, and if a certain incompatibility existed "between the thoughts of Diderot on the one end and social and cultural life on the other, one cannot deny that Diderot is incomparably more at ease in the society of his time than Rousseau." [58] He now

[54] *Confessions*, bk. vii, *O.C.* I, 348; bk. viii, *O.C.* I, 389. Cf. Jean Guéhenno, *Jean-Jacques: En Marge des Confessions, 1712–1750* (Paris, 1948), 226 ff.

[55] Proust, *Diderot et l'Encyclopédie*, 341–2.

[56] Antoine Adam, "Rousseau et Diderot," *Revue des sciences humaines* (1949), 21.

[57] *Ibid.*, 22. In a few pages Adam gives an excellent analysis of the relationship between Diderot and Rousseau. He also attributes to Grimm's thought more substance than is usually the case (22–3).

[58] Herbert Dieckmann, Introduction to his edition of Diderot, *Supplément au Voyage de Bougainville* (Geneva, 1955), xciii–iv. Dieckmann

joins the "enemy." Hobbes and Voltaire, the philosopher and the man of affairs, now seem to him to be telling the truth about human nature and government. The economists are also providing data which make attractive, at least for certain practical purposes, the idea of utility and that of a society based on the satisfaction of individual interests.[59]

In his *Apologie de l'Abbé de Prades,* Diderot in effect abandons Rousseau on many of the issues on which they had expressed parallel views.[60] From then on the disagreement deepens, even though a kind of debate continues. The *Droit naturel* is Diderot's answer to the *économie politique,*[61] but Rousseau's answer to the *Droit naturel* is never published. The dialogue ends with the break of 1757.[62] By then, the end of friendship is

---

adds that Diderot met this residual incompatibility by the device of "soon stopping the publication of those of his works which expressed his personal thought and which he had most at heart" (*ibid*). Or as Vernière writes in his tormented appraisal of Diderot's politics, his eulogies of Catherine the Great are public, while his criticisms remain hidden (Diderot, *Oeuvres politiques,* edited with Introduction and notes by Paul Vernière [Paris, 1963], xxxvi).

[59] Diderot's anxiety for money and what he did for it make Vernière think of Rousseau, "of his poverty, of his pride filled with defiance towards the powerful of this world" (*ibid.,* xxxvii).

[60] Adam, *Diderot et Rousseau,* 26–7.

[61] René Hubert, *Rousseau et l'Encyclopédie* (Paris, 1928), 26–29.

[62] On the quarrel that ended Rousseau's friendship with Diderot, Grimm, and the other members of the "holbachian conspiracy," and that started Rousseau on his introspective path, the authentic text of a key item has now become available: *Histoire de Madame de Montbrillant,* Texte intégral publié pour la première fois . . . par Georges Roth, 3 vols. (Paris, 1951). In a careful and judicious summing up (I, vii–xlii), Roth recounts the extraordinary history of this manuscript known since it was first "published" in Paris in 1818 as the *Mémoires et correspondance de Madame d'Epinay.* In its first version, it was a primary source of the legends and the fantasies that grew around Rousseau in the nineteenth century, until Frederika MacDonald published what Roth calls her "capital" work, *J. J. Rousseau, a New Criticism,* 2 vols. (London, 1906), the

matched by a contrast of ideas which is not eliminated by Diderot's restlessness when confronted with the outcome of the theories and practices of his friends, both philosophers and kings. Two points will be retained as of special importance.

Natural man and the state of nature appeared to Diderot as something that could be retrieved. Having accepted, unlike Rousseau, existing social arrangements, which might be improved upon but never set aside, Diderot felt that in exchange for his surrender to the pressures of the immediate world, he should find an alternate world, not outside of history or of time, but available here and now. His *Supplément au Voyage de Bougainville* portrays Tahiti as a model of perfect and happy life, as the island where man could seek refuge. Here are two worlds. They are both real, and man can take his choice. But they are separate and without any influence upon one other. Having given up the possibility of a revolutionary transformation of the world in which he lives, Diderot points to the remote islands as the alternative. This lack of any dialectical tension between the two worlds or between the present and the future, Rousseau finds unacceptable: the past is gone, but we hold the future in our hands. No escape or transfer is possible and we must deal with the society in which we live.[63]

---

fruit of the first critical inspection ever undertaken of the manuscript, its insertions, corrections, falsifications. Also indispensable are the two works of Henri Guillemin, "Les Affaires de l'Ermitage," *Annales,* XXIX (1941–1942), 59–258, and *Un Homme, deux ombres* (Geneva, 1943). A balanced and, we may hope, final judgment on the matter is provided by Jean Fabre, "Deux Frères ennemis, Diderot et Jean-Jacques," *Diderot Studies,* III (Geneva, 1961), 194–203. Fabre makes the admirable point that what Diderot and Madame d'Epinay concocted was no more than a secret weapon that was never used and whose authorship was not concealed.

[63] The most sensitive analysis of this issue is that of Dieckmann, "Introduction," *op. cit.,* lxxxv–xciv. Speaking of Rousseau, Dieckmann distinguishes between the real and the ideal states of nature: "The first is

Diderot's determinism often lacked the will to action, or a belief in the autonomy and the moral freedom of man to create his own surroundings. His letter of 1756 to Landois shows this clearly. Free will is a meaningless word and "there cannot be any free beings. . . . We are only what is determined by the chain of events." When we act, "the motive is only external, foreign." What deceives us "is the prodigious variety of our actions, added to our habit from birth of confusing the voluntary with the free . . . if there is no freedom, there is no action deserving praise or blame. . . . There is only one set of causes, properly speaking: physical causes." [64]

Rousseau was then writing in the *Nouvelle Héloïse*: "I hear a great deal of reasoning against the freedom of man, and I despise all these sophisms, because a reasoner can well prove to me that I am not free, the internal sentiment, stronger than all his arguments, will forever deny them; and no matter what decision I take in any deliberation whatever, I am convinced that I am free to take the contrary decision. All these subtleties of the school are vain, because they prove too much . . . to listen to those people, even God is not free, and the word of freedom has no meaning. . . . They begin by supposing that every intelligent being is purely passive, and then deduce from this supposition consequences to prove that he is not active. . . . We are supposing that we are active and free; we feel that we are." [65]

---

placed in the past; it has been lost. The ideal state of nature, on the contrary, continues to exist within us, but buried, hidden, repressed and rejected. By reference to the present this ideal state is the norm by which the condition of civilization is judged; at the same time, it is projected into the future as the goal towards which mankind must aspire" (lxxxix).

[64] Letter to Landois, June 29, 1756, in Diderot, *Correspondance*, Roth, ed. (Paris, 1955), I, 213-15.

[65] *La Nouvelle Héloïse*, i, 7, O.C. II, 683. Roth quotes part of this passage in a footnote, and raises the question of whether Diderot's letter was an answer to it (Diderot, *Correspondance*, I, 213). Bernard Guyon,

Against these radical differences on the way in which real history and ideal history were to be related and the role and freedom of man in arranging for a possible meeting of the two, other contrasts appear small.[66] What must be underlined, however, is Diderot's refusal to be narrow-minded or dogmatic. "He is neither Franklin nor Babeuf," [67] and he cannot forget Rousseau. Diderot was never quite at ease on the materialistic and deterministic foundations of his thought. The publication in 1773 of Helvétius' *De l'Homme* moved him to a strong refutation of a book whose principal thesis he could well call his own. But Diderot finds that materialism alone cannot deal adequately with human nature. The complexities of man escape a philosophy which Helvétius pushes to excessive generalizations. Rousseau is wrong and Helvétius is right. But this is not enough: "Rousseau's principles are false and his consequences true; while your principles are true and your consequences false." Diderot rejects Rousseau's view of man and society, but in the end Rousseau's view of man *in* society is preferable. Rousseau's philosophy is

---

in his annotations to *La Nouvelle Héloïse,* feels that in it Rousseau is alluding to *De l'Esprit* by Helvétius, who was at one with Diderot. But Guyon seems to agree with Mornet "who invites us to see in 'those people' and 'the school' not just one man, Helvétius, but an entire group of enemies of freedom. Must we go back to Spinoza? Perhaps, but we feel through these lines a polemical wind aiming at persons who are close, living, dangerous, at whose head Helvétius, d'Holbach, Diderot, are marching" (*O.C.* II, 1779).

[66] Proust, *Diderot et l'Encyclopédie,* makes a number of interesting points on Diderot's distinction between strong and weak, as against Rousseau's between rich and poor (372); on the general will (388–9; cf. infra, p. 172); on Diderot and physiocracy (466–7); on the support by Diderot of the "interests of a property-owning enlightened elite to whom a monarchy, politically absolute and liberal in thought and in the economic domain, was useful" (510).

[67] Vernière, in the Introduction to Diderot, *Oeuvres philosophiques,* IV.

made up of "bits and pieces," while Helvétius has a system. But "perhaps I would rather be him than you." [68]

Not only is the theory badly developed: it is badly applied in practice as it leads Helvétius to a defense of enlightened despotism. The arbitrary government of a "just prince" is always bad. The right of opposition is sacred: "Without it the subjects are like a herd whose protests are despised, on the excuse that it is being led toward fat pastures." [69] And the view that boredom is an evil almost as bad as poverty, is the view of a "wealthy man who has never had to fight for his dinner."

Rousseau cannot be dismissed. Diderot makes one final move to get closer to Rousseau and to repudiate his own world. The year is 1781 and Grimm is the target. In a letter unearthed by Dieckmann, [70] Grimm appears as a career man, without taste, reduced to the sad condition of servant of the powerful. In general, says Diderot, men of letters offer a pitiful sight. Voltaire is a coward. Linguet is a liar. And why is Rousseau so much better than the rest? "Why is Rousseau eloquent and Linguet only a rhetorician? Because, consequent to certain principles, I feel that the first is true, even when he speaks falsely, while the second, without principles, is false, even when he speaks truly. Rousseau lies only in the first line; from the first line to the last

[68] Diderot, *Réfutation suivie de l'ouvrage d'Helvétius intitulé l'Homme, Oeuvres philosophiques*, 575–6. Vernière writes "Against the 'behaviorism' of Helvétius, Diderot relies not only on Montaigne and the entire tradition of humanism, but also on the new sciences which reveal the infinite complexities of the world of life" (558). Fabre, "Deux Frères ennemis" (204–7) is very illuminating. The *Réfutation* was written in 1774.

[69] *Réfutation*, 619–20. The prince praised by Helvétius was Frederick. Already in 1771 Diderot had launched a violent (but private) attack on this particular pet of the philosophers in his *Pages contre un tyran* (*Oeuvres politiques*, 135–48), first published by F. Venturi in 1937.

[70] Cf. his *Inventaire*.

Linguet is a liar." What Grimm is doing is to expose to public contempt those of our citizens "whose enemies have of all time occupied the temples, the palaces, and the tribunals." [71]

"Death has been merciful with Diderot. It has given him time not to forgive or to repent, not above all to forget, but to choose." [72]

In the end, then, the issue was not chiefly one of personal conflicts, but of ideas: "The confrontation was between two conceptions of the world." [73] Rousseau became the enemy, because he was challenging current ideas about progress. The result was "a continuing systematic attempt on the part of the philosophers to discredit him." [74] The opposition was a deep one, as Amiel saw nearly a century ago: "He was for God against d'Holbach, he was for providence against Voltaire, he found a soul in man against La Mettrie, he was for moral freedom against Diderot, for disinterested virtue against Helvétius, for spontaneity against Condillac, for the rights of the heart against

[71] *Lettre apologétique de l'Abbé Raynal à M. Grimm,* in *Oeuvres philosophiques,* 631–3. Diderot offers a bit of advice to Grimm: "You can continue to curry the favor of the powerful . . . but do not be their apologist." For, when judged by the tribunal of God, Grimm could be thrown "into the cauldron where both the protectors and the damned race of the protected will roast for all time." Diderot must, however, agree with Grimm's possible answer that "it is better to be roasted in the other world than in this one."

[72] Fabre's conclusion of "Deux Frères ennemis," 213. Fabre ends with a final anecdote of 1782 when, in re-reading his *Lettre sur les aveugles,* Diderot "gives back to the heart all his rights. In this secret domain Jean-Jacques has of necessity his place." And so Diderot writes: "I could cite a blind man who arranges his flowers with the delicacy claimed by J.-J. Rousseau when he was confiding to his friends, seriously or in fun, his plan of opening a school in which he would give lessons to the flower-girls of Paris" (*ibid.*).

[73] Guillemin, in *J.-J. Rousseau et son oeuvre,* xxix.

[74] De Jouvenel, "Rousseau the Pessimistic Evolutionist," 84.

Maupertuis, against the communism of Morelly, against the absolutism of Hobbes." [75]

Indeed, Rousseau's protest is directed "against the very essence of contemporary society." [76] Against the prevailing corruption, he wants to protect his freedom and independence. Against greed and wealth he wants to be poor. Against unbelief and skepticism, he is anxious to reaffirm a belief in God and a faith which his communion with the *encyclopédistes*, "far from weakening, had only strengthened." [77]

Both Rousseau and the *philosophes* saw in Hobbes the fountainhead of eighteenth-century utilitarianism. Man was a mass of appetites to be satisfied, showing his fundamental traits already in the state of nature. Contemporary thinking envisaged in essence a manipulative state which by skillfully allowing satisfaction of those needs maintained peace and progress. Rousseau, even under conditions of a "perfect hobbism," which, however, he felt could never be realized, saw only tensions, degeneration, and crisis as its consequences. Both sides saw despotism as inevitable: one imagined it would be exercised with a light hand, such as would not hamper the growth of freedom, of culture, science, and wealth. The other identified in it a demoralizing factor, favoring the grossest cupidity and destroying the possibility of a self-reliant citizen democracy.

The century had started with a steady development of hobbesian utilitarian individualism, adapted to the still strong mercantilistic residues of the times. Mandeville's *Fable of the Bees* [78] had appeared to nearly everybody as a wonderful way of recon-

[75] H. F. Amiel, "Caractéristique générale de Rousseau," 44–5.

[76] Starobinski, J.-J. *Rousseau, la transparence et l'obstacle*, 44.

[77] *Confessions*, bk. viii, O.C. I, 362, 380, 392.

[78] First published in abbreviated form in 1706; first full edition, 1714; second edition 1723; French translation 1740. The modern edition is by F. B. Kaye (Oxford, 1924).

ciling the individual autonomy needed to satisfy private interest with the retention of a guiding public hand. Mandeville was not a precursor of *laisser-faire*. The title page slogan, "private vices, publick benefits" meant that "private vices, by the dexterous management of a skillful politician might be turned into publick benefits." "They are silly people who imagine that the good of the whole is consistent with the good of every individual." [79]

This is the political and economic society Melon has in mind in his essay on commerce of 1734. We are dealing with a corrupt world, and the legislator must exploit human passions for the profit of society. Luxury is the necessary consequence of a properly policed society. Indeed, by fostering it, we can hope to eliminate some of the negative aspects of human behavior: drunkenness is now limited to the countryside, where luxury is still absent. Luxury provides well-being, and this is necessary for the multitude which cannot be kept happy with glory alone and spartan virtues. There is the economic argument, too, that the poor are nourished and kept working by growing luxury. Whatever might be said about religion trying to destroy luxury, the state must exploit it. [80]

Rousseau found these ideas shocking and said that they represented a total reversal of western thinking. Voltaire liked them so much he put Melon to verse in *Le Mondain* two years later. [81]

[79] Mandeville, *A Letter to Dion* (1732), edited with an Introduction by Jacob Viner (Los Angeles, 1953), 36–7, 49. Viner is convincing in his demonstration of the mercantilistic leanings of Mandeville. He also reminds us that Helvétius, in *De l'Esprit*, echoes Mandeville when he writes that personal interests would lead to a good society only if "manipulated with skill by a clever legislator" (15).

[80] J. F. Melon, *Essai politique sur le commerce* (Paris, 1734), ch. ix, "Du Luxe," 129–30, 132–6, 150–1.

[81] In 1737 Voltaire followed with the *Défense du Mondain* and the *Lettre à M. le Comte de Saxe*, both apologies for luxury. In 1738 he wrote the *Observations sur MM Jean Lass, Melon et Dutot, sur le commerce, le luxe, les monnaies et les impôts*. Voltaire likes Dutot even

When Hume's essays were first translated into French in 1754, his more moderate arguments on economic man and luxury and his reservations about Mandeville were masked by long footnotes added by the translator, quoting Melon or indirectly attacking Rousseau, who by then had made his views known. It was ridiculous and useless, said the translator, to attack sciences and praise ignorance or to go about dressed like a "quaker." What Melon has written on luxury disposes of all these arguments.[82]

Without question the Hobbes-Mandeville-Melon-Voltaire line of thought, this extraordinary mixture of philosophy, economics, and literature, offered the most attractive explanation and justification of current life. Even a moralist such as Vauvenargues, in a *Discourse on the Inequality of Wealth*, written in 1745 but unpublished until the end of the century, spoke of natural men as "monsters," destroying one another through "frightful slaughter." Early man was indeed the "shame of mankind," given to "impious customs." When, later, inequality of wealth was established, it was on "just foundations." All that was needed to make rich and poor equal was the obligation of charity.[83] The voices raised against the all-encompassing sweep of doctrines and practices of this kind were few and faint. Fénelon could say that luxury corrupts a nation;[84] Claville that an excessive attachment to wealth is the most tyrannical passion.[85] Morelly could link greed and property and suggest that an

---

better than Melon. Dutot's work, *Réflexions politiques sur les finances et le commerce,* was a "hard money" man's answer to Melon's "inflationary" tendencies: cf. Paul Harsin's Introduction, xvii–xxi, to his edition of Dutot, 2 vols. (Paris, 1935).

[82] David Hume, *Discours politiques,* 2 vols. (Paris, 1754), II, 81–3. Melon is quoted at II, 52, 63, 75, 85, 92.

[83] *Discours sur l'inégalité des richesses, Oeuvres complètes* (Paris, 1806), II, 201, 202, 205.

[84] *Plan de gouvernement* (1711), *Oeuvres* (Paris, 1824), XXII, 595.

[85] *Traité du vrai mérite de l'homme* (Paris, 1734), 308–11.

ideal republic would abolish property.[86] But no echo of these voices could be heard. Montesquieu himself was ineffective, because the *Persian Letters* were then more important than the *Spirit of the Laws*.

The physiocrats might be opposed to luxury for reasons Rousseau could in part make his own: it weakened the only productive class, that of agricultural workers.[87] But their approach to economic problems was in the mainstream of the times, and Quesnay wrote in his article on Grains in the *Encyclopédie* that expensive bread would keep small people working hard and away from laziness.[88] Whether the physiocrats, by saying that only land was profitable, were trying to achieve a static agricultural society or whether they were trying to develop modern economic policies, they were certainly satisfied with traditional despotic political forms, softened only by a partial introduction of judicial control. In any case, they stood opposed to the revolutionary thought of Rousseau, hidden from view by his seeming defense of an obsolete economic system.[89]

Apart from the specific content of doctrines of utility and of pragmatic political arrangements, Rousseau judged the world around him as one of deception, one to be measured in the light of the contrast between the shiny surface and the infernal depths of the human soul, the appearance of politeness and the being of crude selfishness. Late in life, he looks back on his former friends

[86] Cf. Grimm, *Correspondance littéraire*, II, 219.

[87] M. R. de Labriole-Rutherford, "L'Evolution de la notion du luxe depuis Mandeville jusqu'à la Révolution," *Studies on Voltaire*, XXVI (Geneva, 1963), 1034.

[88] Henri Denis, "Deux Collaborateurs économiques de l'*Encyclopédie*: Quesnay et Rousseau," *La Pensée* (Sept.–Oct., 1951), 46–7.

[89] Fetscher, *Rousseaus Politische Philosophie*, offers this summary: The physiocrats used traditional political forms to achieve revolutionary economic goals while Rousseau pushed revolutionary political forms to maintain traditional economic and social relationships (257).

and asks: Am I forced to choose between a "rootless and fruitless morality," "pompously displayed in books or in some noisy actions on the stage, but of which nothing ever penetrates the heart or reason," and a "secret and cruel morality, internal doctrine of all their initiates to which the other morality serves only as a mask?" [90]

No such choice was possible in a world in crisis, in which progress meant the disappearance of artisans, the beginnings of modern industry, and the extension of mass poverty; in which cities and mines were making life unfit for human beings; in which land "enclosures," held up by Rousseau to the contempt of mankind, were driving the peasants to ruin and to vain protest.[91]

[90] *Les Rêveries du promeneur solitaire,* 3e Promenade, *O.C.* I, 1022.
[91] Morazé, *La France bourgeoise,* 76.

III

Rousseau Seeks His Way

WE are in the orchard of Madame de Warens in the countryside of Savoie. Rousseau is ill and considers himself to be near death. Indeed, it is because he thinks he is dying that he feels compelled to commit some of his thoughts to paper, in poetic form. Were he to enjoy good health he would feel a sense of responsibility for his activities and he would have to work for the good of society. But since his life is coming to an end, he is entitled to do what he pleases. "How many people repleted with wealth and brimming with health do just that throughout their lives?" In any case, Rousseau tells us, we shall have to see whether those who may criticize my poetry are ready to employ me to do something better.[1]

At twenty-five, Rousseau already feels the vague hostility of the society he knows he will have soon to face. His years at Les Charmettes are the years of innocence, solitude, and peace, of happy days spent in a pastoral landscape of murmuring waters and flowering trees. He has learned to look without regret and envy at the "frivolous taste of senseless mortals." His mind is groping for the order he knows is still missing from his life.

[1] *Le Verger de Madame la Baronne de Warens*, Avertissement, *O.C.* II, 1123–4. *Le Verger*, published in 1739, was probably written in 1737.

Geneva is still present in his mind as a fixed point to which again and again he will come back in spite of the difficulty of fitting the small and no longer democratic community into his ideal views of man and society. Geneva is the dear fatherland which must be protected from its present follies and brought back to the wisdom of the old ways. Geneva can still avoid slavery and recover the ancient spirit of community. Her citizens will be happy if by recovering the faith of their ancestors they will try to be as free as they were.

He has spent these years of peace and happiness reading a great deal [2] and reflecting on the mistakes of men and on the good and bad things they do. And in *The Orchard of Madame de Warens* he summarizes his thoughts. He has tried to enter into the hidden principles which move the universe. He has observed nature, which has appeared to him touching and always pure in the *Cleveland* of the Abbé Prevost. He is helped in this task by Socrates and the divine Plato. With Leibniz, Malebranche, and Newton he can examine the laws of bodies and of human thought. In reading Locke he can see the development of the history of ideas. He has also been fumbling with Descartes and his aberrations. The Latin classics from Horace to Plutarch to Cicero occupy a large place in his reading, as do the modern from Pope to Barclay to Fénelon. Claville and Saint Aubin are also included. He finds Voltaire moving and his writings will always be dear to his heart. But, Rousseau adds, "my taste will always refuse any frivolous essay whose author only wishes to please the spirit. He can well abound in brilliant antitheses, he may well spread flowers everywhere. . . . My heart rather than my spirit has to be satisfied." [3]

[2] "I soon realized that all these authors were in nearly constant contradiction among themselves. . . . My head was confused and I was making no progress." Rousseau then decided to read only for the purpose of accumulating a "store of ideas" (*Confessions*, O.C. I, 237).

[3] In 1735 he reassures his father that he has developed a system of study to add to his fund of useful knowledge as well as to "form my heart

He is not frightened by poverty, a condition which he finds natural to him. He asks what is the reason to do good in his century. Is there anybody worthy of being rescued from the ranks of the poor? Is it possible to be honest and poor? Isn't it better to use wealth in order to enjoy the pleasures of life rather than to be charitable? The conclusion is that it is much better to let the rich follow these "frightful sentiments," to stay altogether clear of their influence, and to be ready, if necessary, "to face poverty." [4]

From the beginning, then, Rousseau is haunted by the theme of poverty and wealth and has no sympathy with the widespread notion of his times that there are advantages in poverty and that the poor ought to be happy in the knowledge that they are making it possible for the rich to carry on. In a letter written in 1741 to Bordes, his friend then, his adversary later, he suggested that there was no wisdom where poverty ruled: "Under the weight of hunger, defeated worth allows virtue to be extinguished in a sad heart. So many pompous discourses on the happiness of indigence are clearly born in the midst of plenty: clever philosopher, careful always to preach the virtues he does not need." [5]

Later, Rousseau was to maintain the opposite theory that only in the poor can the authentic qualities of man be kept alive. Here he is still puzzled by the paradox of poverty exalted by the rich and the false piety of men who praise what they refuse to accept for themselves. He is ready to face poverty, but he is worried about the degradation it entails.

In any case, he had resolved to use as his guide the work of Father Lamy, *Entretiens sur les sciences*,[6] having been impressed

---

to wisdom and virtue," And in 1736 he tells another correspondent that the purpose of his studies is that "of forming my heart and of cultivating my spirit" (C.G. I, 32–4, 47); C.C. I, 31–4, 42.

[4] *Le Verger, O.C.* II, 1124–9.

[5] Letter to Bordes, 1741, *O.C.* II, 1131.

[6] *Confessions*, bk. vi, *O.C.* I, 232.

by Lamy's views on history. History was useful above all to fortify one's own resignation before the follies of man and the tribulations of life. From history, Lamy writes and Rousseau transcribes in his *Chronology,* "we recognize the malignity and misery of men, their vanity, we learn the contempt with which we must consider wealth and we learn that great fortunes lead often to terrible catastrophes." [7]

The "illustrious" Fénelon, on the other hand, has views on history to which Rousseau objects, for they introduce a cosmopolitanism which is of little value. Rousseau is convinced that history must be "one of the principal parts of the study of an honest man." And when Fénelon writes, "I love mankind more than my country, my country more than my family and my family more than myself," he is expressing sentiments which ought to be common to all men.

But to Rousseau this cosmic vision lacks the concreteness which must be attached to the historical experience. How useful to his community is the man who harbors such humane but ill-defined notions? And he asks: "Are we permitted to ignore the things that are of interest to us and to our families? Should we not be fully informed of our own affairs, and is there one man of common sense who would refuse to take any part in what goes on around him?" [8]

It is with these questions in mind that Rousseau faces the problems of education and writes the two essays of 1740 and 1743,[9] in which he gives us an anticipation both of some of his

[7] Quoted by Rousseau in his *Chronologie universelle, ou histoire générale des temps,* dated circa 1737 and first published by T. L. Dufour, "Pages inédites de J.-J. Rousseau," *Annales,* I (1905), 213–20. Lamy is quoted at 217.

[8] *Ibid.,* 215.

[9] *Projet pour l'éducation de M. de Sainte-Marie* (1740), *Oeuvres de J.-J. Rousseau,* ed. E. A. Lequien (Paris, 1821), XII, 3–27; *Fragment du mémoire présenté à M. de Ste Marie pour l'éducation de son fils* (1743), *C.G.* I, 367–79.

later ideas on education and of the *Discourse on Arts and Sciences* as well.

The problems of education are external and internal. They are external insofar as they relate to the specific task of making the young man a member of his society. They are internal—and these are the most important problems—as they relate to the proper training and development of the mind of the student. The ultimate end of education is to make of the student a "perfect man."

The best way of dealing with the external requirements of education is to make sure, from the earliest possible moment, that the young person is not cut off from the world and does not follow a solitary path which will inevitably make him unfit for life. Hence, the need to encourage active participation in the activities and intellectual exchanges of the groups within which the student finds himself. And this exposure to the world cannot take place at too early an age.

Whether Rousseau is himself a teacher capable of carrying out education along these lines he cannot say. He is aware of certain traits of a negative kind, chiefly of his inability to engage actively in that social intercourse he is recommending, because essentially he does not care for the opinion of others. Hence he finds it very difficult to acquire an inclination to social life. Although Rousseau accepts the requirements of the social life of his times, he does not accept the extreme way of that life. He feels that the student who will enter society should be able to control himself.

There is general agreement that the purpose of the education of a young person is to make him happy. But the central issue is how to attain that happiness. Rousseau sees a choice confronting the educator: he may try to satisfy the passions of his pupil, or he may try to moderate them. His decision cannot be in doubt. The immoderate satisfaction of pleasure is in itself a source of uneasiness and unhappiness. The only way is to check passions and to remember that the convenience and the tranquility of others are

[65]

to be taken into account. It is not possible to behave as if one is alone in the world. No rational man can believe that he can satisfy his desires without limit.

But the major task confronting the educator is the development of the mind of his pupil, and here Rousseau proposes as the proper task of education the development of the heart, the judgment, and the spirit, in that order. It is only from right sentiments, buttressed by reason, that a mind capable of dealing with the problems of life can be formed. How wrong are those educators who think that the accumulation of information is the only object of a good education. Rousseau agrees with Molière that "a learned idiot is more of an idiot than an ignorant idiot." Common sense comes before the abstract constructions of reason: "It appears indeed that common sense depends much more upon the sentiments of the heart than from the enlightenment of the spirit and it is a fact that the most learned and enlightened people are not always those who conduct themselves best in the affairs of life." [10] What matters is "to think rightly rather than to know much." [11]

In the light of these principles, what is a proper curriculum of studies? There must be no cluttering of the mind of the young with a multiplicity of precepts about religion and morality. It is not in this way that the pupil can acquire "solid principles which will guide his conduct for the rest of his life. . . . Rather than tiring his memory with the detail of laws and duties, one should dispose his spirit and his heart to know them and to appreciate them as the occasion will arise."

The same rule applies in the teaching of history and geography, where the dryness of a mere chronological treatment should be eliminated. In any case, modern rather than ancient history should be taught. Also to be eliminated as useless are rhetoric, logic, and scholastic philosophy.

[10] *Oeuvres*, 1821 ed., XII, 16.
[11] Letter to d'Eybens (spring 1740), *C.G.* I, 124; *C.C.* I, 116.

The sciences, while not to be neglected, cannot "take precedence over morals," especially in a lively and restless mind. For they are of no use to man if he doesn't learn how to think straight first. "If he has had the misfortune of allowing his heart to be corrupted, sciences will be in his head as weapons in the hands of a madman." (The same thought reappears ten years later in the *Discourse on Arts and Sciences,* where science is attacked as a "dangerous weapon.") Of course, some teaching of mathematics and the natural sciences will be required. But it should never outweigh the teaching of morals and of natural law, because only the knowledge of "the principles of good and evil and of the foundations on which rests the society whose member he is," is worthy of an honest man.

Always, in any case, the teaching of history will have to be the core of the right plan of education: "I will not lose sight of history as the principal object of all his studies and as that whose branches reach out the furthest over all other sciences." [12]

As Rousseau raises history to such a lofty position among human sciences, he is forging a link with Vico, both the early Vico (the defender of humane sciences) and the Vico of the *New Science* (the champion of history, because we know what we do), whose final version was even then in the making. There is the same polemical note against scientific education at the expense of a humanistic one; the same complaint against the attempt to make of man, who is a moral being, a machine subjected to the rules of mathematical thinking; the same conclusion: the placing of history on the highest rung of the ladder of human sciences, as history was the creation of man and therefore the most certain and valuable tool available to man and through which man would know himself.[13]

[12] *Oeuvres de J.-J. Rousseau,* 1821 ed., XII, 13, 12, 26.

[13] In the *Project on Education* there is a favorable reference to the Abbé de Mably's views on history, published in 1740 in the *Parallèle des Romains et des Français.* Pierre Grosclaude (*J. J. Rousseau à Lyon* [Paris,

The reading of a French translation of Pope's *Essay on Man* inspires Rousseau, in 1742, to write one of his most significant statements of these early years.[14] It is about the "chain of being" and the happy life. He does not like Pope at all on the former; he likes him very much on the latter.

The attempts to establish an unbroken continuity from the lowest to the highest forms of life, and beyond, are bound to fail: "In spite of all the efforts of Montaigne and Pope to ennoble instinct, there always remains a furious leap from there to reason." And just as the link between animal and human life breaks at this point, so the chain does not end with God, because reason will never find a relation between the creator and his work, the infinite and the finite.

But how overwhelmingly moving is Pope in what he says (not once but twenty times, we are told) about the conditions of happiness: "That vice can never be happy. That virtue delivered to sorrow knows greater happiness than vice in the midst of pleasures." And "what is needed according to Mr. Pope, beyond virtue or the peace of the heart which is its fruit, to satisfy fully the happiness of man? Only two things, health and what is

1933], 46–49) suggests that it was in this way that Rousseau first started to think about the problems of progress in arts and sciences and of luxury as they affect the condition of man. In his *Parallèle*, Mably had expressed himself strongly in favor of progress and luxury and the arts. But this was a position taken by all writers of the time and it is difficult to say whether it was Mably, or Melon or Voltaire who appeared to Rousseau as their strongest advocates. Rather what is unique is that by the time Rousseau wrote his first *Discourse,* Mably himself had altered his stand and come close to Rousseau in some essays on the Greeks and the Romans which he published in 1749 and 1751 (Grosclaude, 50). The question should then perhaps be put in reverse: Was Mably won over to a critical view of arts and sciences as a result of Rousseau's influence?

[14] Letter to de Conzié, January 17, 1742. This letter was discovered and published in 1962 by Jean Nicolas, "Une Lettre inédite de J.-J. Rousseau," *Annales historiques de la Révolution française* (1962), 385–96, text of the letter 389–96. The letter is also in C.C. I, 132–43.

necessary. Happy is the heart moderate enough to be satisfied! It is a sad spectacle to see men on earth rush after honors and chimerical goods and therefore abandon the veritable sources of happiness to which Mr. Pope tries to lead them."

Rousseau agrees entirely with what Pope is saying. But he also realizes that, if he follows Pope's advice, he will never be able to secure a foothold on the shore of fame and comfort he had dimly perceived in Lyon the year before, as tutor in one of the houses of the powerful. But he is reconciled to his fate and closes the letter by quoting, eight years before inscribing it on the title page of the *Discourse on the Arts and Sciences,* Ovid's verse: "Barbarus hic ego sum, quia non intelligor illis." [15]

When at the same time Rousseau addresses a long letter in verse to one of his friends, Parisot, there is no reason to believe that he is taking a different line. The contrast is always the same between contemporary civilization and his Genevan upbringing and the semijansenistic rigidities of his moral outlook. Rousseau's verses are evidence of the continued anxiety caused by the world with which he feared he would have to come to terms. He could not forget the outlines of an ideal state, made up of equal citizens, all sharing in the exercise of sovereign power and all aware of their duties, of the sacrifices they are going to be called upon to make, and of the heroic stature which because of this they are bound to acquire. But before his eyes are paraded the very different pleasures of taste, all the attractions of an opulent life.

This is what Rousseau tells his friend: his life is now miserable and enslaved, but his youth has been influenced by other ideas and he has been taught that he has to love his fellow men

---

[15] *Ibid.,* 391, 393, 395–6. In his interesting presentation of the letter, Nicolas reminds us that in his 1756 letter to Voltaire on Providence, Rousseau was to express an identical view on the chain of being (387); and adds that here for the first time Rousseau brings together his thoughts on nature, virtue and happiness (388).

and that he has to obey the laws of the community. He has also been taught that even though he was merely a weak and obscure citizen he had a right to share equally in the exercise of the supreme power of the city because he was a member of the sovereign. No doubt had been left in his mind that such a noble privilege had to be defended and safeguarded with the heart and the dedication of a hero and the virtues of a philosopher. He had therefore learned that the divine gift of freedom can be a fatal disease when given to evil men. In Geneva he had been nursed on these principles, not to press even for legitimate rights, but to learn how to obtain the best magistrates and how to secure the wisest laws.

The contrast offered by societies in which arts and sciences dominate is striking. Whatever "power art had produced is quite soon destroyed by luxury," while the greatest force of democracy is in its weakness: "We live without regret in a humble obscurity but at least within our soul we live in freedom." In Geneva "arts are not the support of our republic: to be just is the only politics." In words recalling those of the dedication of the discourse of 1754, Rousseau adds that Genevan magistrates, without any exhibition of glittering uniforms and luxury, are, however, not lost in the mass of the citizens. They stand out, but because of what they do.

On the other hand, he now was enjoying "more polished friends and a less savage climate together with some innocent pleasures." It is right to learn to practice virtue without excess. He is overtaken by pessimism. Why should he try to be a new Don Quixote: "It would not be good for society that there should be less inequality among its classes. . . . Destiny has regulated the estates on earth and it will surely not change them for me." [16]

[16] Letter to Parisot, July 10, 1742, O.C. II, 1136–44.

The letter to Parisot may show the uncertainties of someone who has not yet found his way. But it seems too much to say that Rousseau evokes his egalitarian and republican memories for the purpose of rejecting them. They are still very much alive. The silk manufacturers of Lyon and their "innocent industry" [17] are there, and the elegant life of the cities may be exciting. But this is not a permanent accommodation on Rousseau's part or a renunciation of the democratic community.[18] In spite of the doubts besetting him, he knows that a choice must be made and that the search must be continued to find Pope's happiness in which the simple necessities become, in the letter to Parisot, "a good book, a friend, freedom and peace." The possibility of making the choice and of finding that happiness still eludes him in 1742.

He will have to spend wandering and unsatisfactory years in the midst of a world he increasingly rejects. From Paris to Venice and back to Paris; writing *Les Muses galantes* and *Les Fêtes de Ramire* and earning Voltaire's appreciation; composing articles on music for the *Encyclopédie,* at the request of d'Alembert; earning his living as an employee of men of great wealth. This is a "sad and slow career," Rousseau laments in 1746, in which "vain and tumultuous projects" are forever promising him "happiness and wisdom." So much planning for nothing. The reason is that ambition is at the root of it. "Man, satisfied with the necessary, has little fear of adverse fortune. . . . Woe to the contemptible mortal who in his insatiable soul nourishes an ardent thirst for gold."

[17] Letter to Bordes, 1741, O.C. II, 1131–2.
[18] Pierre Maurice Masson, *La Religion de J.-J. Rousseau* (Paris, 1916), I, 133, agrees with this view. Starobinski ("Tout le mal vient de l'inégalité," *Europe* [Nov.–Dec. 1961], 142) takes a contrary view and suggests that Rousseau's vows of democratic faith are no sooner uttered than they are withdrawn, in an act of acceptance of civilized life and the frivolities of mundanity.

The desire for wealth is not the only evil surrounding civilized man. He also behaves as if his own interests were the only important ones: "Woe to all violent men, to all mortals left untouched by anything except their own felicity." Man also wishes to appear different from what he is: "They all mask their weakness and call wisdom the inclination they have adopted." [19]

But the moment when Rousseau will feel free to say loudly what he thinks, and to declare himself for what he is, is perhaps approaching. On the eve of the summer of 1749 and of the "illumination" of Vincennes, Rousseau drafts what was supposed to be the first issue of a journal. He seems to anticipate the moment of liberation. In his new role of critic he will say what he thinks of the literary world, indeed of the world at large. He uses a mocking and satirical style, such as would be required by *Le Persiffleur*, a proposed critical journal of review of new books after the English models which Condillac, Diderot, and Rousseau were to publish together. But the wit, and the flare for sudden and dramatic contrasts that will stamp all of Rousseau's literary career, are here, as well as a disenchanted and independent attitude toward the contemporary writers and jesters, the scribblers and the dispensers of useless information, who will soon be arrayed against him.

The arrows point straight and true. Rousseau has never wasted his time reading anything printed in the contemporary journals nor has he lost any time in the study of sciences. He repeats again what he had told the father of his Lyon tutees: to be able to judge, one does not have to be learned. What is required is to think straight and be able to write.

His character is unstable. He moves from one extreme to the other. His mood varies, but there are certain fundamental consistencies: "The reappearance of the same objects usually renews

[19] *L'Allée de Sylvie*, O.C. II, 1146-9.

in me reactions similar to those I had the first time I saw them."
He is always the same with the same person. He saw himself as
alternating constantly between his two hebdomadal souls: one
week he would be "wisely mad," the next he would be "madly
wise," with madness always underlying both weeks. But this was
the madness that enabled him "to stand always for truth." [20] This
is the concluding sentence of *Le Persiffleur.* A few months later,
in the *Discourse on Arts and Sciences,* he was to take his stand.

[20] *Le Persiffleur, O.C.* I, 1106, 1109–10, 1112.

IV

Rousseau Faces the Enlightenment

The Statement

UNTIL 1749 Rousseau had only some plays and poetry and a *Dissertation on Modern Music* (1743) in print. Almost nothing political had reached the eye of the public. Some good formulations of his thoughts had occurred to him, however, and the time had come to state them openly, even if he had to do it in a way which might be considered paradoxical, or worse, by his friends. The issue to which Rousseau intended to address himself was nothing less than that of the relation between the nature of man and the institutions of civilization. The theme proposed by the Academy of Dijon, *Has the Restoration of the Sciences and Arts Tended to Purify Morals?*, gave him the chance he needed.[1]

As we open the *Discourse on Arts and Sciences,* the tension is apparent. Rousseau is caught in the heady atmosphere of the eighteenth century and is almost overwhelmed by it. His friends,

---

[1] *Discours sur les sciences et les arts* (1750), O.C. III, 1–30. For the celebrated account of the "happy chance," which enabled him to break the ties keeping him "bound to a society which I esteemed so little," cf. Rousseau's second letter to Malesherbes, January 12, 1762, O.C. I, 1135–6.

his readings, the excitement of the age, press on him. He appears to be carried away by the promise of the times as they open up an endless vista of human progress and felicity. Man is living in a new historical era. Life has changed in a few generations and the account man gives of himself is a source of emotion and wonder.

What we are witnessing is the spectacle of man lifting himself, through his own efforts, above the void of the past. He is, through the use of his rational lights, dissipating the darkness in which nature had enveloped him. True, this was a protective darkness intended to keep man away from the dangers inherent in a full use of his own potentialities. But the results have been remarkable and man has reached to the outermost regions of the universe and with giant strides encompassed its endless reaches.

This is a grandiose and moving effort on the part of man. What would be even more striking and far more trying would be the attempt by man to retreat from these outer boundaries of knowledge and come to grips with himself and with the task of understanding his own nature, his duties, and his ends. No sooner is Rousseau caught in the forward sweep of his times than he recoils from its frightening horizons and proclaims as the most difficult and as the most important issue that of dealing with the inner self and of identifying the proper tasks of man in society.

The question is whether or not those philosophers who have claimed the leadership in the enlightenment of mankind are engaged in this endeavor. Rousseau makes it clear that he believes they are not, as one looks at the substance of the writings of the most influential among them. What they teach the multitudes is wrong: "One holds that there are no bodies and that everything is appearance. Another that there is no substance other than matter, or any God but the world. This one suggests that there are neither virtues nor vices and that moral good and evil are chimeras. That one that men are wolves and can devour one another with a good conscience." [2]

These are the views of Berkeley, d'Holbach, La Mettrie, Mandeville, Hobbes [3]—the views of philosophers who have pushed man far above his early state of innocence to conquer the world and to reach for the stars. Can they be trusted as guides to carry to a successful conclusion that essential re-examination of human nature which Rousseau is proposing? The answer is no. Given the role assumed by the sciences, the risk we run is to be confronted forever by the dangerous dreamings of Hobbes and Spinoza and their followers.

Rousseau feels the beauty of an age of discovery and promise but finds wanting the intellectual leaders who could take man toward a new Garden of Eden. In what the philosophers say there is no wisdom but only idle declamations and catastrophic paradoxes, for they are undermining the foundations of communal life and are destroying virtue. And among all the paradoxes, those advanced by writers who presume to strengthen man by destroying the foundations upon which alone his life can be built are most dangerous and are to be most strongly resisted. The tension between Rousseau and his age had, as we have seen, started well before this fateful summer of 1749. Here it was made manifest beyond a doubt, and was never to falter.

If Rousseau begins as a man of his age, by assuming that everything has to be questioned and that the search for the answer to the problems of man's life cannot be successful if it rests upon the blind acceptance of the inheritance of the past, he at once adds that the answers provided by contemporary political

[2] O.C. III, 3, 6, 27–9. As a rule, the English translation used for the *Discourses* will be that of Roger D. and Judith R. Masters: Jean-Jacques Rousseau, *The First and Second Discourses*, edited, with Introduction and Notes, by Roger D. Masters (New York, 1964).

[3] Identifications in O.C. III, 1254–5.

philosophers are not the proper ones and that society needs something quite different.

The way to the heart of the problem seemed to Rousseau to lie through an open challenge to some of the universally accepted assumptions of the times, chief among them the significance of material progress for human happiness. Thus, the basic theme of the first *Discourse* became that of the relation of arts and sciences to human nature. Rousseau did not consider his answer a paradox; he felt, rather, that his fellow philosophers themselves were engaging in idle paradoxes. By contrast Rousseau was stating what appeared to him a fundamental truth. He also felt it was his own and that no doubt should exist about the sincerity of his position. The evidence of the years before 1749 appears to confirm the view that this was not an improvisation. The reality of the commitment to his point of view seems strengthened by his life and thought after 1749.

Rousseau's contempt for the literary manipulators, the prideful scientists, the poetasters and cheap philosophers, crowding the scene in search of popular applause and mass following, is unlimited. Their presence in such great numbers is harmful to civilization. How much better would society be had these bad poets and inferior mathematicians devoted their energies to the simple and necessary occupations that are needed to sustain life, such as clothmaking, a calling in which they might have excelled.

As for himself, Rousseau fully realizes that if his ideas are to survive beyond his times he must speak a language that will not be understood, for he is not concerned about pleasing the witty and fashionable members of the Paris salons. Rousseau is not writing for those who are influenced by the views of their contemporaries: "To live beyond one's century one must not write for such readers."

There Rousseau stands: in the age of lights but setting out to write about man in a way which will appear surprising and incomprehensible, using the tools provided by the arts and sciences, and that reason which man has strengthened in himself over the centuries, in order to challenge the assumptions and to deny the purposes universally accepted around him. Well he could repeat, quoting again the same verse of Ovid on the title page: "Barbarus hic ego sum quia non intelligor illis." This was to be a prophetic view of Rousseau's own life.

The weakness of civilization lay in the widening gap between being and appearing. Man was being deceived about what he really was by the way he was made to appear to himself and to others. Everything conspired to make this deception an ever more important element in the life of man, who had reached a stage in which urbanity of custom seemed to make intercourse among men easy and fruitful, a stage in which all virtues appeared to flourish. But urbanity was a surface gloss hiding a different reality, and those shining virtues had no substance: "How pleasant it would be to live among us if external countenance were always a reflection of the heart's disposition; if decency were virtue; if our maxims served as rules of conduct." But we should realize that reality is quite different and that strength of character is not to be found under the glitter of the attire of a rich man. The deceitfulness of appearances has been multiplied by the progress of arts. "Before art had molded our manners and taught our passions to speak a contrived language, our customs were rustic and natural and differences of behavior announced at once differences of character."

So great the deception has become that any foreigner visiting Europe and trying to find out what the realities of European life are on the basis of the surface appearances of its quotidian life, of the perpetual mutual exchanges of demonstrations of good will, of the vying with one another of men of all ages and conditions in an anxious game of reciprocal assistance, would arrive at an estimate of the situation which would be the opposite of the real one, so successful has modern civilization been in hiding its more somber realities behind a screen of appearances.

As for Rousseau himself, his decision is made, and that is to remain obscure and to listen to the voice of his conscience, to retreat from the "celestial" spheres to listen to the promptings of his heart, to shed the pomp of appearances in order to seek out his being.

The task was simple as far as he was concerned. But if one wanted to deal with the problems of a given society, then the task was immense and would have to begin with the restoration of virtue.[4]

The loss of virtue leads to wealth and luxury. Wealth and luxury weaken the strength of the political community. The link is certain. The progression is inevitable.

The virtue Rousseau has in mind is the active virtue of the tiller of the soil, of the person who has established his roots firmly on the land which gives nourishment to its children. It is a virtue attached to men reluctant to abandon the bounty and the beauty which nature bestows on those who understand her. Virtue is the strength of the soul with which a life close to nature blesses those who follow it. Virtue is the strength of the body which shows itself in the laborers, the peasants, the humble men who are concerned with the creation and the fashioning of the tools and the aids to life which the riches of the earth provide to mankind. Virtue shows in the life of those peoples, apparently poor and ignorant, but who by rejecting the rash of idle knowledge have maintained their happiness—such as the people of Switzerland today, of Sparta yesterday.

Rousseau's virtue is an earthbound social virtue whose purpose is not the finding of happiness in another world but the

[4] O.C. III, 7, 8.

assuring of conditions of this world which will make communal life possible. Virtue is the thread providing the cohesion, unity, and understanding which in a social state give man the possibility of understanding better what he must do. Virtue is the transparence through which obstacles can be seen and removed. Virtue provides the candid revelation of man's inner feelings and thoughts. The virtuous man does not add layers of deception and greed to his soul. Virtuous—that is, simple—men refuse to speak an artificial language and stand revealed before public sight for what they are. In virtuous societies "men found their security in the ease with which they understood one another." The maintenance of virtue is what makes possible communication among the members of a political community.

The loss of virtue then is also to be lamented because of its social consequences. Man's pride has detached him from all beneficent contact with nature. With the development of arts and sciences virtue has declined. Apparent social ties have multiplied but the real conditions necessary for their maintenance have been destroyed. Luxury has made its appearance, born from multiplying wealth and kept alive by the active search for more. What can be the chances of the survival of virtue if in order to be at one with modern life "it will become necessary to accumulate wealth regardless of the cost?" What will be destroyed will be the inner springs of human nature.

Rousseau sees in business and money the chief preoccupation of his times. In the past, men with political responsibility wrote of morals and virtue. Today these same men talk about commerce and wealth. An economic doctrine has been developed which relates human beings to economic values and judges them in proportion to their economic worth. "One will tell you that in a given country a man is worth the amount for which he will be sold in Algiers. Another, using the same calculation, will find countries where a man is worth nothing and other countries where he is worth less than nothing. They appraise men as herds of cattle." Montesquieu and Fénelon, before Rousseau, had expressed themselves in favor of sumptuary laws. But Rousseau in this attack on the "political arithmetic" of William Petty and the economics of Melon is not looking to any legal remedy for the condition he laments. That condition has much deeper roots and is the result of the gradual development of a civilization whose thinking is colored by certain dominant political and economic doctrines.

The final absurdity can be seen in fixing a man's worth to the state on the basis of his capacity to consume. The greater the consumption of goods, the greater the value of the citizens who are capable of reaching ever fresh peaks of economic attainment. Those who are unable to increase their consumption become the pariahs of the new consumption civilization. The middle of the eighteenth century was witnessing the barest beginnings of the transformation of the economic machine of Europe from quality to quantity, from craftsmanship in the production of goods for purposes largely unrelated to individual needs but closely linked to social values, to mass production of commodities intended for individual use. But Rousseau had a vision of what the future would bring: the very opposite of what was commonly expected by the vast army of philosophers bent upon singing the praise of the world around them.

The future would bring the downfall of those states which saw only advantages in multiplying wealth and consumption and which set their standards and fixed their sights by the satisfaction of those goals. History is witness to the downfall of states caused by excess of luxury. Athens and Rome are only two examples. One could, with no great effort of imagination, bridge the distance of places and the gap of time and feel that what

[81]

happened more than once yesterday is repeating itself "in our countries and under our own eyes." The issues, then, are political ones and of immediate concern.[5]

Modern political societies which have built their institutions on the foundations of commerce have created a modern kind of slavery. This is the slavery of seemingly happy peoples with polished customs and the all-pervasive temptations of wealth, but in which the appearance of perfection conceals an altogether different reality and in which, in spite of the glossy surface, the radical inequality flowing from such a state of affairs is becoming increasingly visible.

"We are deceived by the appearance of good." This is the way in which Rousseau, quoting Horace, begins his *Discourse*. The reality of our society is quite different from what it appears to be. What is, is in effect the result of our betrayal of duty, of our abandonment of the fatherland, of our lack of care for those who are unhappy or our friends. Had we kept faith with duty, country, the poor, and our friends, the result would have been a much simpler society in which arts and sciences would not have flourished but in which social cohesion would have gained and retained the upper hand. Without luxury no art, but without injustice no law needed to repress it; without tyranny no history, but without the weight of history man would have stayed closer to his natural goodness.

The system of education is at fault, for it is a system which goes to enormous lengths to teach the young everything except their duties. Going back to the earlier themes of his *Project on Education*, Rousseau laments the superficial values of an education which weakens both the mind and the body of the student and, by stressing only the sciences and literature, fails to create citizens. We may have poets and painters and astronomers and

[5] O.C. III, 8, 19, 15.

chemists in great numbers, but there will be few men left with the capacity to fulfill the tasks of a responsible citizen in a political society. And the concepts of magnanimity, equity, temperance, humanity, and courage will no longer be understood.

The political consequences will be serious because in politics, as in the moral activity of man, "it is a great evil not to do good." Citizenship is a duty before it is a right. It imposes on the citizen the responsibility of acting in a perceptive way for the good of all. The community without an adequate supply of citizens capable of acting in this way is a weak community. Indeed, "every useless citizen may be regarded as a dangerous man."

Thus, in the end, Rousseau's discussion of the arts and sciences, of the corruption of customs and morals, of the rise of an economy of luxury and of grasping wealth, comes down to the ultimate consideration of what these developments do to good government. Everything goes back to a central political question. We seem to know, Rousseau proclaims rhetorically, a great many sublime things: the movement of bodies, the revolution of the planets, the relations between the body and the soul, which stars have no light. We claim to have penetrated the most remote secrets of the universe. The question is: Had we failed to do so, would we be less well governed? The implicit answer is that if we were capable of a greater concentrated effort on the social problems of the human community man would be better governed.[6]

The task then must clearly be the revolutionary one of creating the conditions which will make man better governed and social life one of solidarity and not one of conflict. The prolonged polemical debate opened by the publication of the *Discourse* was to provide Rousseau with an even better opportunity to state the sweeping implications of his thought.

[6] O.C. III, 7, 25, 17, 24, 26, 18.

The Debate

The publication of the *Discourse on Arts and Sciences* had repercussions that went far beyond what Rousseau himself expected. It suddenly confronted intellectual Europe with a series of extreme assertions for which it was poorly prepared. It lent itself to misunderstanding and confusion. What were the purposes of an attack against the values that appeared to be imbedded without challenge at the core of civilization and culture? Rousseau himself knew that what he had said could bear repetition and clarification. Too much of his criticism of arts and sciences was couched in paradoxical and whimsical language. His criticism of the sciences and of philosophy could be construed as an attack on culture. And he had not had time enough to place his views within a proper social and political context and to relate his analysis to a clear enough summary of the evolution of mankind, the growth of institutions and the necessities of human governance. Rousseau was anxious to make his case, if possible, in such a way that it would reach far and wide and make everybody as clearly aware as possible of the impending crisis.

There were six replies by Rousseau to the criticisms made of his *First Discourse,* seven if one includes the preface to *Narcisse* among them, and, taken together, they were more than twice as long as the *Discourse* itself. They were all written between June 1751 and the end of 1753. Had Rousseau wished to reply to all his critics he would have written many more. But this, in the end, must have appeared to him a pointless task, for in the meantime he had seized another opportunity to develop independently the thoughts that had been forming in his mind: by November 1753 the Academy of Dijon had come to his rescue by providing him with the theme of the origins of inequality.

Some of Rousseau's critics were people with ideas (Bordes and the adviser to the king of Poland), some were petty polemists (Lecat, Fréron, Gautier). Some, finally, were friends who wanted to widen the discussion around Rousseau's ideas (Raynal). Rousseau answered some of them directly, others indirectly, yet others not at all.

The first reply, *Lettre à Monsieur l'Abbé Raynal,* was published in the *Mercure de France* of June 1751, in answer to some observations which were probably due to Raynal himself.[7] This is the briefest of the replies, and it was followed by the better known *Observations de Jean-Jacques Rousseau, de Genève,* also published in the *Mercure* for September 1751, in answer to an anonymous author known, however, to be Stanislas, king of Poland. This is a much longer essay. The third was a letter to Grimm of November 1751, discussing Gautier's refutation published by the *Mercure* the previous October. The fourth, *Dernière Réponse de Jean-Jacques Rousseau de Genève,* was published in the *Mercure* of April 1752 and is a reply to the *Discours sur les avantages des sciences et des arts* by Charles Bordes, published in the same journal in December 1751. It is the longest and the most important of the replies. The fifth, *Lettre à Lecat,* was published as a pamphlet in Lyon in 1752. The sixth and last reply to a second attack by Bordes, *Préface d'une seconde lettre à Bordes,* is a five-page fragment of a more extensive essay which was never concluded.[8]

The years since 1750 had been exceptionally active for Rousseau. He had been a great deal of the time in the limelight and even sometimes at the center of the fashionable salon life he seemed to reject. These had been years of both successful and unsuccessful presentation of his plays, of tension between the pull of the bright culture of his times and the urge to establish

[7] O.C. III, 1256.
[8] All the replies are in O.C. III, 31–107; see also C.C. II, 149–53.

his own private life on the principles he was advocating. The publication of the *Discourse* had faced Rousseau with the issue of his personal life: "How to reconcile the severe principles I had adopted with a style of life which bore very little relationship to them, and how could I, cashier of a collector general of finances, preach with good grace disinterestedness and poverty?" [9]

In March 1751 he resigned his post and henceforth earned his livelihood by copying music. He thus became free to fix the proper order of priorities and to set the stage for the bombshell of the *Discourse on Inequality*. In the end Rousseau proudly announces that his "system" is ready.

Throughout the debate, Rousseau is confident and his replies are sharp and uncompromising. He has no intention of retreating. What he has said in the *First Discourse* is the result of much thought and not of an idle wish to amuse himself with paradoxes, and he is anxious to restate his ideas clearly. What he has said in the *First Discourse* is merely on the periphery of the more complex structure shaping up in his mind. This explains his elation and confidence as he addresses himself to his contradictors. They do not know what he has in store for them for he has barely begun to fight.

He is convinced that his judgment on human nature is right. He is full of hope about his ability to penetrate the mystery of existence and the relation of man to nature, and to

---

[9] *Confessions, O.C.* I, 361–2. Giving up his job with Francueil may have forced Rousseau to give up his children too. But he brought himself to see the problem as part of the larger struggle between rich and poor. A poor man cannot nourish properly his children: "It is the class of the rich, your class, which robs my class of the bread I need for my children." In any case, Rousseau's children would have been brought up as peasants and not as writers or office workers and his action is not due to vicious character but to poverty (letter to Madame de Francueil, April 20, 1751, C.G. I, 308–10; C.C. II, 142–6).

understand the virtues of the common man. He pities the great philosopher (Descartes?) "who thinks of himself as capable of piercing God's secrets and dares to link his vaunted wisdom to eternal wisdom: He approves, he blames, he corrects, he dictates laws to nature and limits to divinity; and while he busies himself with his vain systems and goes to endless efforts to arrange the machine of the world, the laborer, who sees the rain and then the sun in turn bring fruits to his field, admires, praises and blesses the hand from which he receives these graces without attempting to understand the way in which they reach him."

Not all his opponents have the same ambitious views. Some of them are mere children. Others when they are not publicity seekers are guilty of having shrunk the content of the debate from a consideration of morality and goodness to one of fortune and grandeur. One writer Rousseau holds up by name to public scorn: Melon, who was destined to be the first to justify a "poisonous doctrine" about economic man and luxury.[10]

With d'Alembert, Rousseau is more cautious. His views had not been any less critical but Rousseau calls them important. For d'Alembert had asked whether the difference in morals and customs to be noticed among different countries was due not only to the development of arts and sciences but also to the climate of the country, the temper of the people, the economy of the government, the customs and the laws. Any one of these factors might have caused the decadence of morals.

This is what d'Alembert had written in the *Preliminary Discourse* of the first volume of the *Encyclopédie*:

We might perhaps at this point reject the strictures that an eloquent writer has recently aimed at the Arts and Sciences, accusing them of corrupting morals. It would be out of place to agree with such views at the beginning of a work such as this; and even the worthy writer

[10] *O.C.* III, 41, 76, 95.

we have in mind, having supported with enthusiasm and success our undertaking, seems to have given it his approval. Indeed we are not accusing him of having confused culture with its abuses (he would undoubtedly reply that such abuse is inseparable from culture): but we do ask him to examine whether most of the evils he attributes to Arts and Sciences are not due to entirely different causes, which it would be both long and indiscreet to enumerate here. Learning certainly helps to make society more pleasant; it would be difficult to prove that men are better from it and virtue more common: but this is a benefit that can be denied even to morals. Furthermore, must laws be proscribed because they may make possible the commission of crimes whose authors would be punished among savages? Finally, even were we to admit the disadvantages of human knowledge (something we are far from doing), we still do not believe that anything would be gained by destroying it: our vices would remain with us, and in addition we would be ignorant.[11]

Rousseau could not disagree with this statement for it included "great views" and was certainly a part of his own "system." His reply tells us that he is not ready yet at this point to come down to the specific questions of the political structure and of the institutional arrangements and to a discussion of the ways in which these can hamper or facilitate the establishment of morals in a given community. The political problem is part of a larger social problem, of which Rousseau is now trying to disentangle the threads to explain the present condition of man. Once the premises had been made clear and the validity of his overall view of man accepted, then it will be time to consider politics. Then it will be feasible to "examine the hidden but no less real relationships which are to be found between the nature of government and the genius, the morals and the degree of instruction of the citizens." But this is an ultimate objective only and one

[11] "Discours préliminaire des éditeurs," *Encyclopédie, ou Dictionnaire raisonné des sciences, des arts et des métiers* (Paris, 1751), I, xxxiii.

which Rousseau is not prepared to pursue now: everything considered, this is a field of research which in different circumstances he might carry out in Geneva.[12]

Geneva, the symbol of the only modern virtuous people he has been able to find,[13] continues to be the ideal standard in Rousseau's mind. And even before he was ready to identify himself as a "citizen of Geneva" on the title page of the *Discourse on Inequality,* he had called himself a citizen of Geneva in the explanation given in 1752 of the illustration decorating the frontispiece of the first *Discourse:* "The torch of Prometheus is that of the sciences animating the great geniuses; the Satyr who, seeing fire for the first time, rushes to him and wants to embrace him, represents the vulgar men who, seduced by the brilliance of letters, indiscreetly rush to study them: the Prometheus who shouts and warns them of the danger they incur is the citizen of Geneva." [14]

The citizen of Geneva will soon be ready to redeem his promise to d'Alembert and go to his native city to undertake his more specific political research, having beforehand told the citizens of that city of his intentions and of his general views on the organization of the political community.[15] For he still has to proceed to define his views from the beginning, by clarifying an argument which was getting lost in polemical confusion. He is proud of what he has written and even more certain of the importance of what he has not yet said, even though he has no illusions as to his chances of success in reforming mankind. He knows that men "will be no less eager to secure glory and money after I will have convinced them that these two passions are at the root of all their miseries and that men are rendered evil by the former and unhappy by the latter." [16]

He will nevertheless continue on the path he has assigned to

[12] O.C. III, 43.   [13] O.C. III, 42.   [14] O.C. III, 102.
[15] Cf. infra, pp. 157 ff.   [16] O.C. III, 104.

himself, because of an inner urge to state what his understanding of the nature of man tells him is true. He is happy to bring back into the consciousness of man the Gospel:

It is not because of the arts and sciences that the Gospel has spread throughout the universe and that its admirable beauty has penetrated all hearts. This divine book, the only necessary to a Christian, and the most useful of all even for somebody who might not be one, needs only reflection to bring to the soul the love of its Author and the will to accomplish His precepts. Never has virtue spoken a sweeter language; never the deepest wisdom has expressed itself with so much energy and simplicity.[17]

Rousseau was also convinced that he had "discovered great things."[18] His independence and his solitude had given him strength and he now had the right to speak without reticence.

In this interlude between the two *Discourses*, Rousseau wanted to consider the relationship of morals to arts and sciences and the issue of their decline with the growth of a philosophy which was only the fruit of human pride. That this kind of culture should too easily spread is not surprising, "for it is less painful to distinguish oneself through idle babble than through good morals, as soon as it is no longer necessary to be a good man provided one is an agreeable man."[19]

But earlier man lived at a time when the sources of corruption were not there. Rousseau is trying to see through "the obscurity of ancient times and the rusticity of ancient peoples." And what he sees is above all the prevalence of "the severity of morals which is an infallible mark of their purity, good faith, hospitality, justice." Today this is no longer true and polished peoples have

---

[17] O.C. III, 48–9. In the *Fourth Letter from the Mountain* Rousseau was to call his reply to the king of Poland, from which the above passage is taken, as one of his writings which showed his love for the Gospel (O.C. III, 768, 1264).
[18] O.C. III, 103.   [19] O.C. III, 73.

become corrupted and widened the gulf between what they are and what they appear to be.

What a series of paradoxes are offered by our advanced civilization! The fate of religion is a striking example: "Sciences are flourishing today, literature and the arts are shining; what advantages have come to religion? Let us ask the question to the multitude of philosophers who pride themselves in not having any. Our libraries are filled with books on theology and casuists are to be found everywhere. In other times we had saints and no casuists. Science progresses and faith is destroyed. Everybody wants to teach to do good but nobody wants to learn; we have all become doctors and we have ceased to be Christians." [20]

How readily we confuse erudition and wisdom. Our world is filled with critics and antiquarians: "Pamphlets become volumes, books are multiplied but the original question is forgotten: this is the fate of literary polemics: after clarifications contained in endless in-folio volumes one always ends up by losing one's bearings." And just as this "learning" is praised so is "ignorance" condemned.

But there are two kinds of ignorance. One is "the criminal ignorance which extends to the duties of humanity and multiplies vices, which degrades reason, depresses the soul, renders men similar to animals." The other is the reasonable ignorance, "which consists to limit one's curiosity to the extent of the faculties one has received; a modest ignorance born of a real love for virtue . . . a sweet and precious ignorance, the possession of a pure person satisfied with himself and who finds his happiness within himself . . . and does not need to seek a false and vain happiness in the opinion others might have of his lights." [21]

But it is this kind of ignorance which the philosophers cannot comprehend or accept. For they believe that all is well simply

[20] O.C. III, 74, 61, 48.   [21] O.C. III, 54.

because we have given our vices and corruption pleasant-sounding names so that they need not embarrass us any longer. The retreat of man upon himself is not acceptable in a world trying to hide its intentions behind empty manners: "The greater the internal corruption the greater the external tranquility: in this way the cultivation of letters generates little by little politeness. Taste is also derived from the same source. As soon as public approbation is the first condition of literary works, it is natural that those who are engaged in them should consider with care ways with which to obtain it; these are the considerations which in the long run form style, refine taste and spread everywhere graces and urbanity. These things may be, if one wants, the supplement of virtue: but never will one be able to see that they are virtue itself and rarely they will go with it." At a performance of a comedy of Molière, Rousseau is led to admire the delicacy of the audience: "A slightly risky word, an expression merely vulgar rather than obscene, is enough to wound their chaste ears; I have no doubt at all that the most corrupted among them are always the most scandalized." [22]

To see the issue in its proper perspective Rousseau goes back to the beginnings of history and to the nature of man in the original state of nature. This is a time well before that phase in the historical development of mankind which has been selected by theorists as corresponding to the state of nature, a condition which has nothing to do with the already complicated civilized and socialized man who as a rule is taken as the norm of prepolitical man.

Going back to the origins, Rousseau sees nothing to change his views on the goodness of man, or, more precisely, on the qualities of a man incapable of doing evil because the setting was such

[22] O.C. III, 73–4.

that there was no incentive or motive for man to act in an evil way.

There is historical evidence available in the records of both scholars and travelers, all of whom point to the goodness of the savage. But there is also a logical approach which is even more persuasive. In the absence of the scaffolding of institutions and social customs which have grown through the centuries and which have made man what he is, it is difficult to see how man could act as if those institutions and customs existed. In one of the more important statements of this period, in his *Last Reply*, Rousseau writes:

Before the invention of those shocking words, *yours* and *mine;* before the appearance of that breed of cruel and brutal men who are called masters, and of that other breed of men, rascals and liars, who are called slaves; before the appearance of men abominable enough to dare to possess the superfluous while other men are dying of hunger; before the development of a mutual dependence has forced them all to become shrewd, jealous and traitorous; I would like to have someone explain to me what could have been those vices, those crimes with which so emphatically one reproaches them. I am told that for a long time now we have been disabused of the chimera of the Golden Age. Why is it not also said that for a long time now we have been disabused of the chimera of virtue? [23]

This is the chain of consequences which Rousseau sees as the controlling factor in his analysis of the human condition. There are some variations over the years in the exact order of priorities and in the identification of the several links in the chain. But the story remains always essentially the same. The beginning comes with the establishment of distinctions based on claims to property and the social isolation of man which results from those

[23] O.C. III, 80.

distinctions. A protective shell of rights leads to the aggressive assertiveness of man against man. In the ensuing struggle, the natural inequalities which distinguish the individual members of the human race come to the forefront and are used in a destructive game of competition. They succeed, in the long run, in creating two classes of men opposed to one another, the masters and the slaves. What happens next is that as a result of the dialectical process of reciprocal influence both the masters and the slaves deteriorate and each group begins to exhibit its worst traits. It is all of mankind that becomes corrupted as a materialistic conflict spreads its poison impartially among the oppressors and the oppressed.

A further consequence is the growing accumulation of wealth in the hands of the masters to the disadvantage of the rest of human society. And again this is the result of a dialectical process which leads to a further debasing of the nature of the poor, who in order to survive, and given the increasing mutual dependence thrust upon men, are forced to imitate those at the top and, with them, become engaged in antisocial activities under the appearance of acceptable social behavior.

Perhaps the Golden Age has never existed, Rousseau suggests at this point, even though two years later he will refer to the Golden Age as one necessary point of passage, however brief, in the transition of man from the origins to the present. But if the Golden Age vision is rejected, what is rejected even more emphatically is the present possibility of a virtuous life.

In denying both the Golden Age and the empire of virtue, Rousseau's adversaries are refusing to consider the possibility that the way in which men live today has anything to do with the vanishing of virtue. Rousseau is convinced of the opposite—that is, that the conditions of life, the temptations offered by commerce, the very institutions of government, everything in sum, conspire to multiply human weaknesses. The hold of cupidity on man is already great enough, and yet we are strengthening it by everything that surrounds him in his daily life. What will happen, when we push him to the acquisition of riches as the most desirable of human goals, "to accumulate wealth regardless of the consequences?" [24]

The corrupting influence of the system is universal. Rousseau has already said that wealth destroys both the rich and the poor. There is something inevitable about the process which Rousseau calls "genealogical": "The first source of evil is inequality; from inequality wealth is born, for these words poor and rich are relative and wherever men will be equal there will be no rich or poor. From wealth luxury and idleness have come." Luxury becomes both the end product of a degenerative process as well as the symbol, the most visible aspect, of present civilization. Rousseau dismisses as entirely worthless the arguments of contemporary economists that luxury was performing a necessary social function by keeping the poor employed and fed. For without luxury there would be no poor:

Luxury feeds a hundred poor in our cities and causes the death of a hundred thousand of them in our countryside: money which circulates in the hands of the rich and of the artists to satisfy their demand for superfluities is lost for the subsistence of the laborer: the latter goes without dress precisely because the former need gold trimmings on theirs. The wastage of foodstuffs necessary to the nourishment of man is itself enough to make luxury hateful to mankind. . . . We need sauces in our kitchens, this is why so many sick people have no soup. We need wine on our tables, this is why the peasant drinks only water. We need powder for our wigs, this is why so many poor have no bread.

Nor can the question of luxury be solved by proposing to limit luxury, to admit the usefulness of some luxury and to say that

[24] O.C. III, 32.

beyond a certain threshold luxury will not be tolerated. The only acceptable position is that no luxury at all is necessary and that everything is a source of evil which goes beyond what is physically necessary. "Nature gives us already too many needs and it is at the very least highly imprudent to multiply them without necessity and to make in this way the soul of man even more dependent." [25]

It is no less wrong to defend luxury on the basis of historical evolution and of the gradual acquisition of needs which, because of the passage of time, are then no longer considered as luxury. In all ages, Rousseau maintains, luxury, even though widespread, was at least considered as the source of an infinite variety of evils. It was reserved to Melon to support for the first time the doctrine of the economic necessity and of the historical justification of luxury: "I am not afraid at all to fight, alone in my century, these hateful maxims which only tend to destroy and debase virtue and to create both rich and miserable men, that is always bad men."

To say this does not mean that history can be rewritten and that what has happened can be removed and radical readjustments made, suddenly, in the life of men. Rousseau has no intention of "reducing men to be satisfied with the merest necessities," even though they might provide the substance of happiness. He has no wish to "upset present social arrangements, to burn libraries and all books, to destroy colleges and academies." [26] His only purpose is that of determining as far as he can the causes of present discontents, because without a clear notion of how we have become what we are, we shall never be able to change. And change there ought to be.

The task of finding specific remedies Rousseau is almost willing at this point to leave to others more courageous or more

---

reckless than he is. But this is a position Rousseau is unable to hold for very long, because soon we find in the replies more than one concrete reference to problems of war and duty, the needs of political life, and the hard requirements of citizenship.

For the links between morals and customs and political life are close, as are those between culture, arts and sciences, and social problems. The ways in which societies grow, defend themselves, survive or decline, are functions of the moral fiber of their members. There is no escaping the political repercussions of a social system in which goodness has been abandoned for luxury and a hard life of sacrifice given up in favor of the conveniences of life.

The problem of education is primordial. There is no point in teaching young people the many pleasant things which might be useful to them for their amusement once they are grown up. The point is that they have no bearing on the duties of citizenship which must be the starting point of the educational process. For anyone who has been taught to prefer his life to the performance of his duty will soon enough be drawn to whatever tends to make his life easy and agreeable. In this way the citizen will grow with a tendency to be accommodating, hoping to derive from this attitude advantages for himself. The flatterer never overlooks a chance to please and yet his contribution to social life is negative, for he works only with an egoistic end in view. The useful citizen is the one who works for others.[27]

And what does the community need most? Rousseau's adversaries lamented the dismal possibility of a world made up exclusively of workers, soldiers, hunters, and shepherds. But to Rousseau this would be "a spectacle infinitely more beautiful than that of mankind made up of cooks, poets, printers, and musi-

[27] O.C. III, 63, 64, 74.

cians." The latter would be pursuing idle activities, while out of the former, hard-working communities capable of maintaining their freedom would undoubtedly be born, if only we are prepared to eliminate soldiering as a profession: "War is sometimes a duty and is not to be conceived as a profession. Everybody must be a soldier for the defense of his freedom. Nobody must become one to invade the freedom of others. And to die in the service of the fatherland is too beautiful an occupation to be entrusted to mercenaries." [28]

The fact of the matter is that the ideal citizen must not only be far removed from the temptations of the amenities of life, but must be prepared to die for his country. He must also be aware of the harshness of the necessities of political life. It is easy to say that one would admire a powerful and well-governed state, one in which the citizen would not be constrained to the practice of the "cruel" virtues of the early Romans: "It is certainly more convenient to live in a state where each is exempted from being a *homme de bien*. But if the citizens of this state we are admiring were by the unhappy turn of events forced either to give up their virtue or to practice these cruel virtues, and supposing further that they found the strength to perform their duty, would we because of this admire them less?" [29]

Let it be clear that the cruel virtues include the taking of human life by the community if this is necessary to its own survival. They include undoubtedly many others, from hard work to a continuing participation in the common tasks. But the ultimate cruel virtue the citizen must exhibit is his capacity to understand and support the decision which may be taken to deal with finality with those who are threatening to weaken by their action the coherence of the political community. Rousseau, car-

[28] *O.C.* III, 82.   [29] *O.C.* III, 88.

ried away by the rhetoric of his argument, is unwilling to stop short of its most extreme point.

The taking of life seems to be justified both in the case of those who attempt to violate the established pattern of life in a given community and in the case of those who are trying to get away from the community in order to escape some of its burdens. And Africa is the testing ground.

In the first instance, Rousseau sees the issue in terms of the right of self-defense of what Europeans in their supercilious manner tend to consider inferior savage societies, about which we know nothing but which we are tempted to consider as being in need of our civilizing intervention: "Because we have not been able to penetrate into the continent of Africa and because we do not know what is taking place there, we are pushed to conclude that the African people exhibit innumerable vices, a conclusion which should rather be drawn had we been able to export ours."

Against the cosmopolitanism of his century, Rousseau is defending the irreplaceable and unique qualities of each separate culture, for he believes that from the commingling of cultures only further degeneration can come. Since all societies have not reached the same stage of development, Rousseau, given his premises, is bound to say that the least developed are the best and the closest to that ideal state of nature which even if it has never existed and even if we cannot return to it, must nevertheless continue to be the standard of comparison and judgment.

If this is true, the so-called primitive societies of Africa have a right to defend themselves against the intrusion of outsiders. This is what Rousseau would do if he were in charge of any of them: "If I were the head of any of the peoples of Africa, I declare that I would erect on the frontier of my country a gibbet on which I would hang without pity the first European who would dare to cross it, as well as the first citizen who would try to leave it." There would thus be two separate lines of gallows: one reserved for advancing Europeans, the other for fleeing Africans.

Rousseau feels that no further justification is needed for the hanging of Europeans, but the hanging of escaping Africans gives him pause and induces him to deal with the problem in more general terms. For the issue he has raised is that of the right of the community, by all available means, to force the presence and retain the allegiance of all its citizens. This can be justified by Rousseau only on the ground that the community he is talking about is an ideal community in which, in principle, only truth and the common good inspire public action and in which the state is never guilty of an unjust action. If this is the case, then the citizen who tries to run away is someone who wants to pursue evil rather than good. And this is the answer Rousseau gives to the question of why we should be opposed to the exit of a citizen who never intends to come back: "He hurts the other citizens by the bad example he gives and he hurts himself because of the vicious life he wants to pursue. In any case, the law must prevent this: better to see a man hanging than to see him corrupted." [30]

These views imply such a full integration of man with his society that he is deprived of the freedom to abandon it. They must be considered, however, along with two other aspects of Rousseau's thought that he was soon to develop: The first, of the humane view of the nation he was opposing to the cosmopolis, a nation dedicated to the preservation of beauty, of cultural virtues, of traditions committed to peace and restraint vis-à-vis all other nations; the second, to be found especially in the *Political Economy,* of the defense of human life and justice that was to be the essence of the general will.

[30] *O.C.* III, 90, 90–1, 91.

Rousseau is forever caught up in the tension he creates between the awful dilemmas he is setting forth in as shocking a manner as possible in order to awaken his readers to a serious consideration of the problem, and the infinitely happier, if austere, vision of the days to come. But the tide must first be turned.

Rousseau's views of democratic life find another concrete exemplification in his model among the republics of antiquity, Sparta. His critics had challenged Rousseau by drawing on the example of Sparta to support their own arguments. Had all of Greece been like Sparta, what would be left to us today? Bordes had asked rhetorically. Since it would have held arts and sciences in contempt no historians therefore would have been bred and nurtured to transmit its glory to posterity.

Rousseau, in his *Last Reply*, suggests that, had a Spartan been persuaded of the validity of this argument, he would have had to address his countrymen as follows:

Fellow citizens, open your eyes for you have been blinded. I am pained to notice that you are working only to acquire virtue, to practice your courage and maintain your freedom. You are forgetting your most important duty which is that of amusing the idle of future generations. Tell me, what is the possible use of virtue if it is not to be bruited about throughout the world? Of what possible use will it have been to be good men when nobody will talk of you? What will it matter in the centuries to come that you should have died at Thermopylae for the salvation of the Athenians if you do not leave behind, as they did, philosophical systems, poetry, comedies, sculpture? Hurry then to abandon laws which are useful only to make you happy and think only of how to make people talk about you once you will be no longer here. And never forget that if great men could not be commemorated, it would be useless to be one of them.

The condition of human happiness is good laws. The test of statesmanship is whether this condition is satisfied. This is why Rousseau has doubts about Pericles, not as a city planner but as a magistrate. His magnificence and taste is not disputed: "However, we still do not know whether Pericles has been a good magistrate because in the management of states the problem is not that of raising statues but that of the good governance of men." Well-governed men will also become good men. And good men living without splendor and without wealth will be happy men. There is no shorter and more secure way of creating human happiness.[31]

But often the commonwealths of antiquity have offered us venerable images in which "I see men raised by sublime institutions to the highest degree of greatness and virtue attainable by human wisdom." This proves how great can be the role of institutions in shaping the fortune of men. History displays before us the long series of stages of development of mankind. After man has abandoned the state of nature, he meets with successive and different conditions of organized life. In each, institutions exert their influence. In the state of nature man enjoys natural freedom. In varying forms of associated life man enjoys varying degrees of civil freedom. "The different political constitutions form between these two terms as many intermediate steps which begin with the excesses of license and end with those of tyranny." It soon will become obvious that all disorders are "derived more from the constitution of society than from that of man."

What is to be done today will, then, concern primarily the political institutions of a country. But Rousseau is not yet ready to face that task. In those years of diatribes, Rousseau's energies were concentrated on the negative task of criticism of what he thought was wrong with the times. The ultimate ideal is only barely visible in the turmoil of his fight against what exists. The

[31] O.C. III, 84–5, 85.

sophisms of the reasoners must first be set aside. The damage they do is immense.

For if we think seriously about the problems of social man and give up the prejudices of human vanity, we are bound to see that "all these great words of society, justice, laws, mutual defense, assistance to the weak, philosophy, progress of reason, are tricks invented by skillful politicians, all coward flatterers, to dominate the simple-minded." [32] First a clean sweep of the rhetoric; then some thoughts for the future.

In his parting polemical shot, the *Preface to a Second Letter to Bordes*, Rousseau gives us to understand that he has a great deal more on his mind than he has so far said. This short fragment conveys the feeling that Rousseau is completely confident of his grounds. He is no longer overly concerned with the arguments of his opponents: he seems to have gone beyond that stage and to have become the carrier of what, four times, he calls his *system*. [33] Precisely what the system is he does not say, only that it is a "sad and great system, the fruit of a sincere examination of the nature of man, of his faculties and of his destiny." This system is dear to Rousseau, even though it "humiliates" him. But what matters is not, because of vain pride, to make claims for man which cannot be sustained. What matters is not to hesitate to lower man, since we must avoid making a fundamental mistake as to what constitutes man's veritable greatness. By trying to push man toward the stars we are preparing him for his downfall. What we must rather fear is that "by persisting in our attempts to elevate ourselves above our nature we will end by falling below it," or

---

[32] *Fragments politiques,* O.C. III, 538, 540, 478, 475.

[33] As the editors of the *Confessions,* Gagnebin and Raymond, write: "As the polemical debate unfolds, one sees Rousseau's thought, in two or three years, develop and strengthen itself in an altogether surprising fashion. Under the pressure of the adversary, he is going to anchor himself to his ideas and take possession of what he will call his "sad and great system" (O.C. I, 1435–6).

that we may end up by preferring to be "vicious and miserable, rather than poor and uncivilized."

It is a "system" which Rousseau will defend because it is that of truth and virtue and we suffer because we have abandoned it. "The majority of men, having degenerated from their primitive goodness, have fallen into the errors which blind them and the miseries which crush them." It is a "true but painful system" which he could not have revealed all at once. He had to hide his true intentions under a veil of casualness in order to be able to continue at all.[34]

In spite of some obscurity and ambiguity of language it seems clear that Rousseau, in speaking of his "system," is referring to the complex of ideas, many of them grim ones, which had been accumulating in his mind and which he was to set forth in full in the *Discourse on Inequality*. More than to the present as such, he is referring to the concatenation of events which he sees as a "system," leading to the present.[35] Rousseau is aware of the scandal caused by his *Discourse on Arts and Sciences*. After 1750, he implies that he could not reveal all at once a system which would have caused a far greater commotion. The precaution of the gradual unfolding of his views was necessary so that he would be heard to the end. But by 1753 one of his more worthy opponents had become aware that what Rousseau was

[34] *O.C.* III, 103–7.

[35] This interpretation differs in emphasis from that offered by François Bouchardy, the editor of the *First Discourse* and of the replies, who writes that "these somber epithets relate to present facts which he denounces, and not to the conclusion he reaches and, in spite of everything, he hopes will come true" (*O.C.* III, 1284). But Gagnebin and Raymond, speaking of Book VIII of the *Confessions*, suggest a direct link between the "system" and the *Second Discourse*: "It is astonishing that such a small place be reserved to 'ideas,' in years which must have been devoted to very wide readings and to the meditation of the 'sad and great system' whose first account will be given in the *Discourse on Inequality*" (*O.C.* I, 1425).

offering was "a decided system." [36] The time had come to answer the question of the origins and foundations of inequality among men, and this was to be the heart of the revolutionary system he was about to reveal to the world.

There is no open appeal to revolution in the replies. But a revolutionary will manifests itself in almost every line, a revolution will certainly be necessary if an end is to be sought to the present corruption of man. A future "great revolution" may be the only remedy, but we should fear it almost as much as the ills which it might heal. It is both wrong to wish it and impossible to foresee it.

Narcisse

Before proceeding to the "system," let us consider the preface to *Narcisse*.[37] The play had failed after two performances at the end of 1752. But Rousseau would publish it so that he could address himself to the yet unfinished task of replying to his adversaries. This could be done by adding a preface, a document that Grimm found better than the play itself, with "some pages worthy of Montesquieu," [38] and that Rousseau himself later called "one of my good pieces." [39] From it we learn much about the author and about some of the major problems of politics, man and society, property, wealth, the state.

About the author we learn that Rousseau wants to widen and not to narrow the gap which separates him from his "adversaries." Why should those who oppose him not be called adversaries? The prevailing reluctance of writers with different opinions to clarify their respective positions is typical of a century in

[36] Cf., infra, p. 110, n. 45.   [37] O.C. II, 959–74.
[38] Cited by Jacques Scherer, the editor of *Narcisse*, O.C. II, 1861–2. See the whole of Scherer's interesting note (1858–65) on the long history (going back to 1729) of the play and on its interpretation.
[39] *Confessions*, O.C. I, 388.

which nothing is called by its proper name. If an alternative word can be found Rousseau will be happy to use it. In the meantime, he intends to "continue to call my adversaries my adversaries because in spite of the politeness of my century, I am as rough as the Macedonians of Philip."

There is a general conviction that "I do not believe one word of the truths I have upheld." But the test is simple: "It is not permissible to ignore that whenever a man speaks seriously one must think that he believes in what he is saying, unless his actions or his speech should contradict him." Rousseau could believe by 1753 that his thoughts corresponded to his actions and his way of life. He intended to give incontrovertible public evidence of that in case there were still any doubters.

For the moment he challenges the doubters to watch him with care and to study his principles and his personal behavior before they accuse him of contradiction and inconsequence:

If, however, they were to note that I begin to solicit the suffrage of the public or that I am becoming vain because I have written some pretty songs or that I am ashamed because I have written some bad comedies, or that I tried to damage the glory of my competitors . . . or that I aspire to membership in academies or that I am beginning to court fashionable women or that I praise to the skies the stupidities of powerful men or that I no longer am trying to live with the work of my hands, or if I were to begin to hold in contempt the profession I have chosen and were to start to move towards wealth, if they were ever to notice in one word that love of fame makes me forget that of virtue, I beg them to let me know, even publicly, and I promise that I will burn at once my writings and my books.[40]

In the meantime, Rousseau will continue to write books, verses and music, if he can do it, and he will continue to write openly about the world of letters. If in the future someone will

[40] O.C. II, 960, 961, 973-4.

say that this declared enemy of arts and sciences still writes pieces for the theatre, such talk will be "a very bitter satire aimed not at myself but at my century."

But the issues matter more than his person. Rousseau's critics have accused him of opposing the sciences as being intrinsically bad and by themselves the cause of all our vices, and of wanting to proscribe them, to burn the libraries, to close the universities, and to plunge us back into the barbarism of early centuries.

Rousseau considers this a travesty of his position. One may be for arts and sciences in principle, but still be concerned at the way in which culture in general has been used and developed to cause the corruption of morals. This corruption which affecting morals extends to all aspects of human life, individual and social, is too visible to be denied. While arts and sciences are the most obvious symbol of it, there are a thousand other sources of corruption which have contributed to our lamentable condition. History, since the collapse of the commonwealths of antiquity, has been a carrier of human tragedy. The ruin of the Roman Empire, the invasion of Europe, the Crusades, the discovery of the Indies, commerce and navigation, have increased human "disorder." "Whatever facilitates communications between different nations brings to each not the virtues of the others but their crimes and alters for all the morals and the customs which are proper to their climate and to the constitution of their government."

Of course, our historians are hiding the realities of history and the increasing corruption of man. They do not know why or how history is written. For them history seems to be made up of such important matters as "the births, the weddings, the deaths of a few princes; their hunts, their loves, their boring feasts, their sad pleasures and the poverty of their peoples." [41] Perhaps the true

---

[41] O.C. II, 964; *Fragments politiques*, O.C. III, 544.

historian should remove himself to earlier times when the subject matter of history was different and when real men and not mere semblances of men were the protagonists of history, and from that vantage point try to understand better the course of events.

While arts and sciences have become a kind of generic culprit whose responsibility is that of giving "to our vices an agreeable color, a certain honest air which stops us from being horrified by them," there are more immediate targets Rousseau intends to hit.

First of all, that part of the educational system which fails to relate the individual to the society in which he lives. Education has become purely literary. Worse, "we learn all the rules of grammar before we even have heard anything about the duties of man." We are taught in detail of all that has been accomplished until today, "but not a word about what we must do: provided we are capable of eloquent statements, no one will worry as to whether we know how to act or how to think."

This empty and formal education, better suited to provide for the survival of a student in a drawing room than to make him a good citizen, is the result of overrefinement and leads to idleness and to vanity. In the ideal state this would not happen: "in a well-organized state each citizen has his own allotted tasks to fulfill and these tasks are too important and dear to him to leave him the leisure to engage in frivolous speculations. In a well-organized state all citizens being equal no one can be preferred over others as the most learned, not even as the most skillful, but at most as the best." [42]

Directing the state, Rousseau seems to be saying, is too important a human activity to be left to the philosophers. How little does the eighteenth century realize what are the tasks that lie ahead in the management of human affairs and how much less

[42] O.C. II, 966, 965.

optimistic and easygoing an attitude one has to take in order to face the responsibility of keeping political societies on an even keel.

It is frightening to see how much modern political philosophers, from Hobbes to Mandeville and a "thousand others," have tried to distinguish themselves with their dangerous doctrines of contempt for the duties of man and of the citizen. "Our reasoning century" has accepted them all too readily. The danger lies in the relaxation of customs and laws. Contempt for the duties of men breeds contempt for established political ways. "The smallest change in customs, even if advantageous from a certain point of view, always brings prejudice to morals. Customs are the morality of the people." [43] Laws under these conditions become merely negative barriers which may sometimes succeed in preventing the worst but can never create the good society.

The most dangerous thing those who have taken charge of our culture have succeeded in bringing about, Rousseau suggests, is the weakening "of all the ties of mutual regard and benevolence linking men to society." Those who have fallen under the spell cast by our writers see themselves above everybody else. The indifference for mankind grows in the afflicted person in the same proportion as his love for himself. "The family, his country, become for him words empty of significance: he is no longer parent, citizen or man, he is a philosopher."

But there is more to Rousseau's criticism. What he sees at work is a process bound to lead to results which are the opposite of those intended by a philosophy based on interest and utility. "All our writers consider as the masterpiece of the politics of our century a system of arts and sciences, luxury and commerce, laws and other relationships, which, by strengthening among men the ties of society through appeal to personal interest, places all of

[43] O.C. II, 971.

them in a condition of mutual dependence, gives them reciprocal needs and common interests and compels each of them to contribute to the happiness of others in order to achieve its own."

Rousseau suggests the simultaneous development of two contradictory forces. Having said that philosophy weakens social ties based on mutual regard, he now is saying that it attempts to strengthen social ties based on personal interest. One development does in effect lead to the other, "for one cannot indeed strengthen one of these ties without weakening the other." [44]

Any theory maintaining that a strong society can be built primarily upon individual relationships of interest leads to the opposite result by weakening the ties of mutual solidarity which alone can keep that society strong. A foundation of personal interest is not enough to create a community. What is created instead is a potential state of civil war, a condition in which men cannot continue to live together without cheating, treason, mutual destruction. "It becomes necessary never to let ourselves be seen for what we really are: for every two men whose interests can be reconciled there are a hundred thousand others opposed to them." [45] This utilitarian philosophy is the tragic source of

[44] O.C. II, 967, 968 and note.

[45] During 1752–3, Charles Bordes had been busy preparing his own last reply to Rousseau's *Last Reply*. As the writing dragged on, *Narcisse*, with its preface, had appeared in print. Thus Bordes had the happy chance of answering two of his enemy's tracts. His *Second Discours sur les avantages des sciences et des arts,* of 1753 (to be found in Bordes, *Oeuvres diverses* [Lyon, 1783], II, 361–468), is interesting not only because it has the standing of an "official" reply by the academic world of France, but because it shows a rather quick mind that has become convinced that what was being spread by Rousseau was "a decided system" (361). He has easily seized upon two of the most important points in the preface, and tries to disprove both of them. It is wrong to say that for every two men whose interests coincide 100,000 have opposing interests, for the opposite is true (465). And Rousseau's statement that in a well-organized state all citizens are equal is also wrong (463–4). What is true is that wealth and luxury are harmless; to remedy their few evil

"the violence and treason, the perfidies and all the horrors necessarily required by a state of affairs in which every person, while
appearing to work for the welfare or the reputation of his fellow
men, is in effect only concerned with increasing his own above,
and at the expense of, everybody else's."

This is the constitution which our philosophers praise as the
culmination of a century-long flowering of the arts and sciences:
"A strange and calamitous constitution under which accumulated wealth always paves the way for the accumulation of even
greater wealth but under which any accumulation is out of the
question for the poverty-stricken; a constitution in which the
honest man cannot lift himself above his misery; in which the
worst rascals receive the most honors."

Rousseau is well aware that this has been said a hundred
times, but purely in a rhetorical way. While others may have
pointed to these evils Rousseau claims to have discovered their
causes. For all the pessimism of his overview, he is an optimist
because he is trying to prove that "all these vices are not attached
to man as such but to man badly governed." [46]

---

consequences, we should not try to go back to the rusticity of early times,
when equality did not exist in any case (416–20), and where war was
the rule. Progress has meant fewer wars and greater happiness (422–3)
and wealth has become a source of innumerable moral goods, first among
them a love of peace (424–5, 433). As for the poor, they are much better
off today than in the past. One should not describe as unhappy "men
whose work and industry are exercised freely and to their profit; who, born
in truth poor, are at least not deprived of the hope of wealth and are
maintained by the law in the possession of their freedom, the dearest of
all our goods, and of a kind of equality even with the wealthy and the
powerful" (426). Bordes had prefaced his essay with an agreeable
letter he had received from Rousseau in May 1753: "I have learned of
your last reply from M. Duclos who has read it and thinks highly of it"
(359–60). Perhaps Bordes thought that his former friend could still be
won over. In any case, the flattery of Rousseau could not yet do any harm
in the provinces.
[46] O.C. II, 968–9.

The best proof of this decisive statement, which Rousseau was not making for the first time, lies in a comparison between civilized and primitive societies, or, in his words, between European and savage societies. The pseudophilosopher is likely to say that since the European is a man and the savage is also a man, they are both alike and one is not better than the other. But the true philosopher is bound to say:

In Europe, the government, the laws, the customs, the interests, everything forces the individuals to constant mutual treachery: everything makes a vice a duty; their wisdom consists in being bad for there is no greater folly than to make a rascal happy at one's own expense. Among the savages personal interest speaks as loudly as among us, but the message it carries is a different one: the love of society and the care of their common defense are the only ties which bind them. The word *property* . . . has practically no meaning among them: they do not have divisive interests and nothing brings them to cheat one another. . . . It is quite possible that a savage be guilty of an evil action but it is not possible that he should continue to do so out of habit, for this would not help him at all. . . . I say it with regret: the good man is the one who does not have to cheat anybody, and the savage is that man.[47]

Even in societies closer to us in time, not every institution has been contrived to maximize, by the legal sanctioning of private interest, a constant antagonism between their members: "In those remote times in which a barely born and weak right of property was not yet established by laws, wealth was seen only as usurpation and when it was possible to deprive its possessors of it, to take away what did not in effect belong to them was hardly considered theft." [48]

What is to be done? Should the discovery of the "system," of the reasons why mankind had degenerated, justify the plunge

[47] O.C. II, 969–70 note.

[48] *Parallèle entre Sparte et Rome, Fragments politiques,* O.C. III, 543.

into chaos, the violent overturn of present institutions, the burning of books and the closing of universities? The answer is no. Rousseau reluctantly concludes that the semblance of order covering the horrible confusion, the simulacrum of civility hiding savagery, are better than total upheaval. A certain sweetness of custom, the mask of virtue acquired by crime, is preferable to open crime and slaughter. To live among rascals is perhaps better than to live among brigands. Time should be gained to think more carefully on a possible course of action.

V

The Roots of the Trouble

The Recovery of the Past, the Passage of Time, and the Study of Man

IN the eighth book of the *Confessions* Rousseau gives an account of his trip to the forest of St. Germain, where he hoped to find in the wilderness the inspiration he was seeking to cope with the new theme proposed by the Academy of Dijon on the origin of inequality among men.

It was November 1753 and the weather was beautiful. Thérèse, with a friend, relieved him of all cares and expenses, and Rousseau appeared only for the meals.

Throughout the rest of the day, buried in the forest, I was searching, and found, the image of the first times, whose history I proudly traced; I seized upon the small lies of men, I dared lay bare their nature, follow the progress of time and of the events which have disfigured it, and comparing the man of man with natural man, show them, for all his vaunted improvement, the veritable source of his miseries. My soul exalted by these sublime contemplations, . . . I proclaimed with a feeble voice they could not hear: fools, you who ceaselessly complain about nature, know that you are responsible for all your misfortunes.[1]

[1] O.C. I, 388–9.

In this way, we are told, the *Discourse on Inequality* was born.[2] Lost in the forest, Rousseau found the image of the beginning of time and the outlines of the history of man. Whether that history was real, as he wrote in the *Confessions*, or imaginary as he said in the *Discourse*, did not really matter. Perhaps the imaginary history was better. For it led him to the heart of his quest. By tearing aside the accumulated lies of centuries, he could unveil man's real nature and follow through the passage of time and history the changes which have altered it.

When Rousseau wrote the *Discourse on the Origins of Inequality* in 1753–1754 his purpose had not indeed been different from what he describes much later in the *Confessions*. It had already been that of finding beneath the successive layers of civilization the original make-up of man and to trace from it the changes which had caused the present inequalities. He was certain, no doubt, as his previous work had already shown, that as a consequence of the passage of time there had been a loss of much that was good, of much of the natural freedom and equality of man. But he was much less certain of how this loss could be established, or that the task of showing the difference between *l'homme de l'homme* and *l'homme naturel* was at all feasible.

The recovery of the past was imperative and he knew the influence of time was great. But to retrace time to its origins, and from that point follow the evolution of mankind, appeared to him an overwhelmingly arduous task. He was fully aware of it and did not yet have all the certainties of 1762.

He envisaged an unmeasurable gulf separating the past from the present, the first natural state of man from the present civil state. "In thus discovering and following the forgotten and lost

[2] *Discours sur l'origine et les fondemens de l'inégalité parmi les hommes,* O.C. III, 109–223.

routes that must have led man from the natural state to the civil state . . . every attentive reader cannot fail to be struck by the immense span that separates these two states." Furthermore, he was convinced that it was only through an awareness of the slow succession of things that a solution could be found to a multitude of moral and political problems which philosophers could not solve.[3]

But Rousseau did not claim that he could provide the foundation for their solution. He was trying first of all to go back to the origin of time and of the life of man. He was attempting to deal with the original condition of man—with that state of nature about which every philosopher had written with careless ease, by the simple device of transposing to that time the views and needs and aspirations of his own time. Rousseau refused to do this, while at the same time underlining the obstacles to be faced in reconstructing a state of man on a basis other than our own prejudices or our present condition. And yet the fundamental problem remains: that of understanding man before the onset of civilization and of the institutions which had so largely determined his behavior. This was the root of the issue: the contrast between the past and the present. If anything was to be done about the current plight of man, it was necessary to understand how he had got where he was.

The difficulties were great, for our ignorance was complete. The Europeans had been writing about man as they traveled around the world for the past three or four hundred years, but apart from the fact that many of them seemed interested in filling their purses rather than their heads, they had mostly been writing about themselves. Rousseau laments that the story of man has not begun.[4] When the "tourbe philosophesque"[5] tells

[3] O.C. III, 191–2.
[4] His program of field expeditions is not a modest one: "All of Africa and its numerous inhabitants, as distinctive in character as in color, are

us that "men are everywhere the same," it uses a short-cut, useful only to hide the differences among men and the transformations caused by varying economic and political systems. This equality among men perhaps did exist a long time ago, but today has been canceled by national variations due to the way in which men have organized in different manners their own affairs.

If the study of man could be undertaken on a wide scale, a new world would appear in all its variety. We could see mankind in different stages of its evolution, even today. And from a contemplation and comparison of the findings we could learn essential information about the moral and political problems with which we are struggling.[6]

---

still to be examined; the whole earth is covered by nations of which we know only the names—yet we dabble in judging the human race! Let us suppose a Montesquieu, Buffon, Diderot, Duclos, d'Alembert, Condillac, or men of that stamp traveling in order to inform their compatriots, observing and describing, as they know how, Turkey, Egypt, Barbary, the empire of Morocco, Guinea, the land of the Bantus, the interior of Africa and its eastern coasts, the Malabars, Mogul, the banks of the Ganges, the kingdoms of Siam, Pegu, and Ava, China, Tartary, and especially Japan; then, in the other hemisphere, Mexico, Peru, Chile, the straits of Magellan, not forgetting the Patagonias true or false, Tucuman, Paraguay if possible, Brazil; finally the Caribbean islands, Florida, and all the savage countries: the most important voyage of all and the one that must be undertaken with the greatest care. Let us suppose that these new Hercules, back from these memorable expeditions, then at leisure wrote the natural, moral, and political history of what they would have seen; we ourselves would see a new world come from their pens, and we would thus learn to know our own" (O.C. III, 213–4).

[5] O.C. III, 212.

[6] To say that Rousseau was the founder of the science of man is not an exaggeration. He even suggested the modern technique of a foundation-sponsored research project to carry out the necessary field work. "One admires the lavishness of some curious people who have, at great expense, made or arranged voyages to the Orient with learned men and painters, to draw pictures of ruins there and to decipher or copy inscriptions. But I have difficulty conceiving how, in a century taking pride in splendid

If direct observation had to wait, Rousseau's only recourse was to the powers of imagination and of speculative insight. In the search for natural man, the known facts were of little relevance, and imagination had to be used to remove from man the many layers of habits and interests superimposed by time. Rousseau refused to be deprived of the speculative tools which had enabled the scientists to inquire about the origins of the world. He refused to black out the ideas suggested to him by his imagination. He might in this way establish the pattern of change which, starting from what we were in the youth of mankind, has made us what we are today. This, he tells us, has led him to discover and follow paths of inquiry which proved revealing and fruitful. To his mind, what usually appeared as the absurd or comical aspects of the encounters and of the relationships between "savage man" and "civilized man," in Africa, in America, were no longer such, but were like flashes of lightning illuminating the real history of man. They were the essential clues needed to reveal the nature of man in his infancy.

Natural Man, Natural Law, the Original State of Nature and Its End

Unlike other political philosophers before him, Rousseau faces the problems of man in the state of nature by starting from the premise that man in the state of nature was a radically different being from civilized man, and that the main effort must be to get

knowledge, there are not to be found two closely united men—rich, one in money and the other in genius, both loving glory and aspiring to immortality—one of whom would sacrifice twenty thousand crowns of his wealth and the other ten years of his life to a celebrated voyage around the world, in order to study, not always stones and plants, but for once men and morals, and who, after so many centuries used to measure and examine the house, should finally make up their minds to want to know its inhabitants" (O.C. III, 213).

behind the artificial, the new, in order to find the natural, the original, characteristics of man.[7] There is no wavering in the belief that, since man is largely what institutions have made him, and since the result is bad, only by reconstructing as much as possible the way in which the change has occurred and thus identifying the multiple causes of the transformation of man, can any hope be nourished for a redress in the present intolerable state of affairs.

Rousseau's most worthy opponent is Hobbes, a philosopher whose genius and power Rousseau recognized, whose relentless analysis of the harsh and competitive world in which modern man moved Rousseau made his own, but whose vision of natural man Rousseau sharply rejected.

For Hobbes was the typical, as well as the most important, representative of those schools which, when describing natural man in the state of nature, were in effect describing man in an advanced state of social relationships. What they gave us was a pseudoprimitive man already endowed with a multitude of passions and needs which are actually the result of conditions of complex societies, and which presuppose the existence of an elaborate system of laws; a man endowed also with traits and desires which assume the full exercise of reason, something which appeared impossible to Rousseau.

Specifically, Rousseau cannot accept Hobbes' view of the aggressiveness of natural man and of his innate inclination to attack and fight; this would be logical only if there were something to fight about. Nor is natural man miserable, leading a nasty, short, and brutish life. The concept of unhappiness presupposes distress or painful deprivation, unknown to a free being whose heart is at peace and whose body is healthy.

[7] Montesquieu had come close to Rousseau's position by denying to natural man either speculative or rational powers. Cf. *Esprit des Lois*, Bk. I, ch. 2.

Nor, finally, is Hobbes right in ascribing pride to natural man. Hobbes fails to draw the essential distinction between love of oneself (*amour de soi*), a natural pillar of self-preservation, and pride or vanity (*amour propre*), a fictitious, social sentiment which is at the root of all that is evil in civilization:

Vanity and love of oneself, two passions very different in their nature and their effects, must not be confused. Love of oneself is a natural sentiment which inclines every animal to watch over its own preservation, and which, directed in man by reason and modified by pity, produces humanity and virtue. Vanity is only a relative sentiment, artificial and born in society, which inclines each individual to have a greater esteem for himself than for anyone else, inspires in men all the harm they do to one another, and is the true source of honor.[8]

Thus, what Hobbes gives us is a picture of man tangled up in all the contradictions and difficulties of an advanced society, one which makes war the normal condition of man, and his destruction its inevitable consequence. The imposition of government becomes a necessity to stop that war. Rousseau's disagreement is complete, for he reverses the historical vision of Hobbes and places war at the end, not at the beginning, of history. The course of history is not from war to a peace maintained through force by the Leviathan, but rather from relative peace to increasingly bitter social tensions and finally to a condition of latent civil war which can only be stopped from breaking out into open war by the removal of the causes which have brought that condition about.

Hobbes views the establishment of government as a most happy development for mankind and one to be maintained at all costs, for there is no condition worse than that of masterless and dissolute man. Rousseau views government as the potentially admirable fruit of man's sociability, but considers the beginnings

[8] O.C. III, 153–4, 152, 219.

of governments such as they exist today as the consolidation of certain forces and institutions which, if allowed to run their course unhampered, would be fatal to the happiness and freedom of man.

What then is Rousseau's picture of natural man? He tells us that, to reach his conclusions, he had to destroy a multitude of errors and prejudices, and that he had to dig down to the roots of things to prove his main contention that natural inequality is far from having had the importance and influence usually attributed to it. He had to discard all bookish descriptions of the principles by which natural man lived, for these principles were nothing but "rules which, for the common utility, it would be proper for men to accept for their cohabitation." He had to push aside all "scientific books which only show us men such as they have become and not as they were." [9]

By retreating to the superior vantage point offered by "meditation on the first and simplest operations of the human soul," he could begin to discern what appeared to him to be the true characteristics of natural man.

Two are fundamental and "anterior to reason," the fruit of internal, not external, pressure: love of self, or the spirit of self-preservation, and pity. And it is from these two principles, without the concurrence of that of sociability which is a later historical attribute of man, that all the rules of natural law flow: "rules which reason is later forced to re-establish on other foundations when, through its successive developments it has succeeded in suffocating nature." [10]

If self-preservation is readily admitted, pity is less so, even though it is a no less universal and spontaneous quality of man.

[9] O.C. III, 125, 160. Throughout his life, Rousseau will warn about blind reliance on book wisdom.

[10] O.C. III, 125–6. Cf. the skillful comments of Starobinski, *ibid.*, 1299.

But, Rousseau adds, even that most outrageous detractor of man, Mandeville, has acknowledged that pity is a natural virtue and that without it men would have been monsters.

This is a quality of man we still find in abundance in the less developed societies, or among the humbler people. It is a virtue which the modern philosopher, troubled in his tranquil sleep and torn from his bed only by vast dangers to the whole of society, does not feel. But savage man does not possess the cosmic wisdom of the philosopher, and he always thoughtlessly yields to the sentiments of humanity: "In street fights the populace gathers, the prudent man runs away. It is the 'canaille' that separates the fighters. . . ." [11]

To find natural law, then, we must move within the premoral boundaries of human behavior and refuse sternly to identify it with the accepted maxims of common utility of an organized society. The presumed permanent beliefs of mankind Rousseau finds to be nothing but the prevailing beliefs of civilized men, a collection of rules aimed to settle the complicated affairs of men busy in the pursuit of their interests. Rousseau's irony is directed at those who have made primitive man—man without language, without commerce, without property—the possessor of a sophisticated metaphysical system capable of developing alone sublime truth based on abstract reason. In what today we call natural law, we must see no more than the assemblage of those rules thought to be helpful to the maintenance of order in society and which certainly do not reflect the essence of "law" in the state of nature. [12]

In the original state of nature, then, man first of all wanted to keep alive. In the second place, he was controlled by the law of pity, based not on sociability but on a repugnance not linked to reason, to see sufferings in similar beings. Furthermore, he had

[11] O.C. III, 154, 156.   [12] O.C. III, 145–6.

none of that frenzied drive to achieve which might be part of calvinist ethics but not of the nonexistent ethics of original man. What he had was a wish to be free—that is, to be left alone by his fellow men as much as possible. Natural freedom meant isolation and the avoidance of social commitments.

This was the sum total of natural law and it was only after man had left the state of nature that what we today mistakenly call natural law was invented; by then nature was dead.

Within this context, Rousseau has his famous vision of natural man.

He is easily the best, the cleverest being roaming the face of the earth. All available evidence is incontrovertible on this point. The power and skill and speed of natural man has been proved even in historical times. How can one doubt that these were the qualities of the savage tribes who over the centuries have invaded Europe and Asia and easily overturned advanced civilization, all well endowed with customs, laws, and codes. Who can doubt the many eyewitness accounts brought back by modern travelers from all the continents and all recounting the speed of the Ottentots, the strength of the Indians, and in general the superior ability of all the savages with whom the Europeans have come in contact.

These superior physical characteristics went with a lack of other qualities such as those of foresight and planning. The fundamental reason was that natural man had no needs that he could not easily satisfy: the abundance of nature was within easy reach and he lived a daily routine which did not require any thought for tomorrow.

Nor can one say that the limited nature of his desires meant that he was miserable and poor. By the same token he was neither happy nor unhappy. These are sentiments requiring comparisons and standards, moral relationships and identified duties. Natural man was neither good nor bad, and had neither vices nor virtues.[13] The even tenor of his life made him reluctant to abandon it. If one cannot speak of happiness in modern terms, one can speak of a life that satisfied man's essential requirements. Rousseau writes that he has never heard of a savage lamenting his plight or wanting to kill himself, and again the evidence of all travelers is overwhelming in showing the lack of interest of savages for the refinements of European life, their deep attachment to their own way of life, and the eagerness with which all savages who seemingly had been Europeanized went back to it.[14]

The physical strength of natural man has as its main consequence the capacity of being independent. For in the state of nature it is contradictory to say that man is both strong and dependent. Man is weak when he is dependent. In the original state of nature, the strength of each leads to freedom and autonomy. The mobility of man, his ability to find sustenance and shelter, do not lead to aggression and oppression in the sense in which these terms are understood in society. By those terms we

---

[13] O.C. III, 152.

[14] "It is an extremely remarkable thing, for all the years that Europeans have been tormenting themselves to bring the savages of various countries in the world to their way of life, that they have not yet been able to win over a single one, not even with the aid of Christianity; for our missionaries sometimes make Christians of them, but never civilized men. Nothing can overcome the invincible repugnance they have against adopting our morals and living in our way. If these poor savages are as unhappy as it is claimed they are, by what inconceivable depravity of judgment do they constantly refuse to civilize themselves by imitating us or to learn to live happily among us; whereas one reads in a thousand places that Frenchmen and other Europeans have voluntarily taken refuge among these nations, spent their entire lives there, no longer able to leave such a strange way of life; and whereas one sees even sensible missionaries touchingly regret the calm and innocent days they have spent among such greatly scorned peoples? If one answers that they do not have enough intellect to judge soundly about their state and ours, I shall reply that the estimation of happiness is less the concern of reason than of sentiment" (O.C. III, 220–1).

mean a set of relationships from which the weak cannot escape, a set of institutions which give sanction to the greater power of the strong. The loose and free condition of primitive man roaming in the forest, while not preventing encounters and acts of hostility over the possession of the same animal or the same tree, provided a framework within which these conflicts were at once resolved, with each man retreating into the unlimited area of freedom which the state of nature gave him.[15]

The other assumption one must make is that there was no commerce or exchange of goods among natural men. This is true by definition, for if we talk about natural man we cannot say that his life was characterized by the artificial activities of today. Hence, without trade, without pride, or any idea of mine and thine, or any idea of justice, his casual relationships were such as to maintain in full his autonomy and freedom.

Rousseau's summing up is well-known: natural man was without arts, without language, without war, without a family, self-sufficient and free. His intelligence was there, and he was capable of making discoveries, but he could not communicate them: "The invention died with the inventor. There was no education or progress, and generations succeeded one another uselessly; and each one moving out from the same point, centuries were going by with all the grossness of the first times, the race was already old, but man remained always a child." [16]

If this was the original state of nature, it was not the world of a Christian gentleman described by so many philosophers. It was not the world of justice and injustice, of legal systems, of belief in ideas which could only be born in society. The truth is, according to Rousseau, that while everybody has felt the need of reaching the state of nature no one has arrived there: "They talked about savage man but were describing civilized man." [17]

[15] O.C. III, 154, 156.   [16] O.C. III, 159–60.   [17] O.C. III, 132.

The original state of nature might rather be described as one in which time stands still, one in which no cycle of development has set in, or, if there is one within the life cycle of every human being, growth and change are limited to a time span no longer than that of a human life, and always fall back to their starting point with each generation. It is a state, then, in which no revolution or upheaval is likely to take place, a state defined by the rough conditions of equality which nature has placed in man, one in which natural inequalities are quickly resolved by brief confrontations which do not alter the essential pattern. Ties of mutual dependence and of slavery are only the result of conditions which do not exist in the original state of nature, where, each being free of any constraint, the autonomy of primitive man is possible.

The key lesson in all of this, according to Rousseau, wholly apart from any empirical findings, is that a proper conception of the original state of nature has an immense significance of principle. Even if we say that it has "perhaps never existed, that it probably will never exist," it is still necessary to have of it a just notion "if we want to appraise correctly our present condition." [18] It is, then, as a standard of measure, as a model, as a term *a quo*, that Rousseau wants to come to grips with what he clearly conceives as a most hazardous, but most essential preliminary question. The state of nature is not a conceptual tool to be used to *justify* the present: it is a tool we need to *understand* it.

Once this point has been established, Rousseau tries to look at the boundary line of the original state of nature; that is, at the line beyond which man cannot move without entering a state different from the original one. As will become clear, Rousseau has faith in the potential of human progress. Thus, having defined the original state of nature as one in which time stands

[18] O.C. III, 123.

[126]

still, he is aware of the fact that time did not always stand still, and that sometime, somewhere, movement got under way. After a while the frontiers of the state of nature were reached and man abandoned it.

There are three main such boundaries: language, agriculture, and property. The development of language is linked by Rousseau to the establishment of a more settled family life, to the influence the child, in need of help and trying to express himself, had on the parents, as well as to the further relationships between family groups and the necessity of a more complex system of communication to express greater mutual needs. A community with a language is a community which has left the original state of nature, which has already a great deal of history behind it, and has entered a new phase of development no matter how far it may still be from a social state.

In his *Essay on the Origin of Languages*,[19] which is part of the *Discourse on Inequality*,[20] Rousseau contends that while on the one hand physical needs can be conveyed by signs, on the other hand passions, moral needs, the unfolding of reason, must gradually give rise to languages. Languages grow with societies and with the increasing complexities of their needs; they move from the language of poetry and song, which is the language of the earliest societies, to that of the alphabet, a characteristic of peoples already organized in political communities.[21]

[19] *Essai sur l'origine des langues, Oeuvres de J.-J. Rousseau*, Hachette ed., I, 370–408.

[20] The decisive evidence is given by Rousseau himself who, around 1763, in referring to the *Essay*, writes that it was nothing but a fragment of the *Discourse on Inequality* which he cut off as too long and out of place (Pierre Masson, "Questions de chronologie rousseauiste," *Annales*, IX [1913], 45–49).

[21] On music and language, cf. Gossman, "Time and History in Rousseau," *Studies on Voltaire*, ed. Theodore Besterman, XXX (Geneva, 1964), 319 ff.

Agriculture became another of the paths leading away from the state of nature. Earlier, men were scattered over the face of the earth, with the family the only society, the laws of nature the only laws. Rousseau calls these times "those of the dispersion of men."

Since Rousseau recognizes that the family was part of the life of man at this time, he does not have in mind the beginning of human life but a subsequent state, still of complete freedom but one in which a basic nucleus had been organized around the family. This he calls the "golden century" or the "age of happiness." This was so not because men were united but because they were separated: "Each considered himself the master of all. . . . His needs far from bringing him closer to his fellow men separated him from them." The paradox is that while a state of war seemed to prevail, "the whole earth was at peace."

We know why this was so. Needs could easily be satisfied in a noncompetitive world, amidst the abundance of the fruit of the earth. Casual encounters did not lead to permanent conflict. Movement and flexibility were the rule. Hunting and nomadic cattle-raising were the principal occupations. There was no fixed cultivation of the land, since there had been no division of it and no establishment of property rights: "Agriculture is an art which requires foresight. Man in society tries to extend himself, isolated man to limit himself."

Therefore, the turning point, on which everything else depends, was agriculture: "it brings property, government, laws and by stages poverty and crimes." And even the development of agriculture would have been different without the decisive intervention of climates and of great natural events. "Suppose the existence of a perpetual springtime on earth and everywhere the presence of water, cattle and pastures; suppose men coming from the hands of nature and scattered in the midst of all this, I cannot imagine them ever renouncing their primitive freedom and abandoning their isolated and pastoral life, one so well adapted to their natural indolence, in order to impose needlessly upon themselves the slavery, the toil and the miseries which are inseparable from the social state." [22]

Undoubtedly then, great natural commotions, such as earthquakes, floods, volcanic eruptions, and great forest fires, brought men together in order to defend themselves and repair the damages they had suffered. Also the necessity in warm countries of using scarce resources, such as water, brought men together in a way which, over a long period of time, facilitated not only the initial strengthening of the family but gradually the development of those other ties which underlie larger communities.

Before the hardening of human life imposed by an organized agriculture became unavoidable, mankind went through the happiest stage in its development, "where nothing marked the hours, nothing compelled man to keep time, time having no other measurement than amusement and boredom. Under old oak trees, the conquerors of time, an ardent youth gradually forgot its ferocity. . . . There the first festivals took place . . . the solicitous gesture was no longer adequate, voice accompanied it with impassioned accents; pleasure and desire, merged into one, made themselves felt at the same time: That was the veritable cradle of peoples; and of the pure crystal of fountains the first fires of love were born." [23]

Something less noble than love was gradually born too. Culti-

[22] *Essai*, 384, 385, 388, 392.

[23] *Essai*, 392. Are these festivals fulfilling a role of individual differentiation which is the opposite of the collectivistic role of the civic festival of the *Letter to d'Alembert*? (Cf. Starobinski's affirmative answer, *O.C.* III, 1344–5.) In the *Essai* Rousseau was describing the evolution from festivals to civil societies. In the *Letter*, he was trying to recover the lost conditions of community life.

vation began and with it the allotment of lands and the claims to crops by those who had raised them. By then the state of nature had been destroyed.[24] Because property had been born.

With settlements followed by accumulation, a process leading to increasing differences among men, fixed demands on goods were made by those possessing those goods. These claims gave rise to the idea of property. Where property appeared, "work became a necessity, vast forests became smiling fields which had to be watered by the sweat of men and in which quite soon, one saw slavery and poverty grow together with the harvest." [25]

The complexity, indeed the mystery, of this prolonged process did not escape Rousseau. He dealt with it by envisaging a succession of states of nature, from the beginning of time down to a certain moment when the evolution may be considered closed. After this terminal point Rousseau does not deny the reality of continuous change. But it is a change of a different kind. For the loss of freedom is already complete, and what happens later, in the dazzling display of lights of our civilization, is only a shuffling of the chains man has fastened around himself.

What we see of savage life today is not a representation of the original state of nature, but quite certainly the end of a long historical unfolding. Somewhere in between, Rousseau imagined he had caught a brief vision of an age of innocence, of the golden age of Utopia, a state in which with human faculties "keeping a just balance between the indolence of man's primitive state and the petulant activity of our pride," [26] man had enjoyed the longest era of happiness, one which represented the veritable youth of mankind and might have lasted forever.

How far we have come from those happy days. How did we reach the last of society, "where nothing can be changed any

[24] O.C. III, 145.   [25] O.C. III, 171.   [26] *Ibid.*

longer except with guns and money and since one has nothing anymore to tell the people except 'give money,' one says it with manifestos posted at the street corners or with soldiers in the houses?" Language has become useless. To carry out government orders, orators or popular assemblies are no longer needed: "On the contrary, it is necessary to keep the subjects scattered. This is the first rule of modern politics."

And Rousseau concludes: "Therefore, I say that any language which is incapable of making oneself understood to the assembled people is a servile language. It is impossible that a people could remain free and talk such a language." [27]

As he looks ahead, Rousseau is drawn to consider a final state of nature to be found tomorrow at the end of history and at the closing of the cycle of man's evolution. His thought here has the obscurity of prophecy. What he seems to be saying is that with mankind in an extreme state of inequality and oppression under the rule of a master, all notions of good and justice are dissolved entirely. The only law becomes that of the strongest and everything goes back to a new state of nature, "different from the one with which we have started, because one was the state of nature in its purity, while this last is the fruit of total corruption." [28] This must be the point at which Rousseau believes a revolution to be unavoidable. But before that point is attained there lies the entire forward social development of man. Progress must be accounted for.

Progress and Inequality

If language, agriculture, and property have had such far-reaching consequences, it is because man had the capacity to use

[27] *Essai*, 408.   [28] O.C. III, 191.

them in a unique fashion. For he had within himself the potential of "perfectibility" [29] which distinguished him from all other animals on earth.

It is in this potential that Rousseau sees the drama of man: "It would be sad for us to be forced to admit that this distinctive and nearly unlimited faculty is the origin of all of man's misfortunes; that it is this faculty which, over the course of time, has pulled him away from that original condition in which he would spend tranquil and innocent days." [30]

Yet this is what happened. Writing in 1754, Rousseau presents a picture of the progress of mankind all the more startling for being written before the industrial revolution. He is struck with awe by the immense material progress of mankind, its inventiveness and power. Man has been able to raise mountains and fill valleys, to dig lakes and dry marshes, to raise huge buildings and cover the sea with vessels. But the truth is that there is an astonishing lack of proportion between these material achievements and the happiness of man. The conclusion must be that man is pursuing his downfall in trying to secure what the protecting hand of nature had tried to hide from him. [31]

The possibility of perfection is limited or heightened by the role of chance and hazard in the progress of mankind. What has happened, might not have happened. How many turning points in the history of man were in part due to the fortuitous presence of events which might never have happened at all. As we have seen, nature plays a contradictory role, because it is likely that great natural catastrophes—floods, volcanic eruptions, and earthquakes—have forced men to come together for their protection.

Hence, the unresolved ambiguity of nature's role in forcing

[29] A neologism, making its first appearance around 1750. Cf. O.C. III, 1317-8.
[30] O.C. III, 142.   [31] O.C. III, 202.

progress on man. Rousseau is hinting at many things at the same time: progress should never have taken place, progress might never have taken place, progress was inevitable given the nature of man. The latter appears to be Rousseau's overriding belief. The problem then was that of how to reconcile progress with the freedom of man.

The long forward trek beyond the state of nature begins. Man, endowed by nature with the potential of perfectibility, starts on a long journey which is to end tragically for him. Stimulated by necessity, driven by interest, man begins to develop the social drives which during an unmeasured period of time had lain dormant. Once on the move, he could not halt to enjoy the balanced happiness which the very first organized settlements gave him. Man may then have had a sense of solidarity, the joy of family life, a greater feeling of security, without the disadvantages of civil life and the loss of freedom of later, bigger, more organized social structures. The process of change was, however, a continuous one, and Rousseau does not suggest anything about the duration or the real character of this intervening and best age of man.

For there is no going back, once the static conditions of early life have been abandoned. Common interests multiply and gradually man acquires certain ideas about mutual commitments and the advantages to himself in fulfilling them. He learns to distinguish between actions to be carried out alone and actions requiring the help of others. He begins to know from experience that his well-being depends on others for his realization. He also has become part of fixed family groups and determines his actions on the basis of relationships existing among separate families. Each family has become a self-sufficient, if small, society, and each group of families leads to the gradual transformation of a variety of qualities and sentiments which natural man had in himself. Love tends to become jealousy, strength becomes vanity, skill becomes competition. A dialectical process begins which causes a profound transformation in human behavior. Activities, by becoming communal, change their nature. Singing and dancing move from innocence to the stimulation of prideful feelings and a desire to show off to better advantage. The inequalities which nature has placed in man become more keenly felt and seen, and therefore tend to increase.

But these are not the only causes of inequality which receives an extraordinary impulse from the development of the skills by which man provides for his increasing needs and for his new needs, or exploits the inventions which time and chance, and his imagination as well, have placed at his disposal.

Agriculture and ironmongering were the two arts which produced this great revolution, "civilized men and lost mankind." [32] The American Indians, Rousseau tells us, were spared the benefits of agriculture and ironmongering, and for this reason have remained "savages" to our own day.

Regardless of the way in which these two discoveries were made, certain consequences followed inevitably. For both techniques were based on the possibility of greater rewards for greater skills, on the need for organization and the division of tasks—in brief, they made possible the rule of man over man.

Rousseau stresses the multiplier effect produced by the coming together of natural inequalities with the inequalities of "combination." By that is meant the technical inequalities which are favored by the processes of production and exchange, once goods are produced in different amounts by different men and for different purposes. It is at this point that the balance of natural inequalities, which might have been maintained in the original freedom of nature without the enslavement of the weaker members of the human race, is lost in organized society and is lost in a

[32] O.C. III, 171.

way which makes for a widening gulf among men placed in different circumstances.

The widening gulf can be seen in the development of hierarchies and of orders, of types of education and of standards of living, which all make their appearance in civil society, whilst they are unknown in the state of nature with its uniformities and simplicities.[33]

As techniques lead to hierarchies, hierarchies lead to institutions which are the final stage in the sanctioning of inequality. Institutions backed by laws, which are the voice of civil justice, freeze, for a time at least, a fluid process. They mold to their image the activities of men. By telling them what to do, they make them what they are. By providing a guidepost for their actions, they give them their beliefs of right and wrong.

With the appearance of institutions, government is founded, and man has realized his potential for sociability. Man has become a citizen. But what a price he has paid:

Savage man and civilized man differ so much in the bottom of their hearts and inclinations that what constitutes the supreme happiness of one would reduce the other to despair. The former breathes only repose and freedom; he wants only to live and remain idle; and even the perfect quietude of the Stoic does not approach his profound indifference for all other objects. On the contrary, the citizen, always active, sweats, agitates himself, torments himself incessantly in order to seek still more laborious occupations; he works to death, he even rushes to it in order to get in condition to live, or renounces life in order to acquire immortality. He pays court to the great whom he hates, and to the rich whom he scorns. He spares nothing in order to obtain the honor of serving them; he proudly boasts of his baseness and their protection; and proud of his slavery, he speaks with disdain of those who do not have the honor of sharing it. What a sight the difficult and envied labors of a European minister are for a Carib!

[33] O.C. III, 174, 160–1.

How many cruel deaths would that indolent savage not prefer to the horror of such a life, which often is not even sweetened by the pleasure of doing good.

Man no longer knows security, and in effect he is a slave of others. He has reached a condition of inequality which defies any comparison with any natural inequality. Indeed, the inequality of mankind has its roots and draws its power of growth from the development and progress of the human spirit. In the end, it has become fixed and has been legitimized by the rights of property and by the systems of laws.

How can anyone doubt that it is against natural law, as Rousseau understands it, "that a child should rule over an old man, that an imbecile should lead a wise man, and that a handful of people should fatten itself with superfluities, while the hungry multitude is deprived of the essentials of life?" [34]

What an incredible contrast faces us as we compare "the man of men" with "natural man." After untold centuries of sufferings, man has developed his capacity for perfectibility, he is reaping the fruits of the qualities which God has implanted in him alone among other animals. All his faculties have ripened: memory, imagination, reason, the mind.

On the other hand, he is no longer free and independent. Having acquired a multitude of new needs, he is bound to his fellow men, even when he is their master. If he is wealthy, he needs their work; if he is poor, he needs their money; if he is in the middle, he still cannot act alone.[35] Harshness, ambition, treachery, jealousy, become part of man's daily life. Society becomes a forced cohabitation of men of conflicting interests who are moved only by a latent desire to destroy one another at the first opportunity. In the society of man brought to flower in the

[34] O.C. III, 192–4.   [35] O.C. III, 175.

seventeenth and eighteenth centuries, everything is reduced to property and competition. The mask of mutual benevolence hides an ever-present urge to destroy those who may stand in the way of the further acquisition of personal advantages. The multiplication of private needs does not lead to an increase of public benefits, as the economists of the time were saying, but rather to the multiplication of wounds inflicted on private men, to a rise in the tensions of society, to a weakening of the chances of peace and happiness.

In the *Discourse on Inequality*, Rousseau delivers himself of some of his most celebrated utterances. Social man is bad. He is bad because he is forced by the institutional setting to act in a way which is contrary to the interests of other men. Thinking man is a depraved animal. Natural man is a child of intuition and passion. The development of man's rational faculties has taken place within a progressively worsening framework:

The extreme inequality of our way of life; excess of idleness in some, excess of labor in others; the ease of stimulating and satisfying our appetites and our sensuality; the overly refined foods of the rich, which nourish them with binding juices and overwhelm them with indigestion; the bad food of the poor, which they do not even have most of the time, so that their want inclines them to overburden their stomachs greedily when the occasion permits; late nights, excesses of all kinds, immoderate ecstasies of all the passions, fatigues and exhaustion of mind; numberless sorrows and afflictions which are felt in all conditions and by which souls are perpetually tormented: these are the fatal proofs that most of our ills are our own work, and that we would have avoided almost all of them by preserving the simple, uniform, and solitary way of life prescribed to us by nature. If nature destined us to be healthy, I almost dare affirm that the state of reflection is a state contrary to nature and that the man who meditates is a depraved animal.[36]

[36] O.C. III, 138.

The contrast between natural man and civilized man is clear when we consider the consequences of their actions. They are limited for the former, and cumulative for the latter. As Rousseau has often said, a clash in the state of nature is quickly resolved and leaves no permanent harm behind. Clashes among civilized men are not only more frequent because of the closely knit web of existing relationships, they are more vicious in their aftermath. There is the driving force of gain and greed, which pushes man to look first for necessities and then for the superfluous and later still for useless riches acquired at the expense of others.

Forces are at work which support the reaching for limitless power and wealth. There is a nightmarish vision summoned up by Rousseau in which the strongest and most successful man on earth has finally succeeded in getting hold of all the wealth of the world, and having killed everybody else, rules alone over the universe.[37]

Long before this awful state is ever reached, hypocrisy has come to characterize civil life. Rousseau again uses, as he had done in the *Discourse on Arts and Sciences,* the notion of moral dissembling to explain the way in which men live in society and the inequalities by which they are afflicted. If one does not have the qualities and the skills, the wealth and the power, that are needed to acquire the consideration and approval of one's fellow man, it then becomes important to appear to have them or to affect them, and to parade before others as something that one is not. "Being and appearing became two altogether different things, and from this distinction have come the showing off, the tricky treachery, and all accompanying vices." [38]

Life becomes a game with an empty façade of philosophy, of humanitarianism and polite manners, behind which hides a

[37] O.C. III, 203.   [38] O.C. III, 174.

quite different reality. We see the triumph of honor without virtue, of reason without wisdom, of pleasure without happiness. This was certainly not the original condition of man. If society with its inequalities has changed our natural inclinations, the purpose of political philosophers should be that of teaching men how to try to rediscover and practice them. But the state stands in the way.

The First State, Property, and Economic Man

As man was nearing the end of his evolution to civility, the first state was born. Society had to become political society, with certain practical arrangements made to allow it to fulfill what had become its predominant purpose. The absence of some institutional agreement could no longer be endured. Rousseau leaves in no doubt the reason why: the rich could no longer tolerate it.

It is not possible that men should not at least have reflected upon such a miserable situation and upon the calamities overwhelming them. The rich above all must have soon felt how disadvantageous to them was a perpetual war in which they alone paid all the costs, and in which the risk of life was common to all while the risk to goods was theirs alone. Moreover, whatever pretext they might give for their usurpations, they were well aware that these were established only on a precarious and abusive right, and that having been acquired only by force, force could take them away without their having grounds for complaint. Even those enriched by their efforts alone could hardly base their property upon better titles.[39]

At first sight, Locke and Rousseau do not appear to differ very much in the answer they give to the origin of government: it was to secure property. The difference lies in their judgment of its meaning. For Locke it means the translation into a constitutional

[39] O.C. III, 176.

right of a fully validated right based on natural law. For Rousseau, the translation into tyrannical and temporary institutions of a usurpation by the few at the expense of the many.

For Rousseau maintains that what the rich had to defend were gains based on force and on precarious and abusive titles, and that even those who had acquired wealth through their own individual labors could not claim more acceptable titles. All were exposed to the harassment of the propertyless, the vengeance of the poor. It was at this point that what Rousseau with bitter irony calls "the most thoughtful project ever conceived by the mind of man" was put forward by the hard-pressed rich: "It was to use in his favor the very forces of those who attacked him, to make his defenders out of his adversaries, inspire them with other maxims, and give them other institutions which were as favorable to him as natural right was against him." [40]

By appearing to guarantee equality under law, order, and the peaceful enjoyment of individual possessions, they managed to subdue and to persuade those whose interests were quite different. Everybody rushed to be put in irons thinking it was their freedom they were defending.

This is a view which explains the first origins of government and of law purely on the basis of the interests of the possessing class. Regardless of specific historical evidence, "such was, or must have been, the origin of society and of laws." No matter how camouflaged their public announcements were, hiding behind them was the determination of the rich to place themselves in a better condition to defend what they had. The result was an arrangement "which gave new fetters to the weak and new forces to the rich, destroyed natural freedom for all time, established forever the law of property and inequality, changed a clever usurpation into an irrevocable right, and for the profit of a

[40] O.C. III, 177.

few ambitious men henceforth subjected the whole human race to work, servitude, and misery." [41]

Rousseau is aware that this view of the origin of government would be challenged. He therefore lists two alternative theories: the first, the establishment of government by right of conquest; the second, government as the union of the weak. As for the first, Rousseau feels that the right of military conquest cannot give birth to any legal government, since it is based on an act of war which can have no lawful consequences. Until a free choice is possible there is no real body politic.

As for the second, Rousseau finds the words "strong" and "weak" equivocal and prefers "rich" and "poor." This being the case, why should the poor, "with nothing to lose but their freedom," be eager to seize the initiative to give up their one remaining good, to gain nothing in exchange? The rich, on the other hand, being exposed on all sides and vulnerable to attack and injury, could with much greater justification initiate steps intended to protect them. Rousseau concludes by saying that "it is reasonable to believe that something has been invented by those to whom it is useful, rather than by those to whom it is damaging." [42]

A government thus born could not have an easy and constant growth, as it was weighted down by an original sin: its commitment to the defense of property and hence of inequality had irremediably harmed its chances of future development. From time to time a wise philosopher could detect the root of the trouble, but little could be done about it. One kept repairing and changing the patchwork of institutions, while one should have started by uprooting everything that existed in order to build anew.

But this revolutionary clearing of the ground has never been

[41] *O.C.* III, 178.   [42] *O.C.* III, 179–80.

possible, and the resulting gradual evolution of government has been for the worse. The initial property-right laws were followed by the creation of public officials to enforce them, while ultimately institutions which in the beginning had the appearance of legitimacy became the source of arbitrary power.

If we follow the progress of inequality in these different revolutions, we shall find that the establishment of the law and of the right of property was the first stage, the institution of the magistracy the second, and the third and last was the changing of legitimate power into arbitrary power. So that the status of rich and poor was authorized by the first epoch, that of powerful and weak by the second, and by the third that of master and slave, which is the last degree of inequality and the limit to which all the others finally lead, until new revolutions dissolve the government altogether or bring it closer to its legitimate institution.[43]

Human history, then, given its starting point, must proceed along certain unavoidable lines. This is so because "the vices that make necessary social institutions are the same ones that make their abuse inevitable." And the terminal point of this process must be a "new revolution," a phrase Rousseau is using to signify the recovery of human freedom lost by the private appropriation of the common wealth.

One can again go back to the parallel between Locke and Rousseau. With the securing of private property rights, individual liberties were also secured, according to Locke, for the two could not be separated. By contrast, the securing of the former lost the latter, according to Rousseau. But if individual liberty was lost, it could never be alienated, because one can never alienate one's own freedom as one can one's own property. New generations as they are born cannot admit that their forebears have lost for them what belongs to them absolutely and by natural right.

[43] O.C. III, 187.

This then is the real state of the civilized world in which arts and sciences flourish, one in which laws sanction injustice instead of creating justice. It is one which tends to lengthen the distance between whatever qualities and virtues man had and the reality of the daily life. It tends to make man worse than he could be. It gives a higher place to material values and goods than they should have in a well-ordered society. It makes economic man the dominant figure on the human landscape. All the tangled web of wealth, profits, trade, and power is there to enmesh man in a hopeless way. Rousseau is the first great thinker to focus his thoughts on the condition of man as it has been shaped by the uncontrolled conflict of private economic interests.

The drama of the transformation of natural into civilized man is the drama of the poor versus the rich, of the propertyless versus the property owner. The ever-present theme in the age-long history, or ideal history, that Rousseau gives us to explain the origin of political inequality is that of the way in which certain men found it possible to acquire decisive power through the use of economic riches. We have seen how in the initial founding of organized political society and in the shaping of the first government institutions, wealth played a decisive role. This was a "contractual" founding, which had no relationship to the "social contract" of Rousseau's later democratic community. For it was a "contract" between those who had and those who had not, imposed on one of the contracting parties by the other.

The turning point had, of course, come much earlier. It came at that moment, ominous for the future of mankind, when first someone, in the words of Rousseau, "having built a fence around a piece of land, thought of saying, *this is mine,* and found men simpleminded enough to believe him." At that moment the original state of man came to an end, and all the claims to individual control over goods made from then on belong to a period of human history which no longer can be confused with the state of nature. The founding of government represents the end of the process. The much longer intervening period is one in which men of wealth gathered strength and devised the instruments to consolidate it.

As Rousseau contemplates the contemporary world of civilization and means, he is filled with contempt and anger. The decisive contrast is between the poor and the rich. The real strength of man is to be found in the common man, in the people, where natural sentiments can, from time to time, pierce through. In the higher, that is wealthier, ranks of society, those sentiments "are totally stifled, and under the mask of sentiment there is nothing but interest or vanity."

It is therefore not surprising that Rousseau should analyze civilized man in terms of the scope and influence and consequences of his economic activities. The picture he draws is dismal, and all the more striking because, in spite of its having been drawn in the middle of the eighteenth century, it anticipates so many of the issues and difficulties to come. Rousseau looks at economic man in terms of the problems he is creating for himself, for his own domestic political society, and for the relations of that society to other national societies. He looks at economic man in terms of the practices of a money economy based on competition, trade, profits and profiteering, and luxury. He sums up his reflections in one of the ugliest overviews of the conditions of life of modern man.

Where man himself is concerned, the utilitarian view of life has given rise to a devouring ambition, and has pushed man to seek advantages which benefit him not so much as they damage others, and to deepen the break in the personality of man between what he really wants to do and what he asserts he is doing.

A political society based on the acceptance of this individual utilitarianism must be one in which an accelerated trend towards inequality is inevitable. Such a society soon becomes unjust because the inequalities that are increasingly written into the law are not those that could derive from the small natural inequalities found among men. Those alone could find legitimate recognition, in equitable and generally applicable norms, in positive law: "Inequality, being almost null in the state of nature, draws its force and growth from the development of our faculties and the progress of the human mind, and finally becomes stable and legitimate by the establishment of property and laws. It follows, further, that moral inequality, authorized by positive right alone, is contrary to natural right whenever it is not combined in the same proportion with physical inequality." [44]

How soon this trend is actually realized is less important than the identification of its source. In a society whose basis has become wealth, even if in the beginning of time personal traits determined inequalities, "wealth is the one to which they are reduced in the end." Wealth is the final determinant not only of inequality, but of all other power relationships within the community. In the ultimate analysis, Rousseau is saying, wealth rules because "it can easily be used to buy everything else." [45] If this is so, then any political revolution aiming to bring society closer to the conditions of natural man must be one willing to face the problem of the regulation of wealth.

But wealth has not only damaged man and the political society in which he lives, it is also responsible for the wars in which different nations have engaged. For it was only when different national societies were organized that wars began, and mankind witnessed horrors unknown in the state of nature.[46] War, then, is a characteristic of mankind in its later stages of evolution. It tends to increase in intensity with the greater and greater organization and interdependence of man. Man has been moving away

[44] O.C. III, 193–4.   [45] O.C. III, 189.   [46] O.C. III, 178–9.

from the peace and harmless conflicts of its early days largely because of the usurpations which destroyed his original innocence and goodness.

The crisis of the contemporary world, Rousseau tells us, can be fully explained only if we take into account the many new and complicated ways in which wealth and economic power are being used. How far are we from the relatively harmless primitive greed that prompted the first man to put up an enclosure around his field? Ours has become a money economy in which signs representative of wealth have been invented [47]—those signs which Locke considered an invaluable device for the orderly processes of economic accumulation (gold and silver did not deteriorate) but which Rousseau envisages as damaging tools in worsening equalities among men.

For man could now plunge into a frenzy of economic activity such as was not possible before, and engage in trading and producing—roles in which competition, profits, and downright violence to the welfare of the many became the guidelines. Hence, the deepening of the gap between appearance and reality, the appearance of a busy world in which interdependence keeps everybody in line and working for the happiness of others and from which flows his own happiness, and the far different reality. Under the mantle of universal benevolence, there is concealed the increasing hate with which each individual operator views the activities of his competitors. Commerce is based on a desire to inflict as many losses as possible on others. Traders wish for the sinking of their rivals' ships, just as individuals long for the death of their rich relatives.

The profit motive leads to profiteering by speculators on national calamities, on the sick and the wounded in wartime. Wars themselves become the source of great wealth. In the end there is

[47] O.C. III, 175.

no doubt that man profits more economically by doing evil than by doing good, and that this is favored by the institutions on which his society is based. How can one avoid the conclusion, Rousseau writes, that that system is bad which dictates rules of action "directly contrary to those that public reason preaches to the social body?" [48]

The final corruption of developed societies is caused by luxury. Rousseau might agree that luxury was impossible to prevent where men were after their own convenience and the consideration and approval of others. But let there be no doubt that what luxury achieved was to bring to a head the sickness of a utilitarian society and that far from enabling the poor to survive, it was impoverishing the entire community. It was the worst of all the evils that could befall a state, large or small: "To feed the crowds of lackeys and miserable people it has created, it crushes and ruins the farmer and the citizen, like those burning winds in the south which, covering the grass and greenery with devouring insects, take subsistence away from useful animals, and bring famine and death to every place where they make themselves felt." [49]

The specific economic reason on which Rousseau based his stand against luxury was essentially the belief in the superiority of agriculture over industry. Agriculture was for Rousseau both the most important activity of man as well as the least profitable. The two went together in his judgment: it was the most important because it provided the food without which man could not survive; it was the least lucrative because, given the poverty of mankind, it had to produce at prices which could be paid for by the poorest of man. Any economic system, therefore, which drew away the energy of man from the production of the essentials to that of the superfluous would lead to the decline, both economic

[48] O.C. III, 202–3.   [49] O.C. III, 206.

and moral, of the state. With the growth of arts and industries the countryside is emptied and the peasants look for bread in cities, while they should bring it to them. The more we are struck with admiration by the splendor of the great capital cities, the more we must realize that this is happening at the expense of an abandoned countryside.

Happy is the state which has known how to avoid the destructive influence of luxury. In the Dedication to the Republic of Geneva which opens the *Discourse on Inequality,* Rousseau imagines that Geneva has succeeded in doing that. He is glad to think that the so-called gentlemen of taste will have to look elsewhere for "grandiose buildings, beautiful carriages, superb furniture, the pomp of theaters, and all the refinements of softness and luxury." In Geneva they will only find men and a community morally strong because it has avoided the extreme degradation of civilization.[50]

But Geneva was the exception, and everywhere else mankind had reached a phase of development which posed the question of the end of civilization itself, of how long community life was possible under the conditions which seemed to be universally present in the more advanced societies. In these comments on the life of civilized man, Rousseau is describing a world to come, an era to be born of an industrial revolution that was just beyond his horizon. For if it is true that he was polemizing with a society of arts and sciences in which modern industry had made its appearance, this was still an industrial system based on limited production, in which quality and not quantity counted. Even so, his description applies to a full-fledged industrial society and is all the more remarkable as it anticipates the life of man in the mass societies of the middle of our own century.

Industrial workers are forced into unhealthy jobs, in mining,

[50] O.C. III, 120.

in metalwork, in metallurgy, which shorten their lives. In the great cities man is more and more forced to eat monstrous mixtures of improperly kept foodstuffs. He has to heal himself with mislabeled drugs and to suffer the thievery of those who sell them as well as the errors of those who administer them. The large metropolitan centers with their poisoned air multiply epidemic diseases, while the natural strength of man is weakened by the conditions under which he lives. Adding all this up, we can see how high a price nature is exacting from man because of the contempt in which he now holds nature's teachings.[51]

One has only to think of what representative philosophers of the Enlightenment, from Voltaire to Condorcet, were saying on the benefits of progress, to measure the distance which separates Rousseau from his culture. At a time when belief in the marvels of science was leading to the first attempts to build a doctrine of politics in which the coordinated and planned activities of the

[51] "If you consider the mental anguish that consumes us, the violent passions that exhaust and desolate us, the excessive labors with which the poor are overburdened, the still more dangerous softness to which the rich abandon themselves, and which cause the former to die of their needs and the latter of their excesses; if you think of the monstrous mixtures of foods, their pernicious seasonings, corrupted foodstuffs, falsified drugs, the knavery of those who sell them, the errors of those who administer them, the poison of the containers in which they are prepared; if you pay attention to the epidemic illnesses engendered by the bad air among the multitudes of men gathered together, to the illnesses occasioned by the delicacy of our way of life, by the alternating movements from the interior of our houses into the fresh air, the use of garments put on or taken off with too little precaution, and all the cares that our excessive sensuality has turned into necessary habits, the neglect or privation of which then costs us our life or our health; if you take into account fires and earthquakes which, burning or upsetting whole cities, cause their inhabitants to die by the thousands; in a word, if you unite the dangers that all these causes continually gather over our heads, you will sense how dearly nature makes us pay for the scorn we have shown for its lessons" (O.C. III, 203–5).

scientists would be harnessed to produce at a regular and foreseeable rate the inventions and new techniques needed to push civil societies toward dazzling peaks of perfection and happiness, Rousseau was describing an age of anguish and violent passions, an age of revolution in which the machine, urban life, the increasing dependence of man on artifacts, far from being sources of strength and welfare, were creating moral, political, and economic problems whose very existence everyone had as yet refused to admit.

To have anticipated the crisis of the industrial revolution before that revolution had occurred, and on the basis alone of a speculative image of the nature of man to have offered a criticism of the premises of utilitarian individualism—these are two of Rousseau's greatest achievements and a main reason why we read him today.

The "Dedication" and the Ideal State

Emile learns manual work, because "we are approaching a state of crisis, and the century of revolutions." The crisis will arise out of the disorders and conflicts of our civilization, which under a peaceful outward appearance conceals the germs of cruel division, with different classes harboring for each other suspicions and mutual hatred because of the opposition of their interests.

The extreme inequality of conditions will give an opportunity to political chiefs "to stir up all that can weaken men in society by dividing them." Society will be atomized by an exploitation of the deep uneasiness created by social injustice, and leaders will arise capable of using for their ends the resulting conditions. As society disintegrates a revolutionary phase will begin.

Out of these revolutions a despotism will be born to establish itself over the ruins of the republic and its laws. "The times that would precede this last change would be times of troubles and calamities, but in the end everything would be engulfed by the monster, and peoples would no longer have chiefs or laws but only tyrants. From that moment also morals and virtue would cease to be in question." [52]

In this total despotism there would be a dissolution of the human personality and of any rule or institution to which it could cling. This is what Rousseau means by a return to a second state of nature, in which totally isolated men would live in a state of corruption quite unlike that of goodness and innocence of the first state of nature.

Faced by this fearful picture of a totalitarian future, what is there to do? "Must we demolish societies, destroy the distinctions between mine and thine, and go back to live in the forests with the bears?" This conclusion would suit his enemies, writes Rousseau, and he states it himself rather than leave them "the shame of drawing it." [53]

But the real alternatives are only two. For the few who are not committed to social life and who can cut their bonds, a retreat into the wilderness is the best solution. "You can leave your fatal acquisitions, your worried minds, your corrupt hearts, and your unbridled desires in the midst of cities; reclaim, since it is up to you, your ancient and first innocence; go into the woods to lose sight and memory of the crimes of your contemporaries, and have no fear of debasing your species in renouncing its enlightenment in order to renounce its vices."

But for the great majority of men, including Rousseau himself, "whose passions have forever destroyed their original simplicity, and who cannot any longer nourish themselves on grass and nuts, nor do without laws and rulers," this easy way out is impossible.

It may also be impossible because men have been persuaded

[52] O.C. III, 190–1.   [53] O.C. III, 207.

that a divine voice has called all humankind to develop its
faculties and to participate in communal living (what Rousseau
is actually saying is rather more obscure and imprecise: while
man was not born a political animal, he had in himself the
potential of becoming one, and he may feel that he received this
gift from a divine power). They must, therefore, hold their
ground and fight against the surrounding evils.

They will respect the sacred bonds of the societies of which they are
members; they will love their fellowmen and will serve them with all
their power; they will scrupulously obey the laws, and the men who
are their authors and ministers; they will honor above all the good
and wise princes who will know how to prevent, cure, or palliate that
multitude of abuses and evils always ready to crush us; they will
animate the zeal of these worthy chiefs, by showing them without
fear and flattery the greatness of their task and the rigor of their
duty. But they will nonetheless scorn a constitution that can be
maintained only with the help of so many respectable people—who
are desired more often than obtained—and from which, despite all
their care, always arise more real calamities than apparent advantages.[54]

The good citizen who will undertake to do all this in the tragic
days of the extreme crisis which has fallen upon his society will
carry out his activity gladly, and his first duty will still be to the
constitution, in spite of his belief that it is unworkable and will
in the absence of drastic change still yield more harm than good.

These are the dilemmas of Rousseau; a return to the original
state of nature is unthinkable. The road man has followed cannot be retraced. We must cultivate the memory of a lost age, but
we cannot go back to it. The acceptance of an ultimate and
totally corrupt and despotic second state of nature is equally
intolerable. The condition of modern man is a tragic one because
he must fight for improvements and reforms he knows are inca-

[54] O.C. III, 207–8.

pable of achieving the desired results. As he concludes the *Discourse on Inequality*, Rousseau cannot indicate a way out of the dilemma. But at the same time, he is anxious to see whether something can be done.

Much later, thinking back upon these years of the mid-1750's, he wrote: "I saw that everything depended in a radical way upon politics." [55] This is not an expression of despair. If politics occupy the foreground of the social structure, then they are bound to play a primary role in human affairs and might be influenced in such a way as to produce the desired results. If politics express themselves in institutions, then institutions can be changed and shaped to suit the interests of the community. Thus the hopeless despair of man, unable to go back to the first state of nature and powerless to avoid the coming of the second, might give way before the decisive role of politics and the belief that, if it was true that no people would ever be better than what its government made it, a reshaping of the institutions of government might lead to the partial recovery of wisdom and freedom.

Rousseau had in effect been expressing this thought repeatedly and for some time. In the preface to *Narcisse* he had said that the social vices he was lamenting were not so much part of the nature of man as the consequence of bad government, and that he was certain that, in the long run, people were what their institutions had made them.

In the *Discourse on Inequality* he thought he had on balance strengthened the argument of the opportunities open to social man to improve his lot. In an important *Letter to Philopolis*, [56]

---

[55] *Confessions,* bk. ix, O.C. I, 404.

[56] *Lettre de J. J. Rousseau à M. Philopolis,* O.C. III, 230–36. The letter, written in the fall of 1755, was not published until 1782. It was addressed to Charles Bonnet, a Genevan scientist who had published in the *Mercure de France* of October 1755 a criticism of the *Discourse on Inequality* (its text will be found in O.C. III, 1383–6).

written shortly after the *Discourse,* Rousseau had, from a parallel between the aging of man and the shift from nature to society, drawn certain very significant conclusions, vindicating the freedom of man to act politically. Even though society may be as natural to mankind as old age is to individuals, there is still a key difference, namely that "old age flows from the nature of man alone, and that society flows from the nature of mankind, not immediately as you say, but only, as I have shown, with the aid of certain external circumstances, which might or might not have happened, or at least might have happened either sooner or later."

What matters is to be quite clear that it is feasible for man to accelerate or slow down progress and that many of the circumstances that affect us "depend upon the will of man." We have it in our power, then, to influence the course of history and to seize the initiative in order to do so. To give up the struggle to correct what is wrong means to oppose any action whatever: "The most perfect quietism would be the only virtue left to man." This is not possible, and Rousseau was convinced that the *Discourse* had offered very strong reasons against a withdrawal of man to a life in the forest: "I feel too strongly within myself how little I can do without men as corrupt as I am, and the wise man, if there is one, will not today seek his happiness in the midst of a desert. When possible, one must fix one's own abode in one's own country, to love it and to serve it." [57]

Given this primacy of political intervention, and the duty of man to act on it, there was then nothing inevitable about the course of history. What man had done, or tolerated, could be undone. On the foundations of a new constitution, a happier and more virtuous life for man could be built. Once the possibility was admitted that the welfare of man could be linked to this

[57] O.C. III, 232, 234, 235.

political task, the question was that of outlining the frame of this ideal state. What was the nature of a government capable of achieving these results? Which government would keep closest to the law? And what was the content of the law?

Rousseau made up his mind to dedicate the *Discourse on Inequality* to the Republic of Geneva. He was to write in the *Confessions* that he thought Geneva's notions of law and freedom not just enough or clear enough to suit him, in spite of the praise he publicly lavished on them. The moral imperative of the search for a way out, and the practical opportunity of helping his homeland, combined to push Rousseau to try his hand now at the drafting of the requirements of the ideal state. If politics was all, then he should outline the conditions under which political life could produce the results he wanted. In the Dedication this is what he did.

During most of the two centuries since the publication of the *Discourse on Arts and Sciences* and the *Discourse on Inequality,* the so-called individualism of the two *Discourses* and the collectivism of the *Social Contract* have been frequently contrasted. From the very beginning, the early Rousseau was portrayed as favoring a return to the state of nature, as opposed to civilization and culture, and, therefore, opposed to all forms of social life. In the twentieth century, one of the most distinguished of Rousseau scholars, C. E. Vaughan, felt that the second *Discourse* was a landmark of the greatest importance, both for its speculative ideas and for its practical consequences. For "it suggested more extreme forms of individualism than any previous writer had ventured to set forth," and its chief significance, politically speaking, was "to be found in the vast influence which it yielded upon the French Revolution." [58]

If such views be true, it would be an impossible task to

[58] Cf. C. E. Vaughan, ed., *The Political Writings of Jean Jacques Rousseau* (Cambridge, 1915), I, 119.

reconcile the Rousseau of the *Discourses* with the Rousseau of the *Social Contract*. But the point is that no direct comparison as such is possible between the *Discourses* and the *Social Contract*. The purpose of any critical analysis must be that of identifying the successive frames of reference with which an author develops his thoughts. The *Discourses* are in essence keyed to a review of the consequences of certain historical and cultural phenomena. The *Social Contract* presents a rational discussion of what ought to be the principles of a society in which both liberty and authority are to be found.

The *Discourses* are polemical documents in which Rousseau sets about to criticize the position of his adversaries, the utilitarian, materialistic, godless philosophers he saw in the forefront of the Enlightenment. In the *First Discourse* Rousseau is defending the concept of nature as the revelation of divine goodness against the soulless nature of the Enlightenment. There is no advocacy of any return to nature, but a clear affirmation of the superiority of nature over art. In the *Second Discourse* Rousseau takes a stand against Locke and the defenders of theories of the state based on a view of property rights deriving from the state of nature. As a result, he gives a striking analysis of the maladjustments and social troubles of a political system that rests on the legal sanction of economic inequality. His argument is revolutionary because of the frontal attack upon all existing institutional arrangements. It is against "civilization" to the extent that Rousseau is equating civilization with the materialistic paroxysm of his age. It does not deal with the nature of the ideal state because this was not Rousseau's object. The *Discourses* are a manifestation of the jansenistic spirit with its rigorous moralism, its dissatisfaction with the probabilism and compromises of an age which, politically speaking, could readily be satisfied with the despotism of enlightened princes.

In any study of the development of Rousseau's political

thought, the two *Discourses* must be seen as descriptions of what Rousseau *did not want to accept* as a way of life, rather than as descriptions of the ideal organization of society and of the state. They are the latter only by indirection.

Rousseau was keeping alive simultaneously two different levels of discourse: one, more open and exciting, an attack against the world around him; the other, still hidden before 1754 by his polemical offensive, a vision of the nature of political society and the role of the citizen in it.

The "contrast" between the *Discourses* and the *Social Contract* is that between analysis and prescription. In the former, Rousseau tells us what is wrong with the world as it exists and tries to give us the criteria by which we can evaluate ourselves. In the latter, he provides the norms that ought to be followed in a free democratic state.

What is no less interesting, even if only seldom noticed, is that within the text itself of the *Discourse on Inequality,* the same tension exists between the denunciation of the evils of present social life and the outline of the ideal state. It is the tension between the *Discourse* and the Dedication of the *Discourse.* And this is the first time Rousseau gives us an opportunity to look at the two aspects of his thought.

The Dedication is linked to Rousseau's decision to return to Geneva in May 1754. The return to the native city of which he proclaimed himself to be a citizen, was to prove to his friends and enemies that he had accepted in practice for himself the admonition given in the *Discourse* to all but a few to participate actively in political life. Rousseau was going back to the city.

But just to go back was not enough: Rousseau had also in effect committed himself to provide a schema of the ideal state, since he believed that everything flowed from politics and that the right kind of politics could make better men. The best way of providing this schema was to embody it within the *Discourse on*

Inequality with a dedication to the citizens of Geneva, members of the General Council. Written early in 1754, the Dedication is the most complete outline of Rousseau's theory of the state before the *Social Contract*. In the *Discourse* he had retraced the steps that had led to the downfall of men and of the ideals of equality and freedom. In the Dedication he would give his views both of what was needed to recover those ideals and of what were the basic principles to be adopted by a democratic state.

The glitter of the *Discourse* itself has helped to push into the background a political analysis which was intended by Rousseau to restore his purposes to a proper perspective. He must have hoped that after reading the Dedication no one could doubt his commitment to political life. The only remaining difference with his friends would then be limited to the kind of political life and institutions most likely to produce free and moral men.

First of all, the ideal state was one to be grounded in history, with well-defined historical characteristics attached to it. Against the Enlightenment, Rousseau considers a nation's historical heritage an essential part of its strength. Against the generic and uprooted citizen of the world, he outlines the traits of the citizen of the community, one of whose chief virtues is patriotism.

This meant the choice (as Rousseau begins to list the ideal qualities of the community in which he would have liked to be born) of "a small society, that is one built to the human scale." One, furthermore, not "of recent institutions, however excellent its laws . . . I should have sought out for my country some peaceful and happy republic, whose ancient heritage would be lost in the night of time; and whose vicissitudes had been such as to show and strengthen the courage and patriotism of its subjects; and whose citizens, long accustomed to a wise independence, were not only free, but worthy to be so."

This was to be a community isolated as much as possible from the contentions of national wars. His ideal state was not only to be free of any "fiery love of conquests," it was also to be immune from the danger of conquest by other nations through a happy balancing of mutual interests.

This community of historically minded patriots could not, however, be one in which rigid class divisions and privileges tended to perpetuate themselves in the name of history. Rousseau saw the danger of appeals to history and of using history as a chief agent of prescription if by prescription is meant the justification of class positions, of unchanging institutions, or of property rights. The main advantage to be derived from history was rather that of the continuity of the legal and political system. The community itself had to be founded not on prescriptive right, but upon an identity of interests between the people and the carriers of sovereign power. This identity, according to Rousseau, could never be obtained in any society except a democratic one.

As we proceed, we find in the Dedication the principles of the *Social Contract*, those ideals which the reality of the quite different contract of submission so vividly described in the *Discourse on Inequality* had rendered vain: the democratic ideal of a society governed by law, the ideal of the identity between the people and the sovereign, the ideal of a community which does not delegate any of its essential, but clearly outlined, legislative powers, and the ideal of not accepting that rupture and antagonism between the citizen and the state which was assumed to be inevitable by the dominant utilitarian philosophy of his time.

I should have wished to be born in a country in which the interest of the Sovereign and that of the people must be one and the same; to the end that all efforts might tend always to the common happiness. And as this could not be the case, unless the Sovereign and the people were one and the same person, it follows that I should have wished to be born under a democratic government, wisely tempered.

I should have wished to live and die free: that is, so far subject to the laws that neither I, nor anybody else, should be able to cast off their honorable yoke: the sweet and salutary yoke suffered by the proudest of men with the docility which comes from their inability to suffer any other.

I should have sought a country in which the right of legislation was vested in all the citizens; for who can judge better than they of the conditions under which they had best dwell together in the same society? Not that I should have approved of *plebiscita*, like those among the Romans; when the rulers in the State, and those most interested in its preservation, were excluded from the deliberations upon which often rested its security; and in which, by the most absurd inconsistency, the magistrates were deprived of rights which the citizens enjoyed.

Rousseau was aware of the revolutionary implications of such a sweeping grant of legislative powers to the people. It might have been interpreted as leading to an irresponsible, ill-directed, and continuous change of institutions, to a reckless acceptance of attempts to manipulate political life in the name of progress and of the advancement of science. Therefore, having just said that the right of legislation is vested in all the citizens—for they are the best judges of the conditions under which they must live together—Rousseau defines that right with prudence. The common will which was to emerge from the people's legislative deliberations could not be assumed to be established as a matter of course and without deliberate care and effort.

This was to remain throughout his life his approach to the key question of the common, or the general, will: its discovery was a difficult undertaking, one possible only when the community was free from pressure and had a chance to deliberate at length, and when all of its members had succeeded in purging themselves of their egoistic traits and preoccupations. Only then, and this meant seldom, could the general will be expressed.

In the Dedication, writing not in theoretical but in constitutional terms, Rousseau sees the common good reflected in laws which, by taking into account the still valid historical traditions, and by interpreting correctly the present needs of the community, can be accepted as the authentic expression of the people's will.

This is how Rousseau in a key passage establishes the terms of the problem:

I should have desired that, in order to prevent self-interested and ill-conceived projects and all such dangerous innovations as finally caused the downfall of the Athenians, each citizen should not have the power of proposing new laws, according to his fancy; but that this right should belong to the magistrates alone; and that even the magistrates should use it with so much circumspection; the people for their part be so reserved in giving their consent to such laws, and the promulgation of them carried out only with such great solemnity;—that, before the constitution could be upset by them, there might be time enough for all to be convinced that it is above all the great antiquity of laws which makes them sacred and venerable, that the people soon learn to despise laws which they see daily altered, and that by getting accustomed to the neglect of ancient customs under the pretext of improving them, one often introduced greater evils than those whose correction is sought.

Apart from the unusually strong reiteration of Rousseau's belief in the value of custom, and apart from his preference for a legal system with as few laws as possible, the two points of exclusive legislative initiative in the hands of the magistrate, and of constitutional democracy, deserve attention.

The issue of legislative initiative involved Rousseau in the difficult task of reconciling the exercise of direct sovereignty by the people with the need of restraint and care in the actual use of that power. The difficulty could be solved, Rousseau thought, by splitting the legislative process into two parts, one of initiation and one of discussion and approval. We see in the Dedication an anticipation of the much more detailed development of the same theme ten years later in the *Letters from the Mountain,* at a time when Rousseau had broken with the Republic he was now praising. The issue remained throughout the same, the need of the proper and careful formulation of new legislation proposals, and of placing the right of initiation of new laws in the hands of magistrates. The risk of popular legislation pushed through perhaps under the spur of accidents was too great to take, for it would certainly prove the shortest way to a deviation from the general will. The right to discuss, to approve, and to promulgate according to proper procedures legislation which had initially been shaped elsewhere—this right Rousseau reserved to the citizen. If this distributive arrangement was to be viewed as a surrender by the assembly of the citizens, it was a surrender which had to be made in the interests of stability as well as in that of the well-informed exercise of the nation's will.

The second point, likely to strike those accustomed to thinking of Rousseau as the propounder of an unlimited and unruly democracy, is the stress on rules of procedure; that is, on those devices, long identified with constitutional democracy, which place more emphasis on the ways in which decisions are taken than on their substance. Now, it is impossible to discount the interest of Rousseau in substantive matters, certainly not after one has paid due attention to his continuing concern with economic problems, economic justice, the relationships of classes and of the rich and the poor. These are specifically the problem which constitutional systems have been accused of overlooking in their exclusive preoccupation with forms and procedures, and in their belief that, if only every citizen were treated alike by the laws, the rest would take care of itself.

Rousseau refused to let the rest take care of itself. Nevertheless, he was equally unwilling to assume that a society could survive without strict adherence to rules of conduct, even if the general will had provided for an authentic balance of power and wealth, and hence of freedom. How else can one interpret Rousseau's emphasis on the solemnity—that is, the complex procedure—surrounding the promulgation of new laws? This was intended to allow time to everybody to register objections, so that in the end all would be convinced, and the consent given to new laws would have been truly founded on a reconciliation of different viewpoints.

Valid legislation must both be the expression of the general will and conform to constitutional rules. It cannot be class legislation, because it must rest on a common acceptance of fundamental principles. It must be constitutional legislation derived in equal measure from the historical customs of the past and the legal framework of the present.

The Dedication makes yet another important statement. Rousseau was opposed to any delegation of power by the sovereign people to an elected legislative assembly, because of the danger that it could commit the community to a course of action of which the people might not approve. But, as in the case of legislative initiatives, he was also against the idea of a leaderless mass democracy, one which, in the exercise of the totality of its powers, could claim the right to do without executive leadership and, even more, refuse to recognize the importance of the actual design of the administrative structure itself.

Rousseau, whose views on man, property, and the purposes of government were revolutionary enough, could face the much simpler problems of the practical necessities of government without fear of damaging his ultimate goals. A majority of political writers could well say that what was wrong with political institutions was the excess of structures and of rigid hierarchies and of obsolete administrative bodies, and that, if there was to be progress, a great simplification of the machinery of government had to be achieved and change itself made easy. They could equate progress with the absence of authority, and if any thought was given to matters of administration, it was only to decry the fetters that restricted men's unlimited capacity to achieve perfection.

But Rousseau had no hesitation in stressing the dangers that democracy would invite by reliance on precarious and weak authority, and undifferentiated organs of government. He had lifted the purposes of political life and made them much stronger. The tools of government had to be stronger too. The alleged prophet of the return to primitive life is found here preaching the necessity of social discipline and the needs of carefully structured authority in a democracy.

I should have particularly avoided as necessarily ill-governed a republic where the people believing to be in a position to do without magistrates or to leave them with only a precarious authority would imprudently have kept for themselves the administration of civil affairs and the execution of their own laws. Such must have been the rude constitutions of primitive governments directly emerging from the state of nature.

Having thus condemned as unimaginable a system of government which might at most have satisfied the earliest of social groupings which modern man had forever left behind, Rousseau proceeds to outline his views on the needs of today.

I should have chosen a community in which the individuals, satisfied with sanctioning their laws, and with deciding the most important public affairs in general assembly and upon a report of their leaders,—had established honored tribunals, had carefully distinguished among the several administrative departments, electing year after year some of the most capable and upright of their fellow citizens to administer justice and govern the states; a community in short in which, the virtue of the magistrates thus bearing witness to the wisdom of the people, both rulers and ruled would honor one another.

[164]

This then was the outline of the ideal state which Rousseau contrasted with the real one. It was a state to be built on the wisdom of the people, the foundation of Rousseau's faith in the future, on what the common man could do ("those educated and sensible men who, called in other nations workers and populace, are viewed with contempt and under such a false light"). Through their participation in political life, one could create that civic climate which alone might replace the irrevocably lost natural goodness of man.[59]

This then is where Rousseau stood on June 12, 1754. The purpose of most of what he had written had been to liberate man, not for a return to a nonsocial state, but to facilitate his entry into a new political community, and even while he was actively demolishing the foundations of the contemporary world, Rousseau was giving thought to the major premises of the new democracy. His writings show a fairly continuous preoccupation with the task of reconstruction and the blueprint of 1754 is more detailed and complete than has been commonly recognized. Rousseau's conflict with his times flows from a rational appraisal of the foundations of society and of the motives which prompt men to live together. The choice for him is between a utilitarian society of individuals with the state on the outside acting as a policeman, and a society of equals trying by dedicated work to achieve together the common good. The choice he makes is clear all along.

We find in Rousseau's writings of this period the essentials of a modern democratic faith. Economic complexities are not shunted aside. Economic conflicts and their injustices deeply concern Rousseau from the very beginning. He is opposed to Voltaire the cynic, as he is opposed to Voltaire the man of great

[59] O.C. III, 111–20.

affairs, who refused to the state the right of intervention to soften the asperities resulting from the extremes of poverty and of wealth. It is a modern democratic faith because it shows awareness of the difficulties of reconciling liberty and authority, of the need of responsible organs of execution of the popular will, of the care with which popular deliberations are to be taken. The tasks at hand are many and delicate. No assumptions of simplicity can be made. The optimism concerning the essentially sound nature of man is tempered by the emphasis on the indispensable role of leadership. What the separate individuals must seek to achieve in their deliberate search for what is right, is the common good.

VI

The Ideal State

The Problem of the Origin of the State

SOON after completing the *Discourse on Inequality* and its Dedication, Rousseau was asked to prepare the article on political economy for the great compendium of eighteenth-century thought, the *Encyclopédie*.[1] From an overview of the development of mankind and of the tragedies that have accompanied it, Rousseau would move toward the social contract and deal with the issues of the government of man in an ideal system. His new task was that of defining the conditions for the maintenance of the well-regulated political community with much greater detail than in the Dedication.

The novelty of the *Political Economy* lies in the central position occupied by the concept of the general will. The argument develops through an analysis of the origins of the state.[2]

---

[1] *Discours sur l'économie politique,* O.C. III, 239–78. As a rule, the English translation used here will be that of G. D. H. Cole, in the Everyman edition of the *Social Contract and Discourses* (London, 1913).

[2] The content of the *Political Economy* leaves little doubt as to the date of its composition. One is bound to agree with the majority of commentators (from Hendel, *Jean-Jacques Rousseau, Moralist,* I, 98 ff., to Derathé, O.C. III, lxxiii–lxxiv) and to disagree with Hubert (*Rousseau et*

Beyond the family, at a different level of human organization, we find the political community. In order to find it and understand it, the justification for the political community must be set forth in theoretical terms, and most of the common explanations must be rejected as useless. Not only the model of the family, but also the agreement (alleged or real) between rich and poor, the right of conquest or mere prescription are found inadequate. As Rousseau writes in a striking summing up:

There are a thousand ways of bringing together men, there is only one way to unite them. It is for this reason that I am concerned in this work only with a method for the formation of political societies, even though in the multitude of aggregations to be found today under this name there are not perhaps two which have been formed in the same manner and not one which has been formed according to the method I set forth. But I am looking for right and reason and I am not arguing about facts.[3]

The contrast between the family and the political community is a radical one. The authority of the family is natural, while political authority is conventional, the result of quite different specific agreements. The fact that both organizations have an apparently similar purpose, that of making human beings subjected to them happy, is not enough to blur the distinctive line

---

l'Encyclopédie, 58ff.) and say that the *Political Economy* follows the *Discourse on Inequality* and was written around 1754–1755.

[3] O.C. III, 297. This quotation is from chapter v of Book I of the first version of the *Social Contract.* This chapter ("Fausses Notions du lien social") and chapter ii, also in Book I ("De la Société générale du genre humain") are considered, by common agreement of Rousseau scholars, to be among the very earliest parts of the first version of the *Social Contract,* a version whose writing was stretched over a number of years. In style and relevance of argument they belong to the years of the *Discourse on Inequality* and the *Political Economy* (O.C. III, 1416–7). Therefore, for the purposes of our discussion, these two chapters are considered to be part of the *Political Economy* and are discussed with it.

which separates them. Filmer, Rousseau adds, is to be blamed for having stressed the contrary view in the "hateful system" he attempted to set up in the *Patriarcha*.[4] The parallels drawn from relationships leading to the authority of the father, the subordinate position of the mother, the duty and obedience of children, are invalid, since these relationships are absent in political society.

Equally unacceptable is the notion of rights accruing to the rich because of their greater economic power. Such greater economic power may be a fact but it can never give rise to a right: "How can an individual seize an immense territory and deprive mankind of its use except as a result of a usurpation to be punished: for such action deprives the rest of mankind of the land and the food which nature has given them in common." Mere possession is not enough to establish property rights. There are clear conditions to be satisfied before one can recognize rights of first occupancy to anyone:

In the first place, the land should not yet have been settled by anybody. In the second place, the surface occupied should not go beyond one's own subsistence needs. In the third place, possession must be made effective not through a formal gesture but through work and cultivation, the only property signs which must be respected by others. Since the rights of a single man before the social state cannot go beyond this point, and since everything else is only violence and usurpation against the laws of nature, it cannot serve as a foundation of social rights.[5]

If, as a result of an ideal chance, the political community has not yet moved away from an earlier condition in which the distribution of the land among individuals has taken place on the basis of the principles outlined by Rousseau, everything that happens later in the political community is predicated on the

[4] O.C. III, 244.   [5] O.C. III, 301–2.

fullest adherence to the principle of even distribution of the land according to needs. Usurpation has been rejected as creating an acceptable state of affairs in the transition from the state of nature to civil state. To prevent the accumulation of excessive wealth in the civil state becomes the task of the sovereign and of the magistrates. Usurpation has no justification in nature and cannot form the basis of right; accumulation must be prevented from arising in a society governed by the general will.

Both right of war and prescription are equally invalid reasons for establishing the social tie. War, if it is a conflict among societies, presupposes the existence of the political community and cannot precede it. If it is a private conflict it has no relation to the problem under discussion. Usurpation is, of course, possible, but the passage of time cannot give prescriptive sanction to it. There is no lack of authority for this belief, which, however, lacks the support of reason.[6] No tacit consent can validate tyranny.

The only acceptable explanation for the founding of civil societies must be the common utility which the members will derive from it. "Hence, how can we distinguish legitimate states from mobs kept together by force, if not through the consideration of the object or the end of the former or of the latter? If the form of society tends to the common good, it follows the spirit of its founding, if it aims only to satisfy the interests of its chiefs, it is illegitimate." [7] And if Grotius points out that not all political powers are established to favor the interests of those who are governed by them, he is of course justified in fact, but the problem to be solved is one of principle.

False parallels are as dangerous and confusing as false expla-

[6] Derathé (O.C. III, 1419) suggests that Rousseau is thinking of Grotius.

[7] O.C. III, 304–5.

nations. For in dealing with the body politic, we are dealing with something unique and for which ready-made parallels are all too often mistakenly used. One such parallel is that of comparing the body politic with an organism. The temptation, he was to say a year later in the *State of War,* must be resisted, since the body politic is a moral being with a will:

Citizens may well call themselves members of the state. They will never be able to join themselves to the state as real members are joined to the human body; it is impossible to avoid a separate and individual existence for each of them and through which alone he can suffice to his own conservation. . . . Let us consider how much in the aggregation of the body politic public force is inferior to the sum total of individual forces, how much there is, so to speak, of loss of strength in the operation of the entire machine and we will have to conclude that proportionately speaking the weakest man has greater force available for his own conservation than the strongest state for its own.[8]

But already in the *Political Economy* the organic parallel has little attraction for Rousseau. He is aware that it is being made by other writers and he is anxious to counteract any theory of the state which surrenders before the automatic operation of a whole in which the individual moral being ends up by contributing nothing. Therefore, in spite of the help which at a vulgar level of discourse the organic parallel might offer in understanding the functioning of the political body, it is an "inexact" parallel, for there is a difference in kind which must be grasped. This difference stems from the fact that the body politic is moved by what Rousseau calls a general will, described as a will which, "since it aims always to preservation and well-being of the whole and of every part, and is the source of the laws, constitutes for all the

[8] *Que l'Etat de guerre naît de l'état social,* O.C. III, 606.

members of the state, in their relations to one another and to it, the rule of what is just and unjust." [9]

Rousseau and Diderot

At the beginning of the discussion of the general will, the problem of the respective roles played by Rousseau and Diderot in its formulation must be mentioned. It is an issue that looks different from the ones usually met in the history of ideas. For Rousseau himself appears to yield before Diderot. Having given us his definition, he then adds that the source of this "great and luminous principle" is to be found in an earlier article in the same volume of the *Encyclopédie* entitled *Right*. His *Political Economy* is merely a development of it.[10]

This is a remarkable statement and, given the central importance of the general will in Rousseau's thought, it is necessary to try to determine its meaning. The author of the article on *Right* is Diderot. In it, the author assumes that the single individual has been deprived of the right of deciding by himself what is just and what is unjust. Who then can exercise this right? The answer is, mankind. Particular wills are suspect, they can be good or evil, "but the general will is always good; it has never deceived us nor will it ever deceive us."

It is by addressing himself to the general will that the individual can discover the limits of his actions as man, citizen, subject, father, son—the limits, even, of life and death. "You will acquire the most sacred of natural right to everything which is not

[9] O.C. III, 244, 245. Vaughan had tended to stress the organic character of the *Political Economy*. But Derathé cannot agree with him (O.C. III, 1393), and a careful reading of Rousseau bears him out.

[10] O.C. III, 245. Hubert, *Rousseau et l'Encyclopédie*, 51–3, advances the hypothesis that Rousseau's reference was to an as yet unwritten article. This is quite possible, but the question of substance remains.

denied to you by the whole of mankind. Mankind will enlighten you on the nature of your thoughts and of your desires. Everything you will conceive, everything you will meditate, will be good, great, elevated, sublime, if it is in the general and common interest. There is no quality essential to man apart from the one you demand in all your fellow men for your happiness and theirs." Man must therefore repeat often to himself, "I am a man and I have no other truly inalienable natural rights than those of humanity."

For Diderot, then, the issue is that of determining the universal natural rights of man, transcending time and space, and having inalienability as another characteristic. The entire human race becomes the depository of these rights, verified by the general will. But how do we know how to proceed? Where can the general will be consulted? The answer is, everywhere: "in all the written principles of law of all organized nations; in the social actions of savage and barbarous peoples, in the tacit conventions of the enemies of mankind."

This is a general will which is common to mankind in all phases of its development, which is to be found in the actions of peoples that are called savage and yet are already to some extent "social," as well as in written codes of law which presumably only the most advanced societies will possess.

Further, this is a general will that appears to float benevolently above mankind and which rational men can find for themselves. Having silenced all passions, rational man can find in the general will what he can expect from his fellow man and what his fellow man can expect from him. The general will becomes the guide for the conduct of man toward other men, of man toward the society of which he is a member, and of that society toward the other societies. Since of the two wills, the general and the particular, only the general will never makes mistakes, it is clear that for the happiness of mankind legislative power should be capable of expressing the general will, and that we should view with veneration the august mortals whose particular wills bring together both the authority and the infallibility of the general will.[11]

The relevance to Rousseau's thought of this notion of the general will is hardly clear. For Diderot's universalism cannot be the source of Rousseau's idea of the general will, and this in spite of Rousseau's formal acknowledgment. The best evidence is provided by Rousseau himself, who, in chapter ii of Book I of the first version of the *Social Contract*, sets out to destroy Diderot's argument on the general society of mankind. This chapter must have been written immediately after the appearance in the *Encyclopédie* of Diderot's article on *natural right*. It was not addressed to the idea of natural right as such but rather to Diderot's argument concerning the general society of mankind as a source of man's rights.[12]

---

[11] Diderot, "Droit naturel," in *Oeuvres politiques,* Vernière, ed. (Paris, 1963), 32–4.

[12] From Vaughan to Derathé, there has been a persistent debate as to the meaning of this chapter and the reasons why it was not included in the final version of the *Social Contract*. Vaughan suggests that Rousseau eliminated this chapter, "not because it was irrelevant, but because it was fatally relevant, to his argument; because he became aware that, in refuting the idea of natural law, he had unwittingly made a deadly breach in the binding force of the Contract; and because, having no other principle to put in place of the Contract as the foundation of civil society, he felt that his only course was to silence the battery which he had incautiously unmasked against it: in one word, to strike out the refutation, and to let the Social Contract stand" (*Political Writings,* I, 441–2). But in saying so, Vaughan fails to see the necessary distinctions which must be made in Rousseau's treatment of the problem of natural law. According to Rousseau, there are several kinds of natural law: from the "virtual" one, to be found in man not yet engaged in multiple social relationships, to the more fully developed rational one of a later phase in man's development, and containing many elements of social life. One may, in this connection, point to the distinctions made in the first version

There is no general society of mankind, Rousseau maintains. There is no natural society among men.[13] What there is is a gradual evolution such as Rousseau has described in the *Discourse on Inequality* and out of which the necessity of political institutions is born. Having gone beyond his primitive condition, man has acquired increasing needs, and reciprocal help becomes necessary. "From this new order of things a multitude of relations are born without measure, without rule, without consistency, altered and changed continuously by men, one hundred busy to destroy them, against one working to consolidate them." Mankind has left the original state of nature and has entered into a phase of turmoil where peace and happiness appear only fleetingly on the landscape: "Nothing is permanent except the misery which results from all these vicissitudes."[14]

This misery, this inability to distinguish between good and evil, is the result of the increasing sociability of man and of his having developed needs which require for their satisfaction the

---

of the *Social Contract* where the "rules of reasoned natural law" are clearly distinguished from "natural law strictly speaking, based only on a true but very vague sentiment" (O.C. III, 329). Derathé can, therefore, suggest that the burden of Rousseau's argument is only against Locke's views of natural law and not against natural law itself, and that Rousseau's reasons for the subsequent elimination of this chapter included a wish to avoid unnecessary polemics with Diderot and useless repetition of topics he had already dealt with in the *Discourse on Inequality* (O.C. III, lxxxv–lxxxviii).

[13] The original title of this chapter was *That There Is Not Naturally Any Society among Men*. This was later replaced by the title *The General Society of Mankind* (O.C. III, 1410).

[14] O.C. III, 282. This state of misery is perhaps less surprising than appears to Derathé (O.C. III, 1412), because this is not the misery of the state of nature, where in principle it could not exist as Rousseau had said in the *Discourse on Inequality*. By now man has advanced far beyond that stage and finds himself in an intermediate state of nature, preceding the creation of a political society, and itself the source of conflict and usurpation.

assistance of his fellow man. We may perhaps begin to talk about a general society of man at this point, but if we do, we should realize that it performs none of the tasks which should be attached to the concept of society: "The general society such as our mutual needs might generate does not therefore offer an efficacious assistance to man who now has become unhappy, or at most it gives added strength to that man who already has too much while the weak, lost, suffocated and crushed in the multitude, does not find any shelter nor refuge, nor any support to his weakness and dies in the end a victim of this deceitful union from which he had expected his happiness." [15]

In the midst of misery and the further weakening of the weak, the emerging general society of mankind, already far removed from the original state of nature, develops conflicts and wars. The error of Hobbes was not "to have found a state of war among independent men who already had become sociable, but to have imagined this state of war natural to mankind and to have given it as the cause of vices of which it is rather the consequence." [16]

The question is whether this stage in the development of man can produce anything that can properly be called a general society of mankind. Man has now lost the guidance of the sweet voice of nature and no longer considers the maintenance of the independence nature had given him: "Peace and innocence have forever eluded us before we could ever taste their delights." The golden age has remained foreign to mankind, either because it was not recognized when mankind could have enjoyed it, or because it was lost by the time mankind could have understood it. To talk about a general society of mankind at a point when our original innocence has vanished and a possible golden age has been allowed to slip away, but before we have been able to

---

[15] O.C. III, 282. [16] O.C. III, 288.

create the union and the discipline which the new conditions require, is not acceptable.

Without communication, without morality and virtue, no society can be said to exist. Even a general society would require certain precise distinguishing characteristics. It would be a moral being which we would be able to identify as distinct from its members. If the general society existed anywhere except in the systems of philosophers, "there would be a universal language which nature would teach to all men and which would be the first instrument of their mutual communication. There would be a common understanding which would serve to the correspondence of all the parts; the public good or evil would not be merely the sum of the particular goods or evils as in a simple aggregation, but it would be found in the tie which binds them; it would be greater than this sum and public happiness far from being based on the happiness of individuals, would be its source." [17]

If the general society of mankind does not exist, even less can one say that a general tribunal of mankind can function. The existence of a tribunal implies an understanding of the reasons why man's personal interests require that he should submit himself to the general will. This presupposes a capacity for generalizing ideas which is "one of the most difficult and of the latest exercises of human understanding." [18] How can he consult, as Diderot has suggested, "principles of written law, the social actions of all the peoples, the tacit conventions even of the enemies of mankind?"

[17] O.C. III, 284.
[18] Adam Smith knew Rousseau well enough by the end of 1762 to be able to say that this was one of the problems he had faced: "To explain how general names were first formed, as they require abstract thought and what is called generalization, before they can be formed, according to his way of thinking: which he thinks men at first hardly capable of" (Adam Smith, *Lectures on Rhetoric and Belles Lettres,* ed. J. M. Lothian [London, 1963], 3rd Lecture, 22 November 1762, 8).

Rousseau is driven back to his primary position which is that "it is only from the social order established among us that we can draw the ideas of the one we are imagining. We conceive the general society after our particular societies, the establishment of our small republics leads us to dream of the great, and we do not properly begin to become men until after we have been citizens. These considerations show what we must think of these alleged cosmopolites who justify their love of country through their love for mankind, boast of loving the entire world so as to have the right not to love anybody." [19]

A general will established on the basis of a belief in the general society of mankind has no substance. The "luminous" principle acknowledged in the *Political Economy* must be re-thought in terms of the concrete human experience of the partic-ular societies of which men must first become citizens. And Rousseau invites us to engage in this task of the reduction of the general society to the particular society of man: "Even though there is no natural and general society among men, even though men become bad and unhappy in becoming sociable, even though the laws of justice and equality count for nothing for those who live at the same time in the independence of the state of nature while subject to the needs of the social condition, far from thinking that virtue and unhappiness are not for us and that the heavens have abandoned us without resource to the degradation of the race;—let us attempt to draw from our misfortune the remedy which must cure it: through new associations let us repair the intrinsic vices of the general society." [20] Let us, through "perfected art" repair the damage caused to nature by

[19] *O.C.* III, 287.

[20] *Fragments politiques, O.C.* III, 479. The editor, Derathé, considers this fragment as belonging to chapter ii, Book I, of the first draft of the *Social Contract* (*ibid.,* 1518).

"beginning art." [21] Once more Rousseau is saying: let us control the arts to get closer to nature.

The task was that of providing the principles of a political society built to the human scale and not on the generalities of the philosophers. And a will serving the needs of a specific community could not be the all-purpose universal will described by Diderot.

The General Will and the Architect

Rousseau's general will was first of all a political concept to be found only within organized political societies, and was intended to regulate their internal life. It was not merely the source of rights, it was, chiefly, the source of duties. It could not apply to the relations of nations among themselves, each nation in its dealing with others being considered as expressing an individual will. The legislative power was made up of the entire community and it deserved no special veneration. Its task was to express the general will. And not always did the legislative power succeed in doing that. It could fail, and then the expression of its will was not properly called the general will. It had better simply be called "a public deliberation."

Rousseau, then, starts from a point which is at the opposite pole of the cosmic vision of Diderot. Indeed, a general will might first be traced to the subordinate societies in which the members of a political body will organize themselves: "The will of these particular societies has always two relations: for the members of the association it is a general will, for the great society it is a particular will." [22] The general will of these particular societies is the expression of the interests of their members and it will seek to modify the general public will of the body politic. These

[21] O.C. III, 288.   [22] O.C. III, 246.

particular general wills are likely to differ from the general will in direct proportion to the narrowness of the interests of the association of which they are the mirror. Often, under a semblance of propriety, vicious purposes are discovered.

The same interpretation applies to the issue of the general will in larger political entities made up of a number of national entities. A year after writing the *Political Economy,* Rousseau was engaged in a criticism of the writings of Saint-Pierre. All of the Abbé's complicated plans—his "polysynodie," the federalization and fusion of political authority, the rationalization of royal absolutism—could not by themselves facilitate the finding of the general will. To imagine that the greatest good of the state would depend from the greatest good of each of its parts is false.

The greatest good of the state, to be established only through the general will, cannot depend just on the satisfaction of the needs of its members. For in dealing with a body politic we are dealing with a structured complex and it is most probable that individual or partial interests will have to be sacrificed to the interest of the whole. The parallel Rousseau proposes is that of the architect making plans for a palace: "To draw up the plans of a palace it is not enough to dispose each room conveniently. One must in addition consider the relationships of the whole. The most comfortable passages, the most commodious order, the easiest communications, the most perfect ensemble and the most regular symmetry. These general objectives are so important that the skillful architect, for the sake of the whole, sacrifices a thousand particular advantages which he might have maintained in a less perfect and less simple ordering."

Hence, the task of the statesman in charge of the government (that is, the agent who will provide the needed guidance in both determining and carrying out in practice the general will of the people) cannot focus his attention on separate problems of finance, of war, or of trade: "He will relate all these particular issues to a common object and from the proportions which will best suit them, there will flow the general plans whose dimensions can vary in a thousand ways according to the ideas and the views of those who have shaped them."

The problem is that of putting together particular plans so as to have a general plan. It is not an easy thing to decide which of the particular plans is to be preferred. There is no doubt that if each unit of government can maintain its own plan there will be only contradictions in public affairs and embarrassment in their general management: "But the general plan cannot be the plan of this or the other man: in the polysynodie it can only be that of the government and it is to this great model that of necessity must be related the common deliberations of each council and the particular activity of each member." [23]

Rousseau is outlining here some of the difficulties the general will may encounter in the large state with a federal structure. For a federal state organized of necessity on a pluralistic basis, and with a strong role assigned to its many parts, will find that the task of bringing them together into an ultimate common will is not an easy one.

There is, then, a task common to the small community, trying to overcome the divisive will of partial associations, and to the large federal aggregate, trying to reconcile the scattered wills of its component units. For both, it is a task similar to that of the architect. The more one moves in the direction of the higher general will, the more probable will become the establishment of what is just and right. The only authentic general will is the will which expresses the view of the entire community once it has lifted itself above the smaller and conflicting interests of individuals and of particular groups. Rousseau is not expressing himself against the right of association, nor against the possibilities of

[23] *Jugement sur la polysynodie*, O.C. III, 641.

federalism. He is merely pointing out the reality of the selfish interests which subordinate groups are bound to follow and the need of placing the general will of the community above such subordinate wills. Beyond the general will of the body politic, there is nothing.

In the second place, the idea of the general will can help us in classifying political societies, for some of them will have recognized the role of the general will, while others will not have done so. Far from being a universal characteristic, the general will is the distinguishing mark of well-governed societies. States will have popular or tyrannical structures. "The former will belong to every state in which there is between the people and the rulers unity of interest and of will; the latter will of necessity be found wherever the government and the people have different interests and consequently opposing wills."

Hence, the chief characteristics of legitimate states will be that the sovereign power is organized in such a way as to be capable of expressing itself through the general will, while the chief duty of governments, that is of the power entrusted with the task of enforcing the general will, will be that of abiding by it: "As long as the government acts only for the public good, it is impossible that it should attack liberty, because it is only executing the general will and no one can say he can be enslaved when he obeys nothing but his will." [24]

There should be no illusions as to the ease with which the general will can be found. To know what the general will is, one must begin to distinguish it carefully from particular wills—a distinction most difficult to achieve. An understanding of the general will neither comes from heaven nor is absorbed naturally by man. The surrender of one's own personal will is a painful task. And yet it must be accomplished in a political community

[24] O.C. III, 247, and *Fragments politiques, ibid.,* 484.

worthy of this name. It will be accomplished once men understand the miraculous beauty of the law, that "most sublime of all human institutions," which makes man free even if his individual will is restrained. "It is to law alone that men owe justice and liberty. It is this salutary organ of the will of all which reestablishes in right the natural equality among men. It is this celestial voice which dictates to each citizen the precepts of public reason and teaches him to act according to the rules of his own judgment and not to be in contradiction with himself." [25]

Governments, the instruments of the sovereign power which has, through law, expressed the general will of the community, should, therefore, always act under the law and never above it. Governors are never exempted from obedience to the law. It is also their duty to be always aware of the spirit of the law in case decisions have to be taken which have not been foreseen in precise detail by the text of the law itself. If the spirit of the law is not enough to guide governments, then recourse must be had to the general will; that is, to an assembly of the entire citizenry which alone can establish it.

While Rousseau contends that this is the only proper solution in principle, he has serious doubts about its use in practice. First of all, there is the possibility that even the assembled people may be unable to do what they are supposed to do. In the second place, the method is impractical in the case of a large country. It is then perhaps better to try to establish the general will of the community by accepting as a rule the justice of popular demands, as in China, where "it is the constant maxim of the prince to decide against his officers in every dispute that arises between them and the people." [26]

[25] O.C. III, 248.

[26] "Is bread expensive in a province? The intendant is jailed; is there rioting in another? The governor is fired." In the long run this has proved to be the best procedure (O.C. III, 251).

If this is thought to be a weakening of two arguments dear to Rousseau (the role of the citizens acting rationally and in assembly, and the role of the magistrates administering wisely the long-term interests of the sovereign people), let it be added that he was perhaps expressing in another way his belief that the voice of the people was the voice of God, and that it should be heard without captious delays.

These views have also to be balanced against Rousseau's intention of widening the scope and increasing the strength of government action. It is dangerous for "the sovereign to usurp the functions of the magistracy as it is for the magistrate to usurp those of sovereignty." [27] But Rousseau is convinced that modern governments have been far too timid in defining the range of their activities. "It is said that all peoples become in the long run what government makes them: warriors, citizens, men when it so pleases; or merely populace and rabble when it chooses to make them so." Governments have had a tendency to show contempt for their subjects and not to realize the strength inherent in them. If a government wants to rule over men it must make men first. This was a task which ancient governments appeared to understand. It was then that there arose "the many sumptuary laws, the many regulations of morals and the many public rules of conduct." [28]

A society governed by the general will must, therefore, also consider the proper place of a government capable of using that general will for the purpose of building a better society. The general will, mysterious in its origin, difficult in its determination, represents for Rousseau only the beginning of a prolonged effort which must be sustained by a continuous commitment on the part of the magistrates to create daily the conditions leading to responsible citizenship. Rousseau is unhappy to realize that

[27] *Fragments politiques,* O.C. III, 488.   [28] O.C. III, 251–2.

modern governments, "believing they have done everything when they have raised money," do not even conceive that the level or the kind of intervention such as the past had already seen, might be necessary or possible. Just as the degradation of the citizen must be ended, so must the retreat of government from its real responsibilities be halted.

The Support of Virtue

Rousseau has just sounded a keynote, on the needed presence of an active government interested not only in monopolies, as the mercantilistic state was, but also in good citizenship. The problem was how to achieve this end. The answer is, through the support of political virtue—that is, of a quality which Rousseau in the *Political Economy* calls the "conformity of the particular will with the general will," and elsewhere compares to beauty: "Just as we say that beauty is the sum of the commonest traits, we can say that virtue is the sum of the most general wills." [29]

Hence, the task of any government ready to become active is to bring the citizens to see the necessity of defining their individual purposes in relation to the common good of the community. They will thus be "virtuous" and achieve the general will.

In proceeding to this end, the government has dual responsibilities. The first is that of creating the conditions within which the desire to achieve the general will flourishes naturally. The second is that of guaranteeing all citizens against any interference or pressure that would diminish or make impossible the contribution which each of them must make to the attainment of the general will. To instill the love of country and to assure the proper education of the people belong to the former; to protect the essential personal rights of freedom and to create an economically balanced society belong to the latter.

[29] *Economie politique,* O.C. III, 252; *Fragments politiques, ibid.,* 483.

Virtue ought to become a quality of all the citizens if possible. Certainly the effort of the government must be in that direction. Virtue develops as a quality of the mind, when certain communal beauties and values become apparent, and as the fruit of a society which had adjusted to the need and the task of welcoming equally all its members. Virtue is to be lived through the personal experience of a man who can now for the first time realize his strength. Virtue resides in the person placed in a position where he can find it and make of it what he can, once he is aware of his country, has received an education, is guaranteed his rights of freedom, and does not have to use up all his energies merely to survive.

The inculcation of patriotism is the most efficacious way of teaching the citizens to be good: "For, as I have said already, every man is virtuous when his particular will is in all things conformable to the general will, and we gladly will what is willed by those whom we love." Patriotism is the development of a feeling of national solidarity which brings us to consider favorably what our neighbors want so that in our desire to help them achieve their purposes, stimulated by our own attachment for them, we more readily may end up by finding and supporting the general will: "According to the definition I have given of virtue, love of country realizes it of necessity because we are happy to will what is willed by those we love."

Rousseau's patriotism is an elusive concept which runs counter to many traditional views.

First of all, patriotism is different from a mere concern for humanity. "The love of humanity is the source of many virtues, as sweetness, equity, moderation, charity, tolerance, but it does not inspire courage or firmness, etc.: it does not give them that energy which they receive from the love of country through which they can attain heroism."

While the thrust of his argument is not in favor of national egoism, or of an exacerbated nationalism which sets itself above and against the similar feelings of neighboring communities, Rousseau is opposed to the dilution of sentiments which are too valuable in creating and fortifying community spirit to be abandoned in favor of a vague humanitarian feeling: "It appears that the feeling of humanity evaporates and grows feeble by extending itself to the entire globe." If we wish to make peoples virtuous we must begin by inducing them to love their country—a country free and governed by laws, capable of disposing them to the most heroic actions in its defense and concerned with making its citizens happy and good.

The patriotism Rousseau has in mind is something intimate and spiritual, kindled by a way of life and by political institutions, and from which the principles as well as the practice of freedom cannot be removed: "What one loves in one's country, what one can rightfully call the Fatherland, has no reference to our appetites or the habits which flow from them, it is not simply the place, not simply the things; the object of this love is closer to us."

The real love of country flows, then, from the possibility the citizen has of securing what he needs for the fullest realization of himself: "If the citizens will derive from her all that has any value in their existence—wise laws, simple customs, the necessary sustenance, peace, freedom and the estimation of other peoples—their zeal will be fired for such a tender mother. They will not know of any veritable life other than that which they obtain from her, no real happiness other than that of using their lives in her service." [30]

This object of love must be a country in which education will have formed the citizens. It is not the purpose of a public education to kill all passions in man. The magistrate should not

[30] O.C. III, 254, 535–6.

make the mistake of assuming that a man without passion would be a good citizen. The contrary is true. Hence, while the purpose of education is not that of drilling into men's minds what would make them obedient to the commands of their masters, it must be directed to make them consider their existence as bound up with that of the community: "If they were early accustomed never to consider their individuality except in its relations to the body of the state and not to perceive their own existence except as a part of that body, they might at last come to identify themselves in some measure with this greater whole, to feel themselves members of their country and to love it with that exquisite feeling which every isolated man has only for himself."

Addressing himself to the conditions of his own times, Rousseau tells us that if that kind of education is unavailable, it is because there is no concern for the molding of citizens and because once the force of habit has been added to the selfish inclinations of man it is too late to get away from ourselves: "How can love of country assert itself in the midst of so many other passions which suffocate it? And what is left for the duties of citizenship of a heart already divided between greed, a mistress, and vanity?" If anything is to be achieved it is from the moment of birth that one must begin: "If at birth we acquire our rights of citizenship, at that moment we must also begin the practice of our duties." [31]

What is needed to carry out the task is a public authority in charge of education, following regulations prescribed by the government and under the control of magistrates elected by the people. This system is one of the distinguishing marks of a legitimate government. To be entrusted with the responsibility of education is to be asked to perform the highest function in the state. Such tasks must go to those who have proved themselves

[31] O.C. III, 259–60.

worthy in other public offices, to those who "will have deserved this notable mark of public confidence because of ardent and continuous love of country and its laws, through signal services rendered to the state in the course of a long life in the command of armies and in the administration of the greatest affairs of state." [32]

If, under such guidance, "children are brought up in common and in the midst of equality, if they are imbued with the laws of the state and the principles of the general will, if they are taught to respect them above all things . . . we cannot doubt that they will learn to cherish one another mutually as brothers, to will nothing contrary to the will of society, to substitute the actions of men and citizens for the sterile and vain babbling of the sophists." With such an education the government achieves the purpose of "keeping within narrow boundaries that personal interest which so isolates the individuals that the state is enfeebled by their power and has nothing to hope from their good will." [33]

This is one side of the ledger from whose balance public virtue is to flow. Having elicited the patriotism of its citizens and having, through the heavy burden and discipline of public education, successfully brought them to consider the public good above their private one, government must now redeem its own commitments in two other and no less important fields of public policy, where its own actions are decisive.

The first is the satisfaction of the pledge to guarantee the safety and the freedom of every member of the community. The political community would be dissolved "if in the state a single citizen who might have been helped were allowed to perish, or if a single one were wrongfully confined in prison, or if a single trial were to lead to an obvious injustice: for the fundamental

[32] Draft of the manuscript of the *Political Economy*, O.C. III, 1400–1.
[33] O.C. III, 261–2.

conventions having been broken, it is impossible to imagine what right or what interest could maintain the people in a social union."

After the solemn warnings about the general will and the subordination of particular interests to the common good, after the forceful defense of a far-reaching system of public education from which a new man is to emerge, Rousseau, in striking language, poses the issue of the defense of the rights and of the life of the members of the community:

Is the welfare of a single citizen any less the common cause than that of the whole state? If we are told that it is good that one should perish for all of us, I will admire these words on the lips of a worthy and virtuous patriot voluntarily and dutifully sacrificing himself for the good of his country: but if we are to understand that it is permissible for the government to sacrifice an innocent man for the good of the multitude, then I hold this maxim as one of the most execrable ever invented by tyranny, as the most false ever to be advanced, as the most dangerous ever to be admitted, and as the most directly opposed to the fundamental laws of society.

There is no room here for reason of state, for the right of the government to engage in the oppression of single individuals, as if such actions did not matter to the body politic. If those who support similar views are pressed to explain what they mean, they shall be forced in the end to identify the state with a "small number of men who are not the people, but the officers of the people and who having bound themselves by oath to perish for the welfare of the people, would thence infer that the people itself is to perish for their own." [34]

A far different task awaits the magistrates, a task which is both at once one of the most necessary and one of the most difficult: that of "protecting the poor against the tyranny of the rich" by

[34] O.C. III, 256–7.

preventing the establishment of wealthy classes and hence the development of poverty. Nothing matters more, because laws can be properly applied only to the citizens who are found in the middle range of the social structure.

Those who are in such a condition of "mediocrity" can feel the full force of the law. The law will be flouted by the rich who have the power to elude it and will even break its rules, while the law is not applicable to the poor, whose misery puts them beyond its reach. A state made up of rich and poor is a lawless state.

It is essential, therefore, to prevent the worst inequalities in the distribution of wealth. This can be done not so much by taking wealth away from those who have it, but by depriving everybody of the means of accumulating excessive wealth. What is necessary is not to "build hospitals for the poor but to guarantee the citizens from becoming poor." [35]

The most obvious causes of both opulence and poverty are the unequal distribution of the population between cities and countryside, the development of luxury crafts and of trade at the expense of agriculture. As a result, not only will the country be divided between rich and poor, but selfish interest will replace public interest, citizens will show indifference for the common cause and all the springs of government will be weakened. How to avoid all this requires the application of the steady hand of government in the performance of a hundred daily tasks of administration and in the skillful satisfaction of legitimate public needs.

The Satisfaction of Public Needs

By satisfaction of public needs Rousseau means the creation by the state of conditions that will enable all the members of the

[35] O.C. III, 258.

community to secure what is necessary for their subsistence. It does not mean the filling of "private granaries" in such a way as to exempt the citizen from having to work. Work, even in a society of plenty, must always be necessary and never useless. Work is the redeeming feature of a democratic society even if that society has reached, because of favorable developments, a state of economic abundance. Just as abundance must never mean that the few are able to reduce the many to a condition of submission, so it can never mean the other alternative "in which everybody would find easily at hand without work and without effort all that is needed to satisfy his needs." A true state of abundance exists in that country where what is necessary to human life is to be found in such quantity that "each can, through his work, easily accumulate all that he needs for his livelihood." [36]

To maintain an ideal state of abundance the government will have to have available adequate means. Such means are first and preferably to be provided through the public domain. "Anybody who has thought enough about such a matter can hardly fail to share the opinion of Bodin, who considered the public domain as the most honest and the safest of all the means to provide for the needs of the state." [37] Rousseau has hitherto been describing the public domain as consisting mostly of lands, but he now gives support to the views of a modern political philosopher—something he seldom does, except in the case of Montesquieu. He must have felt a strong affinity with the thought of a man who had such a lively sense of the require-

---

[36] *Fragments politiques*, vii, 2, O.C. III, 524. This is the concluding paragraph of a fragment of uncertain date but which on the basis of internal evidence appears to belong to the period of the replies and the *Political Economy*. Cf. Derathé's comments, O.C. III, 1528 ff. One conjecture is that the fragment was written before the *Political Economy*.
[37] O.C. III, 265.

ments of social solidarity and who could give such a subtle description of the public domain: "But besides sovereign power there must always be something enjoyed in common, as the public domain, a public treasury, the buildings used by the whole community, the roads, walls, squares, churches, and markets, as well as the usages, laws, customs, courts, penalties, and rewards which are either shared in common or of public concern. There is no commonwealth where there is no common interest." [38]

This is a notion of the public domain extending beyond the traditionally more limited one, and including controls over the tools of economic and social life which carry a burden of common concern and which the state alone can manage if the common interest is to be protected. Rousseau too places the public domain at the center of the body politic. It becomes the primary source of public revenues, indeed the only source not likely to weaken the true economic system which in the judgment of Rousseau would be upset by policies requiring the introduction of taxation.

But increasing public expenditures lead to social unbalance and to the enriching of idlers. They will multiply wars and the danger of mercenaries. They will result in urbanization and the abandonment of the countryside. To maintain such vast operations the revenues of the public domain will not be adequate.

Rousseau is, therefore, under no illusion as to the possibility of avoiding taxation except perhaps in an isolated agrarian state. Under more normal conditions of political life, taxation can hardly be ruled out; and Rousseau thus devoted a great deal of thought to the question of establishing the principles of taxation. The resulting proposals are conceived in terms of the needs not of a static and simple community, but of a growing and advanc-

[38] Bodin, *Six Books of the Commonwealth,* Tooley ed. (Oxford, 1955), Bk. I, ch. 2.

ing state whose policies, favoring a higher output and a balanced economy, are an important item in the pursuit of its goals of political equality.

The first issue to be solved is that of the taxation of farming land. Rousseau has seized the essence of the practices which had already succeeded in some of the more progressive agricultural countries of Europe. He therefore maintains that land taxation should not be proportioned to the crops' yield and increased as the yield increases, but should be related to certain fixed standards, such as the surface of the land, or, though Rousseau is silent on this point, to some long-range average yield. The farmer will reap the benefits to which he is entitled because of better cultivation methods and greater personal efforts. Work and intelligence will be rewarded and a stronger incentive to remain on the land, one of Rousseau's highest social goals, will be provided. He refers to the example of Holland, England, and China to show that such a system results in the best cultivated and the most productive lands, while, on the contrary, the land is abandoned wherever "the farmer is taxed in proportion to the yield of his field." [39]

It is also better to tax the consumer rather than the producer. In this way fraud is avoided. This is particularly important in the case of sumptuary taxes, where the public exhibition of the payment of the tax by the consumer is an essential part of the enjoyment he derives from his purchase. The consumer of luxury goods is anxious to show himself in the role of taxpayer, since an invisible display of luxury renders luxury useless. The real goal of the state is that of bringing about a gradual converging of all fortunes toward an average. Rousseau has stated earlier his belief that only through a greatly enlarged middle class can a state rest upon a solid foundation and be guaranteed the

[39] O.C. III, 273.

allegiance the rich refuse and the poor are unable to give. The task of reducing the rich to this ideal "mediocrity" is not an easy one. But luxury taxes may be one way in which this goal can be reached. In any case, they are likely to produce favorable consequences under either of two alternatives. The first is that the tax will drive the wealthy to engage only in useful expenses and this will benefit the state. The second is that the wealthy will continue to behave as before. If so, the government will easily secure the means it requires to satisfy the real needs of the state.[40]

Another key principle of taxation is that of taking into account the advantages which each citizen derives from society. In this measurement of the "utilities which each derives from the social state" the first consideration must be an awareness of the fact that the state usually "provides strong protection for the immense possessions of the wealthy man while barely leaving the poor man in the enjoyment of the hut he has built with his own hands." If all the advantages of society are enjoyed by the powerful and the rich, then a legitimate system of taxation must take this fact into account. Hence, "he who possesses only the simple necessities of life should pay nothing at all, while the tax on him who possesses superfluities may, if necessary, take away everything exceeding his necessities." [41]

Rousseau's reflections on the twin themes of the disparity of wealth and of the disparity of social advantage, leads him again to the theme of rich versus poor which forms a flaming thread running through his writings of these early years. This is not a rhetorical theme, since it belongs to the heart of his political analysis. But his rhetoric is irresistible and deserves to be quoted at length.

Are not all the advantages of society for the rich and powerful? Are not all lucrative posts in their hands? Are not all privileges and

[40] O.C. III, 277.　　[41] O.C. III, 271.

exemptions reserved for them alone? Is not the public authority always on their side? If a man of eminence robs his creditors, or is guilty of other knaveries, is he not always assured of impunity? Are not the assaults, acts of violence, assassinations, and even murders committed by the great, matters that are hushed up in a few months, and of which nothing more is thought? But if a great man himself is robbed or insulted, the whole police force is immediately in motion, and woe even to innocent persons who chance to be suspected. If he has to pass through any dangerous road, the country is up in arms to escort him. If the axle-tree of his chaise breaks, everybody flies to his assistance. If there is a noise at his door, he speaks but a word, and all is silent. If he is incommoded by the crowd, he waves his hand and every one makes way. If his coach is met on the road by a wagon, his servants are ready to beat the driver's brains out, and fifty honest pedestrians going quietly about their business had better be knocked on the head than an idle jackanapes be delayed in his coach. Yet all this respect costs him not a farthing: it is the rich man's right, and not the price of his wealth. How different is the case of the poor man! The more humanity owes him, the more society denies him. Every door is shut against him, even when he has a right to its being opened: and if ever he obtains justice, it is with much greater difficulty than others obtain favours. If the militia is to be raised or the highway to be mended, he is always given the preference; he always bears the burden which his richer neighbor has influence enough to get exempted from. On the least accident that happens to him, everybody avoids him: if his cart be overturned in the road, so far is he from receiving any assistance, that he is lucky if he does not get horsewhipped by the impudent lackeys of some young duke: in a word, all gratuitous assistance is denied to the poor when they need it, just because they cannot pay for it. I look upon any poor man as totally undone, if he has the misfortune to have an honest heart, a fine daughter, and a powerful neighbour.[42]

Any society in which this economic cleavage had become a reality can only arrive at a political contract which will not be

[42] O.C. III, 271–2.

among equal citizens but between two classes. And the text of this act of surrender will be, as Rousseau had already said in the *Discourse on Inequality*, a ruthless and simple one: "You need me because I am rich and you are poor; let us therefore agree among ourselves: I will permit you to have the honor of serving me, on condition that you give me the little you have left in return for the pains I shall take to rule you." [43]

But a society tending to an averaging of wealth will be able to enforce a different contract, a social contract, and will also be able to consider the social ends which taxation must have. Taxes that are collected only because they produce revenues are not good. The true statesman will lift his sights and "transform heavy burdens into useful tools so as to predispose the people to believe that such charges had as their goal the good of the nation rather than the yielding of tax revenues." Such would be a tax system which would stop the importation of luxury goods, relieve the poor, and charge the rich. In this way one could, through taxation, "prevent the continuous increase in the inequality of wealth," the enslaving of the workers, and the multiplication of idlers in the cities. [44]

Finally, Rousseau maintains that all personal taxes that "directly attack the right of property and therefore the true foundation of political society" must always be established only with the express consent of the people or of its representatives. While a host of taxes regulating domestic consumption or foreign trade do not require such approval, taxation relating to property rights does. [45]

Because of an apparent Lockian influence, Rousseau's views on private property in the *Political Economy*, have often been contrasted with his earlier views in the *Discourse on Inequality*.

---

[43] O.C. III, 273. Marx places these words in the mouth of a "capitalist" (*Capital*, Vol. I, ch. 30). Rousseau, needless to say, does not use that word.

[44] O.C. III, 275–6.   [45] O.C. III, 270, 277.

At the root of the misunderstanding there is confusion about Rousseau's frame of reference. Property in the *Discourse* is discerned first as an element in the evolution of man, secondly as the source of exploitation in a community imposed by the rich on the poor. In the *Political Economy* property is discussed in terms of the role it must play in the well-organized state.

In the *Political Economy* the issue arises in connection with property taxes and the need of obtaining an expression of consent on the part of the community before they can be imposed: "One must remember that the foundation of the social compact is property and that its first condition is that everyone should be maintained in the peaceful enjoyment of what belongs to him." [46]

The initial impression of Lockian derivation in these words tends, on reflection, to fade away. In the margin of the manuscript, Rousseau has added, "see Locke," [47] as if to suggest that these really are Locke's views. His takeover of Locke's doctrine is, however, a prudent and limited one. There is no statement in the *Political Economy* that property is a natural right to be sanctioned by civil society. Property is merely to be guaranteed by civil society as part of a relationship among men which, having developed fairly late in the evolution from the primitive state of nature to civil society, is only one of the practical considerations to accompany the organization of the political community. That is, accepting the Lockian view that civil society must guarantee property, Rousseau does not accept the prior and essential Lockian concept that property rights are natural rights. He does not repudiate his earlier statements that it was an unhappy day for mankind when the words *mine* and *thine* were first uttered. And the rights of property are limited by the emphasis on the "peaceful enjoyment" each will derive from the

[46] *O.C.* III, 269–70. [47] *O.C.* III, 1406.

safeguarding of his right—a noncompetitive right, built to the human scale.

Furthermore, property rights, as Rousseau makes clear, must serve specific purposes if they are to be protected. First among them is concern for the institution of the family. Laws will be needed to guide the transfer of property from generation to generation and "the spirit of these laws which it is the responsibility of the government to apply, must be that from father to son and from relation to relation the goods of a family should leave it or be alienated as little as possible." What Rousseau has in mind when he says that property rights are the foundation of civil society is that the continuity of the family, and not the protection of speculators, comes first. Clearly he is alluding to land, the basis of his ideal community, and to the perpetuation of family traditions through the ownership of land across the generations.

The second condition he has in mind is that of social stability. The guarantee of property must be accompanied by laws regulating property, because "nothing is more fatal to morals and to the Republic than continuous shifts of condition and of fortune among the citizens; shifts which are the proof and the source of a thousand disorders, which overturn and confound everything." [48] The avoidance of the social chaos flowing from the unregulated and too frequent transfers of property can best be obtained in a society in which, as Rousseau has said, there is a convergence toward modest average fortunes which, almost by definition, do not lend themselves to the practices of a merchant entrepreneurial society.

The property rights Rousseau is so anxious to shelter are those of the small individual property owners of a democratic society of free and equal citizens. In that respect property becomes the

[48] O.C. III, 263–4.

foundation of society. The goods which cannot be taken away are the goods which the citizen and his family are using directly. It is a concept of property which rules out the possibility of the accumulation of wealth justified in theory and sanctioned in practice by Locke. On the contrary, as we have just seen, Rousseau has recommended a policy of drastic confiscation of everything above a certain minimum required for the necessities of life. Such a policy is compatible with Rousseau's view on property but not with Locke's.

Finally, another passage calls for elucidation:

It is certain that the right of property is the most sacred of all the rights of the citizens and in some respects even more important than liberty itself; either because it more nearly concerns the preservation of life or because material goods being more easy to usurp and more difficult to defend than the person, one must respect more what can be more easily taken away; or finally because property is the true foundation of civil society and the true guarantee of the commitments of the citizens: for if material goods were not answerable for their proprietors [personnes], nothing would be easier than to elude one's own duties and to evade the laws.[49]

After the traditional beginning (property more important than liberty and vital to life), comes the deliberately shocking conclusion, that property is given in hostage for the good behavior of the citizen, and guarantees the fulfillment of the citizen's duties toward the state. If property were not answerable for the actions of proprietors, then the temptation to flout the laws might be too great. Property, a usurpation in the prepolitical state, acquires a new role when the citizens agree to form the political community. Property now guarantees both the freedom of the citizen and the fulfillment of his duties. It is limited in its extent and it is inextricably linked to the state. It is not a right that can be

[49] O.C. III, 262–3.

claimed against the state. It is one of the tools that must be used wisely to enable the citizens to do what they must do. It will be one of the important tools the state will use if it wants to satisfy public needs and to mortify private gains.

This may be a distant goal. But there is no reason why man should not work to achieve it. In his *Letter to Philopolis,* as we have seen, Rousseau had turned away from a philosophy of quietism which denied movement and the influence man can exert over his social life. Man must reject counsels of despair. If we say that whatever is, is right, then logically everything was equally right even before the beginnings of governments and of laws, which would therefore lack all justification. Mankind has certainly taken many disastrous turns in the road leading to the present. It would be wrong to try to stay where we are and miss whatever chance may be left us of getting closer to an ideal state. The conclusion is that we can through political action control the way in which we move as a society and that therefore political action is a moral duty.

The Profession of Civic Faith

The Lisbon earthquake sends Rousseau back to Pope's *Essay on Man.* In 1742 he had dealt a first time with Pope: the chain of being was unacceptable as it established a continuity between the human and the divine, but Epistle IV had the right definition of happiness. In 1755 he lamented the use of Pope's "whatever is, is right," if it led to political quietism. Now in 1756 Voltaire forces him once more to take up the same problem.[50]

---

[50] *Lettre à Voltaire,* August 18, 1756, C.G. II, 303–24. R. A. Leigh has now published "the actual text read by Voltaire of Rousseau's letter," which is the text of the Leningrad manuscript: "Rousseau's Letter to Voltaire on Optimism," *Studies on Voltaire,* XXX (1964), 247–309. Quotations will be from this text.

Voltaire, in his *Poème sur le Désastre de Lisbonne,* had called Pope to task for his optimism. How could one say that whatever is, is right, when faced by such immense disasters?

Europe had been shocked by the Lisbon earthquake of 1755. Where was the hand of Providence? Voltaire had found in the immensity of the disaster cause for lamenting the optimism of Pope and Leibniz. Hence, the "paradox" of Voltaire attacking one of the Enlightenment's central tenets, while Rousseau, the harsh critic of the life and thought of his times and a pessimist concerning mankind's past evolution, rallies to the defense of the optimists and of the believers in the justness and beneficence of God.

The paradox strikes Rousseau toward the end of his letter:

I cannot avoid noting, sir, a most singular contrast between yourself and myself on the topic of this letter. Filled with glory . . . you live free in the midst of abundance; certain of your immortality you are tranquilly philosophizing on the nature of the soul, and if your body or heart is suffering, you have Tronchin as doctor and friend. Nevertheless, you see only evil on earth. While I, an obscure man, poor and tormented by an incurable disease, reflect with happiness in my retreat and find that everything is well. What is the source of these apparent contradictions? You have explained it yourself: you enjoy life, while I hope, and hope embellishes everything.

The paradox was only apparent, as Rousseau well knew. The "optimism" of the Enlightenment was based on a faith in progress brought about by science and the philosophical elite, and without much concern for what the great majority of men could do or of what would happen to them. Reason was universal but not everybody was equally endowed with it. The "canaille" could be left to its own devices, to enjoy later the generalized benefits that the rights of men would have brought to mankind. For the moment, institutions, sharp social divisions, grossly unequal distribution of wealth, could all be left as they were, provided freedom was granted to those who had something intelligent to say and priests and kings went about their business without interfering with the forward march of philosophy and of the arts. The orderly state of affairs needed for the progress of mankind was disturbed by such events as the mass slaughter of Lisbon. This interference by Providence in the philosophers' planning required the expression of a suitably pessimistic view, regardless of Condorcet's final vision of near immortality.

The position of Rousseau was quite different. For him ultimate happiness would not come from an automatic unfolding of progress achieved by man in semianarchical conditions of social conflict, but in the recovery of certain qualities which men had gradually lost. In order to believe that this recovery was possible, Rousseau had to have confidence in the capacity of man to see through the imperfections of his current life, and to look to a stage beyond it that was to make possible for him once again the happy life that he once knew. More than to reason and to the flowering of the arts and the sciences, Rousseau felt the need to look inside man himself. More than in the theorems of mathematicians and philosophers, the brilliant elite which had given to life a veneer of balance and perfection which did not correspond to the reality of things, Rousseau wanted to find reassurance in the moral strength of the common man. Rousseau felt that what he saw was comforting, and because of this he could reproach Voltaire the famous, the rich, the honored symbol of the eighteenth century, for a pessimistic view which Rousseau the poor, the harried, the outcast, did not feel. If Rousseau was a pessimist concerning the past and the evolution of man down to the present, he saw the possibility of optimism for the future. "Whatever is, is right" was wrong if used to defend the anarchy of the present, but right if used to understand the design of nature.

What had been destroyed in Lisbon was in effect an artifact, a construction of man. Natural man had never built a big city with edifices of six or seven stories on a narrow strip of land. Civilization and not nature had instilled in man those anxieties and desires which caused the inhabitants of the wounded city to go back to their houses to salvage their belongings and their moneys. Without such civilized habits, very few would have been killed. How is it possible to blame nature and providence for something which is of our own making? And are we also quite certain that those who died in the earthquake would not have suffered greater sorrows and pains had they lived longer?

Of the men crushed under the ruins of this unhappy town, many without doubt have avoided greater misfortunes; and despite the touching description and the aid it gives to poetry, it is not certain that even one of those unhappy people has suffered more than if in the ordinary course of things he had waited in the midst of long agonies for the death which surprised him. Is there a sadder end than that of a dying man tormented by useless cares, oppressed by lawyer and heirs, murdered little by little in his bed by doctors and to whom barbarous priests describe death with relish? As far as I am concerned I see everywhere that the evils to which nature submits us are less cruel than the ones we like to add.

Rousseau can therefore go back to one of his main themes: "The source of moral evil cannot be sought anywhere outside of free, perfected and consequently corrupt man." Civilization and not nature is responsible for our troubles and no matter how skillful we are at multiplying our miseries through "beautiful institutions," we have not yet succeeded in making life unbearable and we do not yet prefer nothingness to existence. The view advanced by Voltaire with the support of Erasmus that very few people would like to relive their lives in the same way is based on a faulty statistical sample. Who were the people consulted by Voltaire? "Perhaps the rich, satiated with false pleasures and ignoring the true ones, always bored with life and always fearful of losing it; perhaps men of letters, of all the classes of men the most sedentary, the most unhealthy, the most reflective and therefore the most unhappy."

Pessimism is perhaps justified if we look at mankind through the eyes of the rich and of the literary set. But preferably one should look at the great mass of the people in order to form a judgment.

Consult an honest bourgeois who has spent an obscure and tranquil life without projects and without ambition; a good artisan who lives comfortably off his trade; even a peasant, not in France where the policy is that they must starve so that we may live, but in the country, for example, where you are or generally in any free country. I dare state as a fact that there is not perhaps in the High Valais a single 'montagnard' who is unhappy with his nearly automatic life and who would not gladly accept, in place even of paradise, the bargain of being forever reborn to vegetate in this way forever.

If we were to do that then we would believe in providence and in God. Rousseau does, and concludes his letter with the famous and moving statement: "All the subtleties of metaphysics can well sharpen my pains, they will never shake my faith in the immortality of the soul.[51] I feel it, I believe it, I want it, I hope it, I will defend it until my last breath." Indeed, all the questions raised by Voltaire are brought back to that of the existence of God, and in God Rousseau believes all the more strongly since "the condition of doubt is a condition too turbulent for my soul."

A belief in the beneficent hand of providence is not only enough to justify an optimistic view of human life, it is a necessity for its proper organization. Rousseau's argument now shifts, to justify a civic profession of faith, built on the foundations of religious freedom—a freedom made strong by the twin guaran-

[51] All other manuscripts and editions: ". . . will never cause me to doubt for a moment of the immortality of the soul and of a beneficent Providence" (Leigh, *op. cit.*, 294).

tees of freedom of conscience and of the right to a disestablished church. No one should dare to control man's conscience, where no one can penetrate: "Do kings of this world have some right of inspection in the other world and are they empowered to torment their subject on earth to force them to go to paradise? Clearly all human government must be limited by its nature to civil duties and in spite of anything that the sophist Hobbes may have said, when a man is a good servant of the state he must not render account to anybody of the way in which he serves God." Works are better than faith if ever a choice has to be made. An irreproachable moral life is certainly worth in the eyes of God "a thousand bizarre rites prescribed by men and rejected by reason." Rousseau would rather appear before God saying, I have done good but have not thought about You, rather than to say the opposite.

Proceeding from these premises and having made them as clear as he can, Rousseau states the terms under which a civic profession of faith should be made. Its first quality lies in its negative character. The profession of faith bans religious intolerance as an attack on the foundations of society. Intolerance is the most hateful of the dogmas to be proscribed and it is necessary to uproot it at its source because some of the most sanguinary fanatics "preach only patience and sweetness when they are not the strongest." Rousseau's definition of intolerance applies to "any man who cannot imagine it is possible to be a good man without believing all that he believes and pitylessly damns those who do not think like him." Equally intolerant and equally to be banned are those who would force the believers to be unbelievers.

The essential character of the profession of civic faith Rousseau sums up as follows:

I would therefore like the adoption in each state of a moral code, or of a kind of profession of civic faith, which included on the positive side the social maxims which everybody would be bound to admit and on the negative side the fanatic maxims which one would be bound to reject, not as impious but as seditious. Thus every religion which could be reconciled with the code would be admitted, every religion which could not be reconciled would be proscribed, and everybody would be free to have no other religion than the code itself.

The ideal state is now complete. Within the walls of the civic code live some religious believers and others whose only rules of belief and conduct would be provided by the code itself. Transcendent and worldly commands would be heard within the boundaries of the community. The difference in language would be nullified by a common adherence to the self-imposed discipline of the democratic state.[52]

[52] As if anticipating the charges that would be pressed against him for his defense of a civic profession of faith, Rousseau tells Voltaire in an early paragraph of his letter: "I know the distinction that must be made between the intentions of an author and the consequences which may be drawn from his doctrine."

VII

Beyond the State

War and Peace

ROUSSEAU'S *State of War*, or, more accurately, *That the State of War Is Born of the Social State*, was published for the first time 140 years after it was written.[1] It is only one or two years removed from the *Discourse on Inequality* and the *Political Economy* and in its ideas is very close to them.

In it Rousseau develops further some of his basic themes concerning the natural condition of man and the requirements of the ideal state, in relation to the problem of war, to refute once again Hobbes's doctrine on the permanent conflict among men in the state of nature.

Such a doctrine not only flies in the face of what we know about the nature of man but is also historically untenable, for "how can we imagine that this species so monstrous and hateful

---

[1] E. Dreyfus-Brisac published it in his 1896 edition of the *Social Contract*. The *State of War* is one of a series of *Ecrits sur l'Abbé de Saint-Pierre*, O.C. III, 561–682, written for the most part in 1756. They are: 1. *Extrait du projet de paix perpetuelle*; 2. *Jugement sur le projet de paix perpetuelle*; 3. *Que l'Etat de guerre naît de l'état social*; 4. *Polysynodie de l'Abbé de Saint-Pierre*; 5. *Jugement sur la polysynodie*; plus a number of fragments.

could have lasted even two generations? And yet this is where the wish, or rather the frenzy, to establish despotism and passive obedience have led one of the greatest geniuses who ever lived." [2]

Even if it were true that man was capable of the unlimited and reckless greed assumed by such views, still "it would not produce that state of universal war of each against all of which Hobbes dares to outline the hateful picture." For there is a contradiction between the two related aspects of Hobbes' assumption, the unlimited urge on the part of man to appropriate everything for his own use and the urge to destroy his fellow men. The absurd conclusion follows that "the conqueror who having killed everybody should have the misfortune to be left alone upon the earth, would enjoy nothing in spite of the fact that he would be master of everything."

The reason for this is clear, Rousseau thinks:

What good would he get from the possession of the whole universe, if he were its sole inhabitant? Who will gather for him the harvest of every climate? Who will carry the fame of his empire into the vast deserts which he will never reach? What will he do with his treasures? Who will consume the food that he has stored? In whose eyes will he make boast of his power? I see. Instead of slaying all, he will bind all in chains, so that at least he may have slaves. That changes the whole face of the argument at a single stroke. It is no longer a question of destruction. The state of war is done away.[3]

To prove that this is so, Rousseau has only to remind us of what he has already said about man in the beginning of time. He is fearful and cowardly, he runs away from danger, he lives from day to day, he avoids enemies and conflict wherever possible, he lacks any desire to conquer for purposes he cannot see. Before he can acquire the soldierly qualities which go with a warlike spirit,

[2] O.C. III, 611.
[3] O.C. III, 601 (Vaughan's translation, *Political Writings*, I, 288).

he must already be a citizen—that is, must already be far removed in time from the original state of nature.

Man has a vivid realization of his own smallness and of the limitations of strength and life which nature has imposed on him. His years are numbered; his physical needs cannot be extended beyond a certain level. And yet, consider the efforts of many philosophers to reverse the true order of things: "Everything brings natural man to rest; to eat and to sleep are the only needs he knows; and hunger alone forces him to give up his laziness. One has made of him, however, a madman always ready to torment his fellow men because of passions unknown to him; on the contrary, those passions exacerbated within society by everything which can inflame them, are treated as if they did not exist in it." [4]

True, small individual conflicts may arise. But they are quickly quelled and they are not wars. The killing of a fellow man to which someone may be led for the sake of self-preservation is an act that horrifies him when he is forced to commit it and that he will commit without anger. This is because natural law is not founded in reason only. We cannot forget an earlier natural law, "engraved in the hearts of man in ineradicable characters and it is there that it speaks more strongly than all the precepts of philosophers." The conclusion leaves no doubt: "There is no general war of man against man and mankind has not been created only to destroy itself." [5]

War must therefore be analyzed from a different starting premise, one which will not ascribe to a weak, relatively isolated man, bounded by the confining traits of his physical nature, guided by the dictates of an original set of principles to which reason has not yet contributed much, actions of which he is totally incapable. War must flow from conditions in which per-

[4] O.C. III, 605.   [5] O.C. III, 602.

manent and intricate and constant relationships among men are in existence. War is a process resulting from decisions which can be taken only when political societies have come into being. War is the result of problems created by political bodies which, unlike their individual members, can grow and change: "The state is an artificial body without any predetermined measure, the size which is appropriate to it is indefinite, it can always be increased and it will always feel itself weak as long as stronger states exist. Its safety, its conservation require that it become more powerful than all its neighbors." States are not deprived of passions, and reason of state is not made up of reason alone: "The essence of civil society consists in the activity of its members, and the state without movement would be a dead body." [6]

These activities are the result of forces released by the establishment of societies and they are linked to the attainment of selfish economic advantages. These become the goals of whoever controls political society: "Land, money, men, all the loot that can be seized, become therefore the principal objects of reciprocal hostilities. This vulgar cupidity will gradually change our ideas about things and war will degenerate in brigandage, while enemies and warriors become little by little tyrants and thieves."

From this follows Rousseau's definition of war as "the consequence of a mutual disposition constantly and publicly manifested, to destroy the enemy state or at least to weaken it by all available means." [7]

The paradox Rousseau is facing has now taken shape. He has been led to believe by all the authors of books on law and morality, by the books of the philosophers and the publicists, convinced as he was by their skillful pleadings, that life in the state of nature was miserable. He has therefore been persuaded "to admire the peace and justice established by civil society, to

[6] O.C. III, 605.   [7] O.C. III, 607.

bless the wisdom of public institutions and to rejoice to be a man since he is a citizen." Thus properly indoctrinated about his happiness, Rousseau closes his books, leaves the classroom and goes out into the world to find confirmation of what he has learned: "I see unhappy peoples groaning under an iron yoke, mankind crushed by a handful of oppressors, a famished crowd overwhelmed by sorrow and hunger whose blood and tears the rich drinks peacefully, and everywhere the strong armed against the weak by the redoubtable power of the laws."

Rousseau is astonished by the fact that this grisly state of affairs is accepted with indifference and without resistance. But it is nothing more than "the tranquillity of the companions of Ulysses trapped in the cave of the cyclops while they were waiting to be devoured." And if this is the spectacle offered by the immediate landscape, lift your eyes and look afar, Rousseau suggests, and you will still be shocked: "I perceive fires and flames, abandoned countrysides, pillaged cities. . . . I get nearer and see murders, ten thousand men killed, mountains of dead, the dying trampled under the horses' hooves, everywhere the image of death and agony."

The conclusion is inevitable. The writers and the publicists have given us a false picture of mankind. What we see today is the fruit of the institutions destined in theory to maintain the peace. Addressing himself to Hobbes, he invites the "barbaric philosopher" to come and read his book on the field of battle. This would put in its proper setting the "horrible system of Hobbes" and would enable us to turn his absurd doctrine around and see that "it is not true that the state of war be natural to man but that war has been born of peace, or rather of the precautions which men have taken to guarantee themselves a durable peace." [8]

[8] O.C. III, 609–10.

If anything is saving men from complete destruction as a result of conflicts and wars, it is the continued presence of those natural sentiments of compassion and benevolence, of those natural inclinations which even today we have not wholly succeeded in destroying. They are there and resist our own prejudices and the vices multiplied by social life. If Hobbes were right, a sensitive man endowed with pity would be a monster and "we would be naturally what we have great difficulty in becoming even in the midst of the depravation which surrounds us."

Even society has failed to kill all that is good in man, responsible though it is for what we are and for the catastrophic incidence of war at the end of the long evolution of mankind toward organized life. Unless this is understood, Rousseau is convinced that we will never be able to consider what has to be done: "The error of Hobbes and of the philosophers has been to take natural man for the man they have before their own eyes and to transplant into one system a being who can only exist in another."

War is linked to the progress of civilization. Man is happy when his soul is sound and his body doesn't suffer. "Those who have nothing have limited desires, those who do not rule over anybody have limited ambitions. But the superfluous awakens cupidity, the more one has, the more one wants. Whoever has much, wants everything." Out of this progression have come the extremes of human passions and civil societies and wars.

Our superficial philosophers look at man as he has been changed and molded by social life a hundred times and they imagine they are observing man. Rousseau concludes the *State of War* on a note already struck in the *Discourse on Inequality*: "They are trying to find out why savages brought among us do not share our passions or our pleasures and do not care at all for all the things we so ardently seek. They will find the answer only through my principles. They know only what they see and they have never seen nature. They know very well what is a bourgeois of London or of Paris but they will never learn what is a man." [9]

Absolutism and a United Europe

If war is something which potentially or in reality exists permanently among sovereign states, then peace might be secured by a weakening of their sovereign attributes and by arriving at some form of confederation or union among them. The possibility is greatest among the European states which Rousseau sees as possessing many common traits. They form among themselves "a kind of system which unites them through the same religion, through the same international law, customs, letters and trade and a kind of equilibrium which is the necessary result of this." [10]

These common traits have become more than an abstract idea. There is a reality of Europe, visible at every point: in the commingling of commerce, in easy communications, in the restlessness of its inhabitants which pushes them to unceasing travel, in the community of studies and knowledge brought about by the printing press and in the general spread of letters, in the multitude of states which their needs should in principle make mutually dependent. It is true to say that these factors have made of Europe, quite unlike Asia and Africa, whose peoples have in common only a name, "a real society with its religion, its morals, its customs and even its laws which it is impossible for any of the peoples composing it to violate without causing immediate difficulties."

But this ideal European society which should have become the reality on the basis of so many important activities and relationships, has remained a sham, for the truth is that daily this "brilliant refuge of sciences and of art" is defiled by conflicts and

[9] O.C. III, 611–2.　　[10] O.C. III, 565.

wars. And one is at a loss to explain "our beautiful speeches and our horrible proceedings, so much humanity in the maxims but so much cruelty in the actions, such sweet religion and such bloody intolerance, a politics so wise in the books and so harsh in the practice, chiefs so beneficent and peoples so miserable, governments so moderate and wars so cruel."

The reason is not far to seek. Our national societies are still so removed from the only possible society under law (and Rousseau means here the society whose model he has just given us in the *Political Economy*), that European society as well is founded on nothing but chance, as it is born from relationships of national societies which in themselves are imperfect. The surface union must degenerate of necessity in quarrels and conflict at the first clash. As he had first expressed in the preface to *Narcisse*, Rousseau underlines again the illusion of safety we imagine can be found in the multiplication of a thousand reciprocal interests and needs. The peoples of Europe "are related at so many points that the smallest movement of one of them must create a shock in the others; their divisions are all the more calamitous that their ties are more intimate so that their frequent disputes have almost the cruelty of civil wars." [11]

This means that the European society, like the national societies that have preceded it, has been founded merely on the calculus of interests. While the brute power of a tyrant within a national society can keep in check opposed individuals who are constantly at each other's throats in the pursuit of their personal gains and keep them apart by the application of the superior strength of the state, European national states are in permanent conflict among themselves since there is no higher system to regulate their affairs. Just as the formation of the ideal state cannot be left to chance but must be the result of a deliberate

[11] O.C. III, 567-8.

decision of man to accept the commitments of political life, so a true European union can neither be achieved nor maintained by the course of chance. Deliberate intervention and not the mere "force of things" is needed to create Europe.

Rousseau is brought to recall an earlier attempt to unite Europe led by Henry IV and Sully. What immense, protracted, and detailed effort had gone into their plan. How much hardheaded reflection and subtle diplomatic work had preceded the beginning of the application of the plan. All this came to nothing under the assassin's blows, but the historical record is there to show the tortuous and difficult paths that lie ahead before the goal of a united Europe can be reached. It was naive of Saint-Pierre to believe that such a goal could be achieved merely by writing one book. The reality of politics is such that Saint-Pierre's plan failed not because it was not good enough, but because it was too good: "The evil and the abuses from which so many people profit come in by themselves; but what is useful to the public can only be introduced by force, since private interests are nearly always opposed to it." [12]

The question is not that of the utility of the project on perpetual peace prepared by Saint-Pierre, which is obvious. The difficulty rather lies in the failure to act, in politics as in morals, on the basis of the conflict between the real interests of society and of man and private interests. The former are deep-seated, not readily identifiable, and cannot express themselves. They can be summed up as a longing for peace. The latter are loudly expressed in terms of national independence and fortune. They go hand in hand with the two chief objectives of kings, which are to extend their domination abroad and to make it more absolute within their own nation. Whatever else they may say is

[12] O.C. III, 599.

mere pretext, a smoke screen of empty slogans intended to deceive the public: "such as the public good, the happiness of the subjects, the glory of the nation, words forever proscribed within the walls of cabinets but so heavily used in the public proclamations that they always herald calamitous orders and that the people groan in anticipation of what is to come as soon as their masters start talking to them of their paternal care for their welfare." [13]

Absolute monarchies, then, are a source of wars among nations and of tyranny within nations, and a great obstacle to a united Europe. Viewing the supporters of benevolent despotism with unconcealed contempt, Rousseau delivers a scathing criticism of royal absolutism and of absolute power in general. The carriers of absolute power aim to reduce their people to an instrument of their fantasies. Nothing of what they do is a recognition of a duty to perform; it is due to the pleasure of issuing commands to a mass deprived of freedom and judgment.

Nowhere is the contrast between reality and appearance greater than here. Ignorant and boring and corrupt rulers are described and treated as invincible conquerors, kings of kings, monarchs of the world, and sacred majesties. The greater the emptiness at the top, the greater is the adulation showered on the occupant of the throne. In this make-believe world, courtesans and manipulators, financiers and men of letters, are all interested in maintaining a system which feeds their vanity and their greed.

How power can be exercised in a system of absolutism is one of the main issues. Rousseau sees the ruler making a division among the affairs of state, reserving to himself the "greater affairs" and delegating to his ministers the "details," that is, the routine affairs of state. The difficulty with this distinction is that

[13] O.C. III, 592.

the "details" are in effect the "essential" sphere of government, while the "great affairs of state," including the gossip of ambassadors, have nothing to do with the welfare of the people:

What matters for the citizens is to be governed justly and in peace. Furthermore, to see that the state be great, powerful and expanding, is the private business of the prince and the subjects have no interest in it. Hence, the monarch must first of all busy himself about the detailed matters which make up the substance of civil freedom, of the safety of the people and even often of his own. Once he has taken care of these matters, if he still has any time left, he can devote it to all these great affairs which are of no interest to anyone, are always born only from the vices of the government and which consequently are nothing for a happy people and very little for a wise king.[14]

Wars, or a foreign policy of prestige and grandeur, are the real purpose of such governments, but the attention to the details of administration alone can establish the welfare of the people and the conditions under which the community will live at peace with itself. But in an absolute system of government, who cares about a good or a bad administration? The happiness of an absolute ruler cannot be "troubled by the miseries of a people he cannot see, by complaints he cannot hear and by public disorders of which he will never know anything." Isolated and concerned either with trifles or with matters of personal interest, the carrier of absolute monarchical power can also be relied upon to be, usually, an imbecile, thanks to the operation of the laws of succession to the throne: "If by a miracle a great soul might be capable of filling the painful tasks of royalty, the hereditary system established for succession and the extravagant education given to the heirs of the throne will always supply 100 imbeciles for every true king, and there will always be regencies, illnesses,

[14] O.C. III, 618.

interludes of delirium and passion which often will leave at the head of the state a mere simulacrum of a prince." [15]

Hence, it follows that the chief characteristic of absolute monarchical government is its instability, the uncertainty as to where power is to be found, and the constant search for ways in which to balance its exercise: "Generally one sees republics change their systems less frequently than monarchies." [16]

If one takes for granted that absolute monarchy is bad and should be abolished or changed, the key problem is how to proceed. According to Rousseau, one of the weaknesses of Saint-Pierre was that he failed to take into account specific existing circumstances, as he merrily went on to build immensely complicated plans. No political speculation on the reform of existing governments is valid until and unless all the relevant historical factors are taken into account. The chances of being able to do something about royal absolutism in mid-eighteenth-century Europe were severely limited by a series of negative factors.

The general climate of opinion and of social sentiments were unfavorable. It was impossible to rely on "love of country, the public good, the desire for true glory," for all these chimeras had faded away long ago and only traces of them were left in a few small republics. More than that, the intermediate bodies which in a large kingdom could perform useful functions had been allowed to decline. Worse still, the French monarchy had tried "to render Parliament contemptible before the people rather than really give its members the authority it feigned to have given them." This was nothing less than a trap by which one hoped to destroy the intermediate powers. [17]

[15] O.C. III, 619.   [16] O.C. III, 642.

[17] O.C. III, 643, 637. This is a clear allusion to the conflicts that in the mid-seventeen-fifties marked the relationships between the French monarchy and the parliaments, which, awakened too late to the implications of royal absolutism, had been trying to regain some of their powers of constitutional control over the king.

In effect, the intermediate bodies raise in principle the question of their survival in an absolute monarchy. This is where Saint-Pierre is confused. He wants to give power to the intermediate bodies but leaves to the king alone the final decision. If there are intermediate bodies between the prince and the people, can, or must, they have a jurisdiction independent of both? If they have a precarious authority and are dependent on the prince, can they ever become an integral part of the institution of the state and have any real influence on its affairs? The alternatives are clear. Either the deliberations of the intermediate bodies soon become empty debates, or royal authority is bound to be altered and a trend toward a republican form of government will get under way. The logic of absolutism, as the history of the French monarchy so well proves, cannot tolerate the survival of really independent and powerful intermediate bodies.

But even assuming that it might be possible to go against history and against the hard institutional encrustations, who is to be found to take the leadership in the reform of royal absolutism? "At a time when a whole nation can concern itself only with idiocies, how attentive can it be to great problems, in a country where music has become an affair of state, what will be affairs of state except songs? When one sees all of Paris in turmoil for a buffoon or a wit, and the business of the academy or of the opera placed ahead of the interest of the prince and the glory of the nation, what can one hope from bringing public affairs closer to the people and transferred from the Court to the City?" [18]

The coming of the day when royal absolutism will be removed from the life of the state is remote. And until that day, royal absolutism will work against a European union. A European Diet "would limit the government of each state no less than its

[18] O.C. III, 638.

boundaries." As princes would be guaranteed against the revolt of their subjects, so would the subjects be guaranteed against the tyranny of the princes. Otherwise, there could be no European Diet: "I therefore ask myself where is a single sovereign in the world who, thus blocked forever in his most cherished projects, would tolerate without indignation the mere thought of being forced to be just, not only with foreigners, but even with his own subjects."

By limiting war, a European union would check the advance of despotism which is strengthened by war and its accompanying enforced discipline and tyrannical financial exactions. How could one hope that princes could submit their disputes to a higher European court if they proclaim might and not right to be the foundation of their power? "A mere gentleman doesn't deign to bring his complaints before the tribunal of the marshals of France and you imagine that a king would bring his before a European Diet?" [19]

The sad truth is that princes view wars as a source of advantages greater than the disadvantages. In war princes hope to obtain exclusive gains for themselves alone, while disaster and death will fall more likely on their subjects. But perpetual peace brings real advantages to all and its generalized benefits hold no interest for princes covetously looking to the immense personal gains to be derived from a successful war.

Nor is it to be imagined that ministers advising the princes could have a different point of view.

The ministers need war to make themselves indispensable. . . . They need it to harass the people under the pretext of public necessity, they need it to give jobs to their henchmen, speculate on the markets and establish in secret a thousand hateful monopolies, . . . they would lose all these advantages as a result of per-

[19] O.C. III, 593.

petual peace, and yet the public never stops asking why, if the project for perpetual peace is possible, the ministers have not adopted it? The public does not see that there is nothing that is impossible in this project except that the ministers should adopt it.

Rousseau extends the blame well beyond the ruling class. Everybody is guilty. Before peace can assert itself, "it would be necessary that the sum of particular interests should not carry the day over the common interests and that each should see in the good of all the greatest good he can hope to achieve for himself." [20] This is a remote and chancy possibility. If it is not realized, then peace and union might have to wait for violence or revolution. But on this basis "who among us could dare suggest if this European league is to be desired or to be feared? It might perhaps cause a greater evil all at once than it might not prevent for centuries."

In the end, the only conclusion—seemingly dictated by Rousseau's prudence—is that reform is impossible while revolution is feared. Once old customs and the structure of the state are changed, the consequences will be immeasurable. "Let us evaluate the danger of once setting in motion the enormous masses which compose the French monarchy. Who will be there to check the shock that will have been given, or forecast all the effects which it can cause?" [21]

But on the conditions necessary for the establishment of a European union, Rousseau is clear. What fortune has started, reason may achieve. Let us see how "the free and voluntary society which unites all the European states, by acquiring the strength and solidity of a real political body, might become a real confederation."

These are the conditions: (1) no great European power can be excluded from it; (2) there must be a single source of

[20] O.C. III, 595.   [21] O.C. III, 600, 638.

laws; (3) there must be a coercive power; (4) it must be indissoluble. In Rousseau's words, European union will be possible when "the confederation be so general that no considerable power will refuse to join it; when there will be a judicial tribunal capable of establishing the laws and regulation which must oblige all the members; when there will be a coactive and coercive force to constrain each state to submit itself to the common deliberations, either to act or to abstain from action; finally, when it will be strong and durable enough to prevent its members from seceding at will as soon as they will fancy the existence of a particular interest contrary to the general interest." [22]

Union will be possible when the states will understand that the terms which bring individuals together in the social contract, in an act of renunciation and of freedom, apply also to a contract among national entities and will achieve for them the same objectives and peace as well.

[22] O.C. III, 574.

VIII

The Roots I Have Cut

Wealth and Human Happiness

THERE is a little-known essay left for our consideration in this reconstruction of Rousseau's early thought. It is an "extraordinary text" in which Rousseau warns us of the "dangers lying in wait for the wealthy man: greed, avarice, temptations of all sorts and above all the taste for oppression and violence. With an astonishing warmth of heart and vehemence, he denounces not only the individual immorality caused by wealth, but also the social injustice it generates." [1]

This is the *Discourse on Wealth*, a message addressed to an imaginary correspondent, Chrysophile, [2] which forms a fitting conclusion to the many years of public discussion and anxious private debate on wealth and happiness and the relations of economic factors to political life. [3]

[1] Bernard Gagnebin, in his general introduction, "Les Ecrits politiques," to *O.C.* III, xxv–vi.

[2] *Discours sur les richesses,* par J.-J. Rousseau, publié pour la première fois par Félix Bovet, Paris, 1853, 24 pp. The *Discourse on Wealth* has not since been included in any of the editions of Rousseau's works. It has not yet been published in *O.C.* It is, however, reproduced in Appendix II of Iring Fetscher, *Rousseau's Politische Philosophie* (Neuwied, 1960), 266–75.

[3] It has **not** been possible, so far, to date with precision the writing of the *Discourse*. Its first editor, Bovet, attributes it, with very persuasive

The issue taken up by Rousseau in his letter is whether the acquisition of riches is justified if the purpose is to do good. He knows that this is an argument advanced many times to defend the accumulation of wealth: if the end purpose is good, then whatever a person does in order to acquire the means to do good is justified. Rousseau rejects the argument on the grounds that a contradiction is involved in trying to achieve good by indulging in all the vices which destroy it. Anyone attempting to proceed in this way is beginning under such a handicap that it is most doubtful whether the end can ever be achieved.

You want to do good but you begin by doing evil: "I would like, you say, to be rich so that I could use well my wealth, and if I desire to have property it is to do good with it and to help the unhappy. As if the first good were not that of not committing evil. How is it possible to enrich oneself without contributing to the impoverishment of others, and what would one say of a charitable man who begins by plundering all his neighbors in order to have later the pleasure of giving them alms."

The immense gap between poverty and wealth must also be taken into account. There is a time gap to begin with, and it is not clear in what way this prolonged interval between initial poverty and ultimate wealth can be filled. The plan may indeed be to do well once wealth has been attained, but a serious problem is what to do while wealth is being accumulated: "It is not enough to envisage the end of one's voyage if one does not make inquiries about the route to be followed." Also, death can intervene before the ultimate goal is reached, and, if so, it may take place at a moment when the efforts to accumulate wealth have produced only evil. For one cannot reasonably expect that time will stand still while the efforts to become rich are under way.

---

external evidence, to the years 1749–1756. Bouchardy thinks that it was written "probably after 1754" (O.C. III, 1244). Strong internal evidence would seem to suggest the years 1753–1756.

Nor can it be assumed that during that time there will be no poor people to help, no unhappiness to remove. Will it be necessary, on being approached by a desperate man about to be crushed by misfortune, to say: "My friend, my sense of humanity compels me to let you die because I have not yet accumulated the 100,000 pounds of income I need in order to assist you. . . . Come back in thirty years when I will be wealthy and you will see how large will be my beneficence."

Another issue is that of the limits to be placed on the accumulation of wealth. At what point will it be possible to say that added wealth is no longer necessary and that on the morrow charity will begin. The risk of this approach is that the desire to accumulate wealth, once fired, will continue until the end of one's life and that one will die buried under gold, the victim of avarice, without having accomplished any good at all.

But the worst difficulty is that in trying to do good through the accumulation of riches, man undergoes a qualitative transformation and becomes unable to do what he set out to do in the beginning. How is it possible, Rousseau asks, that a man, having spent a lifetime in the ruthless task of accumulating a fortune, will at the end of his life open the heart and mind to pity and generosity? "My friend, if you want to be a man only in your old age, obtain nature's guarantee that you will get there, lest, deluded in your expectation, you stop life before reaching goodness or die not having lived." For, Rousseau tells his imaginary friend, this is the real issue: "You are today poor and honest. But do you know what you will become when you will be rich? Don't you know that in spite of everything your ideas and your principles will change with your situation and that, in spite of yourself, when you will no longer be what you are today, you will no longer think as you do today."

For the rich man will not be able to remove himself from the influence of the environment in which he lives, from the thoughts of the people he knows, and from the temptations to which he is subjected. The environment of poverty leaves open the road to honor and to truth. But it is idle to imagine that the same will be true for those who move among the rich. Once Chrysophile is rich it will be necessary for him to choose either "to live as a wealthy man and be pitiless, or to live as a poor man and be ridiculous. . . . But today in the station where God has placed him he can live modestly without shame and practice goodness without having to fight."

Rousseau considers the rich incapable of expressing the sentiments of natural men or of participating properly in social life. The rich man in effect is no man at all. The alternative is: "He could be a man but he wants to be rich." Having undergone a process of self-destruction, he can harbor only cruelty. The rich will "look without pity upon the unhappy poor, crushed by continuous work, unable to get from it more than a bare sustenance which merely serves to prolong their misery. The rich man does not consider it at all strange that profit be in inverse proportion to work and that a mean and voluptuous idler should fatten upon the sweat of a million downtrodden people exhausted by fatigue and need. This is where they belong, he will say, for they are born to that estate, habit levels everything, and I am not happier under my canopy than a peasant in his hut, no more, he should add, than the cattle in their barn."

The rich man does not limit his contempt to the poor who surround him in the midst of the advanced civilization in which he moves. His contempt goes beyond Europe to those "savage climates, whose inhabitants without work and without needs live in a state of continuous indolence; then the rich man tenderly laments the fate of these unhappy people deprived of the only happiness, which is that of preparing for others the comforts of life. And he could not understand how one might live in a country where there are no honest rich charitably sucking the blood

[227]

of the people. Indeed, how can one fail to prefer the bright destiny of those who are our slaves to the idleness of the savage who is utterly useless as far as we are concerned?"

Yet this parody of man, this nonman, is deeply insecure. He has power and has most of the world at his feet, and yet he is unhappy and afraid. He may well multiply "iron doors, locks, chains, guards," he may well erect everywhere scaffolds and other instruments of torture, he may even endow chairs at universities where "only approved doctrines will be taught," or unceasingly place on his payroll new writers capable of describing "the theft committed by the poor as ever more infamous and the theft of the rich ever more respectable." All this will be to no avail, for the inevitable reaction will be to corrupt those with whom he is in touch. He will be poisoned by those who are supposed to serve him, and everything will acquire shapes contrary to reality. In the end he will be defeated: "Your doors will be broken down, your locks will be smashed, your coffers will be forced open."

How different are the poor, and how worthy. They are free. They work. They can do good today and not in an uncertain future, for they have retained the qualities which in man lead to goodness and solidarity. Once poor it is much better to continue to be poor: "Rather than to try to enter basely the class of the rich, stay in the class of people of merit and leave between these two classes the eternal separation established by nature."

The class of merit is an all-embracing one, based as it is on traits which nature implanted in its members. Whether small or large, it embodies those human qualities we must defend, if ever an order closer to nature is to established. The gulf which separates the two classes cannot be bridged, and the ultimate aspiration must be the elimination of the rich. The danger, given the conditions of contemporary civilization, is that the rich might overwhelm the poor and succeed in extending their habits and their social views to the entire community.

How sad it was that the rich should have found ready supporters among philosophers and men of letters. Once more Rousseau sees the intellectuals and the philosophers of his time as being responsible for the acceptance and defense of the institutions which have led to the present state of affairs. He taunts them, those "vaunted wise men," for they do not realize on what contradictory grounds they stand. They are nothing but "cowardly adulators of wealth, even more cowardly detractors of poverty, who most prudently know how to accommodate their philosophy to the taste of those who pay for it." [4]

A number of other scattered texts can be related to this period of Rousseau's life. While they lack the white fury of the *Discourse on Wealth*, they continue to show the same deep concern for the political and social consequences flowing from economic maladjustments and the behavior of the rich.

Two of the longest fragments deal with luxury, commerce, and the arts.[5] Rousseau now wishes to treat the issues of the economic system not, as he has done up to now, from the point of

[4] All quotations are from the Bovet edition of the *Discourse on Wealth*, 11–22.

[5] Vaughan (I, 341–9) publishes them as if they were a single fragment. Derathé, on the other hand (*O.C.* III, 1528–9), feels that there are two, written at different times, the second being probably another version of Fragment vi, 8 (*O.C.* III, 512–4), which was written in 1762 as part of an answer to an inquiry of the Economic Society of Berne. It is true that, as Derathé points out, there are some striking similarities of composition between this fragment and the answer to the Berne questionnaire. On the other hand, Derathé himself (*ibid.*, 1531) points to parallels between this fragment and similar passages on wealth and poverty in the *Political Economy* and the *State of War*. In substance, it seems legitimate to treat the fragments as a unit and as reflecting the views of Rousseau in the mid-fifties.

view of morals, but from a new point of view, that of the prosperity of the state. Rousseau, who feels he has been wrongly charged with untenable and flimsy paradoxes on the role of the arts and sciences, wants to prove that it is rather his critics who have cut themselves off from history in their philosophizing on such questions as luxury.

Throughout history luxury has been viewed with hostility and suspicion. The ancients were against luxury and enacted sumptuary laws to curtail it. It is true that later degeneration saw the triumph of luxury and the consequent destruction of the state. But even then writers continued to be against luxury. It was the paradox of Rousseau's century that for the first time philosophers had come out in favor of luxury, defending what the wisdom of the ages had always condemned. Therefore, "in refuting this soft and effeminate philosophy, whose comfortable maxims have brought to its support so many partisans, I am only joining my voice to the cry of all the nations and pleading the cause of common sense as well as that of society." The responsibility for this state of affairs Rousseau is willing to place at the feet of two men who, "in trying to acquire celebrity through singular opinions capable of flattering the taste of their century, have thought today of upsetting all the economic maxims of old political writers and of substituting for them an entirely new system of government, so attractive that it was very difficult not to be seduced by it." [6]

What these economists and philosophers are doing has become normal in a century in which individual interests are to be pushed and in which "no one is concerned any longer about the

---

[6] Of the two men, one is easy to identify as Melon, whose views on luxury Rousseau had already denounced in his *Last Reply* of 1752 (O.C. III, 95). The second could well be David Hume, as Derathé suggests (O.C. III, 1529). Hume's discussion of luxury, a bit distorted by his translator, had been published in Paris in 1754 (supra, p. 58).

public good." As the concern for the public good has declined, easy answers have been provided to the question how to make people happy, such as that the fostering of the arts, the increase of trade, the accumulation of money, would produce happiness. But even in the system Rousseau is attacking, if trade is useful to bring about the prosperity of the state, it is not in itself the "essence of its prosperity, for I do not believe that anybody has ever advanced as proof of the happiness of a nation that she is made up of workers and merchants." [7] As for gold and silver, they are not an index of wealth since they have merely symbolic value with reference to the goods which they help to exchange.

This proposition is self-evident in Rousseau's mind on the basis of the following hypothesis: "Let us suppose that after long and painful efforts a people has finally realized its goal, [that is] it has ruined all its neighbors and accumulated as much gold and silver as is to be found in the rest of the world. And let us see what would be the consequences of this public prosperity for the private happiness of the citizens." There are two alternatives. The first, that this gold will be evenly distributed among the citizens. Then no advantage will accrue to anyone because no one will be able to show off his wealth. If all that gold were to be destroyed overnight, its loss would not be felt.

But Rousseau wishes to waste no more time in dealing with "so chimerical a hypothesis as that of the even distribution of wealth: this equality cannot be admitted even hypothetically because it is not to be found in the nature of things." Thus the second alternative is the only real one, of the unequal distribution of gold. In an established society any initial inequality will be augmented. Money breeds money and unsocial behavior. Conditions come about which "cost the honor and life of the

[7] O.C. III, 518–9.

poor, and make the glory and fortune of the wealthy. To a cruel man covered with gold, the poor man who in order to buy bread steals a crown is a rascal who will be hung—while honored citizens tranquilly drink the blood of the artisan and of the laborer, and the monopolies of the merchants and the speculations of publicans are described as useful skills and guarantee to those who practice them the favor of the prince and the admiration of the public."

To these bloody images already to be found in the *Political Economy* and the *State of War,* Rousseau now adds an attack against "monopolies" supported by government, while repeating the judgments about the exploitation of the masses we found in the *Discourse on Wealth.* This monstrous inequality is enforced by public authority, and while the rich appropriate to themselves the substance of the people, the people are reduced to slavery. Hence, it follows that "the wealthier a state is in money, the greater the number of the poor and the greater their sufferings." [8] The real conditions of happiness are to be found in freedom and work, in the opportunity, that is, made available to all, of securing without undue difficulty and through work everything that is needed for sustenance.

The chances that this will happen without deliberate effort, Rousseau viewed as very scant. Too many people are anxious to abandon "mediocrity," that happy medium where well-being is found, in order to reach for wealth, which then becomes an intolerable source of unhappiness. [9] Too few are ready to work hard and make the choice between a life of leisure and a life of freedom. Perhaps a great upheaval is not only unavoidable, but must be invited. On revolution, Rousseau's position has remained ambiguous, even though he had analyzed the human condition in truly revolutionary terms. But now, at the end of his

[8] *O.C.* III, 521–3.   [9] *O.C.* III, 502.

Discourse on Wealth, we find a one-line fragment: "Shake with a nervous arm this frightful giant." [10] The wrongs of modern civilization are perhaps not going to be redeemed in any other way. Nothing, Rousseau appears to be saying, but a radical shock will be enough to destroy the power of the forces responsible for the plight of man.

Waiting for the Tree to Die

In 1756 the first cycle in Rousseau's thought comes to an end. It had begun in the orchard of Les Charmettes. It ends in the temporary peace of the Ermitage. The ceaseless turmoil of the intervening years has died down, for the moment. And Rousseau can look back in an introspective mood and try to recall his achievements and the fact that a period in his life is closing.

The purpose of this book has been to show how much of decisive importance Rousseau had said in the course of these twenty years, how indeed most of what he was to say later in his major works is to be found in this early period of vigorous polemics and creative thinking.

By 1756 Rousseau had stated his oppositon to the culture and institutions of the contemporary world. He had found them wanting, incapable of guaranteeing peace and certain to lead to wars and revolutions. He had attempted to get to the heart of the matter by pointing to the contrast between being and appearing, the disease of modern man. He had become convinced of the superiority of natural man over artificial social man. He had, therefore, painstakingly attempted to push aside the many layers which in the course of time civilization had superimposed upon natural man.

[10] *Discourse,* 24.

Of that original state of man, Rousseau had a simple vision, followed by a more complex one of a second state of nature in which man had achieved, perhaps, a golden age of happiness. Whether or not these images had any historical reality was not the first concern of Rousseau. Their appeal was that they provided a model and a foundation from which a useful analysis of human nature, past and present, could be developed, to arrive in the end to what mattered most, the definition of a citizen.

He had from those premises evolved certain views about the state in its harsh realities and traced the origin of the present difficulties to a fundamental injustice in the relations among men committed by the rich against the poor. He had also further outlined at length the requirements of the ideal state needed to build a free society of equals. He had at this point discussed the nature and purpose of the general will, the responsibilities of the citizen and of the state, the causes of war and the possibility of peace. He had portrayed the moral and social consequences of undue wealth and given the outlines of a civic faith which would bind the community together.

All this had been done in a deeply religious mood, with the conviction that there was a latent greatness in man which could be brought out once more, in part at least, through a parallel improvement of the institutions by which man was governed and of the capacity of man to look at himself within the larger framework of a common purpose. He was not an optimist, because he knew that the recovery of greatness was difficult once man was corrupted; but he was confident of the future and reproached Voltaire for his pessimism and told him that, on balance, it was a good thing to be alive. He feared revolution and yet at times could not see how it could be avoided. He was firmly convinced, above all, that he possessed a truer image of man than his contemporaries, and that the philosophers and the men of letters lived in a world of make-believe, their vision darkened by selfish preoccupations and a readiness to accommodate themselves to the dictates of a deadly, even if benevolent, despotism.

The end of this first phase of Rousseau's thought is accompanied by a few autobiographical pages written in the winter of 1756:

> The polemist of the years following the publication of the *Discourse on Arts and Sciences* (1751–1753), the fiery adversary of French music . . . turns around to consider the beginning of his career and his pugnacious and a bit mischievous activity. His clear-sightedness, his serenity even with a shade of modesty, but with the assurance of someone who knows his value, have two principal causes: the first is that having henceforth given up polemics, he can detach himself from a past still close; the second is that having written the *Discourse on the Origin of Inequality* (spring 1754), having recovered in Geneva his citizenship and the religion of his infancy, he has the feeling of having reached a turning point. Hence, the condition of moral and intellectual equilibrium of which this piece bears witness, a condition which would be broken in the spring of 1756, when Jean-Jacques, suffering from an "emptiness of his heart," will launch upon a new adventure.[11]

What he has done so far, Rousseau tells us, has been to try "to go back to the sole and fundamental principle" which should serve to resolve the problem of man and of society. He has tried to look to man himself and to find in his constitution "the true system of nature." This has been called "my system," even though in order to establish it "I did nothing more than to remove from man what I was demonstrating he had himself added." This had been his effort throughout nearly his entire life and he was convinced that he had reached the truth.

[11] Gagnebin and Raymond, *O.C.* I, 1836. The text of the *Fragment Biographique* is in *O.C.* I, 1113–9. Its attribution to the winter of 1755–1756 was first made by Th. Dufour and is now confirmed (*ibid.*, 1836).

The position of his adversaries could not be any weaker,[12] for they had proceeded with inconceivable thoughtlessness. Rousseau does not think he was ever refuted, because truth cannot be refuted. But not even a serious attempt at debate was undertaken. His adversaries' arguments went never beyond "three or four school commonplaces." They showed clearly that they were writers "in bad faith who were driven by their interests to speak against their better judgment," writers who could "maintain that letters are the foundation of the state." This, Rousseau had never believed. At the beginning of his literary life he had told his friend Parisot that in Geneva arts were not the support of the Republic.

What Rousseau has proved to himself is the futility of such literary debates, which he has no intention of continuing. He is pleased that he has probably upset the bright intellectuals and artists who may even have feared for their livelihood, as if Rousseau's attacks against arts and sciences could endanger their financial security. Rousseau wants to reassure them. "The century of wealth and laziness cannot possibly do without their talents and in times so corrupt there is no question of morality." They can go about their business, "these idlers who abound in Paris and who, because they have nothing to do, appoint themselves the arbiters of the beautiful they have never felt and spend their life talking about music they do not love and about paintings they do not understand."

Rousseau is going to dismiss these people from his mind. He feels relaxed and happy. He still has the friendship of a man he greatly admires, Diderot.[13] He is sustained by the thought of the

[12] There were only two exceptions. A great prince, the king of Poland, and a friend, Bordes, who had criticized Rousseau in "two discourses filled with spirit and ideas and very agreeable to read," even though what he did was just to give "a pleasant coloring to vulgar errors."

[13] O.C. I, 1837.

conversations "of this virtuous philosopher whose friendship, already immortalized in his writings, makes the glory and the happiness of my life, of this astonishing universal and perhaps unique genius, whose worth is ignored by his century, but in whom the future will have difficulty to recognize only a man." Perhaps a few, the best, among the philosophers will find it possible to continue to work with him, in spite of all he has said against them and about the culture of their century. This is not likely, however, once they have really understood what he has done.

For the quiet of Rousseau's mind comes from his certainty that he has done something no one has yet realized. His enemies are under a radical misapprehension if they think that he has been merely playing with literary images and has amused himself by touching upon the foibles of culture and civilization. Rousseau knows that what he has done is something more important: he has struck at the foundations of contemporary life and institutions. He has seen his adversaries rally to the defense of what Rousseau knows is dead: "For two or three years I had the pleasure of watching them ceaselessly water the leaves of the tree whose roots I had secretly cut." [14]

[14] O.C. I, 1114–9.

IX

After 1756

Barbarus hic ego sum . . .

TWENTY-TWO years were left. They were first filled by the creative outburst that produced the *Nouvelle Héloïse,* the *Emile,* and the *Social Contract.* They were then used for the painstaking measurement of the real and the possible against Rousseau's ideal standards of men, society, and government, carried out in the *Letters from the Mountain,* the *Project of a Constitution for Corsica,* and the *Considerations on the Government of Poland.* They were finally devoted to a never-ended and obsessive effort of introspection and justification (who am I, what have I done, and why?) in the letters to Malesherbes, the *Confessions,* the *Dialogues,* and the *Dreamings of a Solitary Walker.* At the end, Rousseau felt as much as ever that he was an alien in his world, and in the *Dialogues* he went back for the third time to the epigraph he had first used in the letter to Conzié years earlier: "Here I am, a barbarian, for I am not understood."

Throughout this infinitely complex literary output, the deeply rooted themes of Rousseau's thought appear and reappear in all their subtlety and splendor of language, their variety of presentation and striking novelty of forms. They remain essentially unchanged in their social, political, and economic aspects and show

[238]

an unbroken continuity with what Rousseau had said in the years up to 1756.

The effort to make himself clear never lets up. Rousseau is aware of the distinction one must make between the intentions of an author and the consequences and interpretations which may be drawn from his doctrines.[1] He knows that readers will misunderstand what he has written.[2] After the *First Discourse* he had been judged a man of paradoxes; after the *Letter on French Music,* an enemy of the nation; after the *Discourse on Inequality,* an enemy of mankind; after the *Letter to D'Alembert,* a defender of Christian morality; and the opposite after the *Emile.* And yet, "I have always remained the same." [3]

Hence his overwhelming urge to defend himself, to show that, as a believer in austere republican institutions and legal liberty, and as a defender of the laws, he could not be described as a seditious manipulator and a supporter of license. He could not accept the accusation of wanting to destroy the order of society, just because he had refused to declare sacred laws that were responsible for the most disastrous disorders and miseries of mankind.[4]

He felt that in spite of what men of letters, "paid from the fat

---

[1] Letter to Voltaire, 18 August 1756, C.G. II, 305.

[2] Rousseau had written in the *Polysynodie* that aristocracy was the worst of sovereignties. He must have doubted that this would be clear to his readers, for a few years later, having in the meantime written the *Social Contract,* he added a footnote to the yet unpublished manuscript of the *Polysynodie:* "I could wager that one thousand persons will find here yet another contradiction with the *Social Contract.* This proves that there are still more readers who should learn to read than there are authors who should learn to be coherent" (O.C. III, 645). Prophetic words!

[3] *Lettre à Christophe de Beaumont* (1762), in *Oeuvres complètes de J.-J. Rousseau,* ed. L. S. Mercier (Paris, 1792), XIV, 10–11.

[4] *Rousseau juge de Jean Jacques, Dialogues,* 1772–1776, O.C. I, 887.

of the people," [5] said, the solitary prophet could do a great deal. In essence, what he had attempted to do from the very first was to criticize our stupid admiration for the instruments of our unhappiness [6] and to suggest on the contrary that nature had made man happy and good, but that society was depraving him and making him miserable. At the same time, he had been anxious to show that "human nature does not go backward, . . . that one can never return to the times of innocence and equality once one has left them," and that his key objective was not the acceleration of the process of crisis and revolution, but only, if possible, the slowing down of the process of corruption: "Thus his goal would not be that of bringing large populations and great states to their first simplicity, but only to stop, if it was possible, the progress of those [peoples and states] whose smallness and situation has preserved them from a rapid advance toward both the perfection of society and the deterioration of the species." [7]

Rousseau has been able to gain his insights, he tells us, because he has found in himself the traits of original man, because of what he was and because of the life he lived. To the analysis of his life, his emotions and dreams, Rousseau devotes, as we now well understand, some of the more important pages of his work. He had always been preoccupied with himself. But it was "the new life," made real through his gradual retreat from the world, that provided him with a better chance to be himself and find in this way the true meaning of human existence. [8] It was when he left his books unpacked, and refused even to have a pen and a desk, and "instead of these sad papers and of all this printed stuff, I would fill my room with flowers and grass," [9] that he

[5] Fourth Letter to Malesherbes, 28 January 1762, *O.C.* I, 1143.
[6] *Dialogues, O.C.* I, 934.   [7] *Ibid.*, 935.
[8] *Les Rêveries du promeneur solitaire*, 1776–1778, *O.C.* I, 1014–5.
[9] *Ibid.*, 1042.

would really think about the human condition. A chain of ideas would then be set in motion which would assemble and place before his imagination visions of peace in the midst of simple and good people.[10] Then perhaps the reconstruction of an ideal world could begin, and the distance which separated it from the real world be measured. He could be lost in dreams which could be a state of pure contemplation, or the result of the observation of small things, or of still objects.[11]

He could in this way find happines, a happiness not made up of a succession of fugitive moments of intense enjoyment, but consisting rather of a steady state where time stood still: "If there is a condition in which my soul finds a basis sufficiently solid to rest there in its entirety and gather there all its being, without having to recall the past or envisage the future; where time be nothing, and where the present lasts forever without however marking its duration and without leaving any trace of its passage, without any other sentiment of deprivation or enjoyment, of pleasure or pain, of desire or fear, than alone that of our existence, and that this sentiment alone could fill the soul in its entirety—as long as this condition lasts, whoever finds himself in it can call himself happy, not of an imperfect, poor and relative happiness, such as one finds in the pleasures of life, but of a sufficient, perfect and full happiness which does not leave any emptiness in the soul which has to be filled." [12]

In this way Rousseau described himself and the way in which he had come to grips with the problem of man and society. But if contemplation and withdrawal had given him the sense of human existence, he knew that the solitary and contemplative life was not acceptable for the majority of men, who must, Rousseau tells us, lead an active life to satisfy their ever-renewed

---

[10] *Ibid.*, 1073.   [11] *Dialogues, O.C.* I, 816–7.
[12] *Rêveries, O.C.* I, 1046.

needs.[13] If Rousseau could find happiness sitting by a murmuring stream, the kind of happiness that can be created within a social group was still his concern and injustice in public life still angered him.[14]

What Rousseau keeps forever reminding us is, in effect, this: in solitude he has found the clues he needed to analyze the problems of multitudes of men living together in society. "Thus, here I am, alone on earth." [15] He has become the symbol of the alienation of man cursed by society. In the end he must consider this as a privileged position giving him a considerable advantage above everybody else in looking at the evils of institutions and of progress. This sense of loneliness and of rejection by society does not lead to pessimism. There is here both a sequel and a parallel to his earlier statement that he had by his work cut the roots of the tree everybody still thought was flourishing.[16] At the end of his life, in the *Dreamings of the Solitary Walker,* he can say that "everything must in the end find its proper order, and sooner or later my turn will come." [17]

The Road We Have Traveled and the Choices before Us

The opening sentence of *Emile* is the key to Rousseau's world: "All is well on leaving the hands of the creator of things, all degenerates in the hands of man." Nature gives us not only beauty,[18] but goodness. Nature, in its magnificence, untouched by man, does not herald "slavery and domination." [19] Nature

---

[13] *Ibid.,* 1047. Raymond's comment is that Rousseau the citizen always establishes the "priority of action over feeling" (*O.C.* I, 1801).

[14] *Rêveries, O.C.* I, 1066, 1057.

[15] The opening words of the *Rêveries, O.C.* I, 995.

[16] See supra, p. 237.   [17] *Rêveries, O.C.* I, 1010.

[18] Cf. the *Nouvelle Héloïse, passim.*

[19] Third letter to Malesherbes, 26 January 1762, *O.C.* I, 1139.

offers us laws which, if followed, could prevent slavery and domination: such is the "sacred imprescriptible law which speaks to the heart of man and his reason" starting from the principle of political equality among men and which only a "feudal barbarism" could abolish by cutting off from the body politic "its most numerous and sometimes most healthy part." [20]

We already know that Rousseau sees the present condition of man as the end of a long process which began with the abandonment of his original condition as nature had created it. Now Rousseau peers once more into the past and he sees three stages in the evolution of man. The first is that of man in the state of nature: "He does not conceive of his own well-being as opposed or conforming to that of anyone. Nothing attracts his hate or his love; limited to mere physical instinct, he is nothing." The second state is one which perhaps witnessed the only real happiness of man. Some ideas of relationships, of justice and of moral duty begin to appear. Personal interests cross each other: "But as long as the clash of interests is less than the aid offered by intelligence, men are essentially good." But the third and final stage is at hand as progress multiplies social relationships and sharpens the opposition of strong particular interests, "when a turbulent love of self becomes vanity, when opinion, making the whole world necessary to each man, makes them all born enemies of each other." [21]

Since this is the stage reached today by human development, then, in Rousseau's eyes, social relations, progress of ideas, and culture are to be held accountable for having made man what he is—that is, bad. Bad men are not found in the desert, but in the

---

[20] *Considérations sur le gouvernement de Pologne, 1770–1771, O.C.* III, 973. Cf. Fabre's comment (*ibid.*, 1760) on Rousseau's natural law and his approach to the problem of the poor: no ostentatious philanthropy, but political power.

[21] Letter to Beaumont, *Oeuvres complètes,* ed. Mercier, XIV, 28–9.

world. How wrong had Diderot been in accusing Rousseau of being a bad man because he was a solitary man.[22] The beginning of badness comes to life and is exalted in society, where evil is born. And beyond society, the institutions that have grown out of it bear specific responsibility for the corruption of men.[23]

How has Rousseau convinced himself that this is so? He claims to have observed man all his life and to have perceived what he calls a "secret opposition" between the constitution of man and that of our society. A tension and an irreconcilable condition which increased public calamities in proportion to human progress and the complexity of human affairs. He also claims a certain vision of life which his progressive alienation and detachment from his fellow human beings have given him and him alone. There was the vision of Vincennes to which he returns in the *Dialogues*. What he saw was "another universe, a true golden age, societies of simple, wise and happy men"—a universe in which he could fulfill "in hope all his visions, through the destruction of the prejudices by which he had been conquered himself, but from which he believed in that moment all the vices and miseries of mankind to derive." [24]

In writing to Malesherbes he gives animation and substance to the dream. He fills this imaginary world with human beings after his heart, by moving "under the shelters of nature men worthy of inhabiting them." Rousseau then crowds this golden century of his fantasy with all the happy events of his life, and with sadness looks upon "the true pleasures of humanity, pleasures so delicious, so pure, and by now so far from man." [25]

These were but fleeting visions in the midst of a hateful world,

---

[22] *Dialogues*, O.C. I, 788–9.

[23] *Ibid.*, 790, and second letter to Malesherbes, 12 January 1762, O.C. I, 1136.

[24] *Dialogues*, O.C. I, 828–9.

[25] Third letter to Malesherbes, 26 January 1762, O.C. I, 1140.

where everything was in effect the opposite of what Rousseau had imagined. But they served one fundamental purpose in Rousseau's political philosophy: to strengthen his conviction of the necessity of a standard by which to measure accurately man's present condition, of a goal which could provide norms for the changes that had to be introduced in that condition. This, then, was the justification of the search for the ideal state of nature: not to find in it a justification of institutions and relationships as they existed in the historical present, but the inspiration necessary to change them. The vision was only a vision; the state of nature may never have existed. This ideal man was perhaps a fanciful one. It did not matter: "This man does not exist, you will say. So be it, but he can exist as an hypothesis." [26]

Without this hypothesis, Rousseau clearly believed, no one could cope with either the general or the specific evils of our society. That those evils were all around us it was difficult to deny. But Rousseau further believed that they could, in part at least, be done away with by operating within the framework of existing society. What was essential was to understand how man had become what he was and to go back in history in an attempt to find out what he might have been, had history taken a different course. There was nothing inevitable about history. There was only the inevitability of certain consequences flowing from given premises. And there was the inevitability of change.

As the vision blurs, the mind has to focus on the reality of things. That reality is such that it has affected the individual, the family, and all social relations. Man suffers from a universal disease: the inability to be himself and appear for what he really is. This dissembling is caused by our social order. Everybody lies when he maintains that he is ready to sacrifice his interests to the

---

[26] Letter to Beaumont, *Oeuvres complètes,* ed. Mercier, XIV, 61.

public good: "No one wants the public good when it is not in agreement with his own." [27] All will preach modesty and declare themselves satisfied with a "mediocre" or average condition, but the only real passion will be for luxury and gold.[28]

The family has equally been affected by progress. Since natural sentiments have been silenced by extreme inequality, the iniquitous despotism of fathers is responsible for the unhappiness of children and for the habit of forced marriages. Again, if public morality is to be improved, one has to go back to the assumptions under which parents operate.[29]

All social relations are poisoned by the fact that "for a long time now the society of man has offered only a false appearance without reality, without truth." [30] It is a society in which a gain for one person is bound to cause a loss for somebody else. "This relationship is in the essence of things, and nothing can change it." [31] Thus Rousseau once more rejects the doctrine of the automaticity of social adjustments and relationships. Rather than creating happiness for all, they create more and more unhappiness as their complexity increases. For this is the result of the egoism inherent in the constitution of societies, and nothing can change it until that constitution is changed.

Rousseau is persuaded that we can change it if we want to—that while progress has inevitably brought about our sad state, change is possible if the accepted premises of that progress are changed. Men have the freedom of making a choice and it is up to them to decide whether they wish to choose. Rousseau's purpose is to show men *how* to choose, "by teaching them to distinguish reality from appearance, and the man of nature from the fictitious and fantastic man" who is the fruit of our institutions and prejudices.[32]

[27] *Ibid.*, 29.   [28] *Considérations*, O.C. III, 960.
[29] *Nouvelle Héloïse*, O.C. II, 24.   [30] *Dialogues*, O.C. I, 729.
[31] *Emile*, Garnier ed., Bk. II, 99.   [32] *Dialogues*, O.C. I, 728.

For, beyond the broad generalizations, Rousseau had singled out specific causes for the decline of society. And it is to the reciprocal influences of three of them and to each of them in particular that he attributes special responsibility. They are the population upheavals which have led to the abandonment of the countryside in favor of cities, the way in which culture has affected the behavior of opinion-forming elites in urban centers, and finally the economic system itself.

To the tragedies of urbanization and the beauties of life on the land, Rousseau devotes many famous pages in the *Nouvelle Héloïse*, which remains his classic treatment of that problem.[33] The movement away from the land he sees as a complex process deriving from the pressures of public opinion, of a literature which has been holding up to contempt country life and of a political system favoring cities and centralization. Thus huge numbers congregate in a few cities, leaving the rest of the territory a desert. Thus Europe rushes toward its ruin.[34]

Worse even than the resulting population imbalance is the conformism in thought created by urban life, where a few men think while the majority ape them, where coteries fight one another, each protecting its own privileges and interests, and no one is concerned with the common good.[35]

This analysis flows from Rousseau's extraordinary bias in favor of a life close to nature. The natural condition of man is to cultivate land and live on its fruits. Every effort must be devoted to those arrangements that will keep the maximum number of people happily and properly exploiting the soil. Land is an economic resource that provides a never-exhausted source of

[33] Cf. especially, on mountains, I, xxiii; on urban life, culture, and the particular problems of Paris, II, xiv–xxvii; on the structure of a self-sufficient community at Clarens, IV, x; on authority and equality in a peasant democracy after Rousseau's heart, V, vii.
[34] *Nouvelle Héloïse, O.C.* II, 20.   [35] *Ibid.*, 234.

human sustenance, of security and of peace, of continuity and enjoyment in the life of man.[36]

This happy picture is clouded by the corruption of the political system in an advanced civilization, where the rich exploit the peasants: "One nearly regrets to be a man, thinking of those whose blood we drink." [37] It is a system that leads the rich to abandon the country because of the greater chance of indulging in luxury in the cities, and at the same time drives the harassed poor to send their children to the cities to be relieved of the expense of maintaining them. The hope is that the children may escape the curse of their father.[38]

How absurd a system which makes it impossible for the best form of social activity to survive. But where things go well, the sight of a well-cultivated land with free workers on it is so exciting that "one forgets one's century and one's contemporaries." [39]

The corrupting forces of the times were the men of letters and the culture they provided. For them Rousseau had only contempt; he knew that what he was doing was "trampling under foot the opinions of his century." He really could not be surprised that he was paid back with a total rejection of his ideas.[40]

The quarrel had, of course, been a long and tiresome one. The accusations were sweeping and could be summed up in the refusal by Rousseau to accept the rule of reason to the exclusion of the wisdom and happiness that come from an appreciation of the emotions of the heart. In their cold rationalism men of letters had lost touch with the real people around them: "Stay clear of those cosmopolites who go far to seek in their books duties they refuse to fulfill around them. There is a philosopher who loves

[36] *Ibid.*, 551.
[37] *Ibid.*, 603. See also at 515–6 for the consequences of a free or tyrannical government on agriculture.
[38] *Ibid.*, 534–5.   [39] *Ibid.*, 603.   [40] *Rêveries, O.C.* I, 1020.

the Tartars so that he does not have to love his neighbors." [41]
What the culture of our time has forgotten is that national customs differ and the imposition of uniform standards of life is a
source of corruption, for it is impossible that habits be the same
for people living under different conditions. [42]

The literary men themselves are corrupt and venal to the
bone. They are responsible for doctrines which, "while flattering
the happy and the wealthy, crush the unfortunate and the poor,
removing from the former all checks, fear and restraints, from
the latter all hope and consolation." [43] The main charge of Rousseau, apart from his dislike of a literary class at the service of the
powerful, [44] is expressed in a letter to Mirabeau written in 1767.
The literary men, Rousseau says, pretend that "human reason
goes on forever perfecting itself, since each century adds its
lights to those of preceding centuries." Rousseau believes, however, that "human understanding has always the same measure, a
very narrow one at that, and that it loses at one end all that it
gains at the other, and that prejudices forever reborn take away
from us acquired lights which cultivated reason cannot
replace." [45]

The ultimate contradiction lies in the fact that these philosophers, seeming to believe in the perfectibility of man, were
tireless in showing contempt for human nature, which, according to them, was bad in the beginning and had become better
only under their tutelage. The philosophy of the Paris salons is
thus a humiliating and sad one, which downgrades the common

[41] *Emile*, 9.
[42] Letter to the Maréchal de Luxembourg, 20 January 1763, C.G. IX,
7. Here Rousseau uses corruption to mean a change brought about by an
alien culture. By definition such a change must be bad.
[43] *Dialogues*, O.C. I, 842.
[44] "I sell the work of my hands, but the productions of my soul are not
for sale at all" (*ibid.*, 840).
[45] Letter to Mirabeau, 26 July 1767, C.G. XVII, 156.

man, who apparently needs nothing more than to absorb its wisdom, and in political matters must be guided by a benevolent despot.

These philosophers furthermore have become skillful in manipulating public opinion in such a way as to benefit their interests. They apply a "consequential and methodic spirit" to the task. Ever since the philosophical set organized itself in a body its leaders have been the arbiters of "the destiny of individuals, and hence of that of the state." [46]

In conclusion, as Rousseau points out in one of his last writings, the third walk of the *Rêveries,* the reason why he has been forced to reject the philosophy and the culture of his time is that its representatives are providers of a certain morality which Rousseau cannot accept: "This rootless and fruitless morality which they pompously display in books or in showy theater pieces without ever reaching either the heart or reason; or else this other morality, secret and cruel, the internal doctrine of all their members, to which the other serves only as a mask and which alone they follow in their conduct." [47] These are the moralities of utility and of private pleasure and gain, which Rousseau from the first had felt would lead at an accelerated pace to the downfall of the society of men who had accepted them as its main guide. The first parades under the appearance of social concern, but is unable to provide for the common good through the

[46] *Dialogues,* O.C. I, 965.

[47] *Rêveries,* O.C. I, 1022. Jean Fabre's comment on this passage is: "Rousseau distinguishes here the morality which the philosophers of his time admit, which is roughly that of social utility—if he judges it to be 'rootless' it is because it can only be the result of reflexion, if he judges it to be 'fruitless' it is because addressing itself only to the interest of the partner, it is incapable of creating a real moral sentiment—and the 'internal doctrine' which they do not admit, according to which it is profitable in all things to seek one's pleasure and to follow one's inclinations" (O.C. I, 1786).

reconciliation of individual goods; the second authorizes in effect the most extreme license in the pursuit and attainment of private profit, regardless of consequences.

This was a culture not only linked but also enslaved to an economic system in which it found large advantages and which it was therefore supporting as the necessary foundation of the community. Rousseau was convinced that all this was wrong and that a catastrophe such as that described at the end of the *Discourse on Inequality* was inevitable if men continued to be "more favorable to wealth than to prosperity." [48] Clearly prosperity had nothing to do with the accumulation of wealth. Through culture Rousseau comes back to the economic system.

In the second part of the *Nouvelle Héloïse,* Julie tells us how little we know about the economic system and speaks of the hidden forces that make it go. It is baffling to all in Paris that, together with such great wealth, there exists a poverty deeper than in the countryside where there are no millionaires. She considers this question well worthy of research by Saint-Preux. It will probably be better to unravel the history of economic life "in the garrets of the poor." There, rather than in the mansions of the Faubourg St. Germain "one finds out through what secret iniquities the powerful and the rich take away the last black bread from the oppressed, whom they feign to pity in public." [49]

But if the workings of the economic system are still hidden from public view, its consequences are clear. The first is the moral evil wealth creates, even when the intentions of the owner are good. Going back to what he had said in the *Discourse on Wealth,* Rousseau reminds us that not only can the rich man not buy pleasure through money, but that whatever good he will try to do could better be done if his wealth had earlier been divided rather than allowed to accumulate in his hands and that "the

[48] *Considérations,* O.C. III, 1004.
[49] *Nouvelle Héloïse,* O.C. II, 303.

good which he believes to be able to accomplish through it rarely matches the real evil of which one must be guilty in order to acquire it." [50]

Apart from past evil, there is the present continuing evil of repressed civil war, which an unbalanced distribution of wealth will create. The rich attract enemies and create tensions which are the opposite of social order and peace.[51] Rousseau disagrees with Helvétius, who had suggested that without personal interest there would have been no general interest, hence no just or unjust actions.[52] The present economic system is one of deepening antagonisms between two classes, so that the idea of the state and of the community degenerates. How can a proper political order exist if there are "people swimming in opulence and people the most abject. Is it between these two extremes, one made to buy, the other to sell itself, that one must seek love of justice and laws? Through them always the state disintegrates: the rich holds the law in its pocket, the poor prefers bread to liberty." [53] Indeed, political power can be distinguished in its exercise by reference to the uses of wealth: "Civil power is carried out in two ways: one legitimate through authority, one abusive through wealth." [54]

And formal equality is nothing in states where wealth can exert such abusive authority. For equality becomes a mere semblance and illusion: "It serves only to keep the poor in his poverty and the rich in his usurpation. In reality laws are always useful to those who own and damaging to those who have nothing. Hence it follows that the social state is convenient to

---

[50] *Dialogues*, O.C. I, 671.   [51] *Ibid.*, 921.

[52] P. M. Masson, "Rousseau contre Helvétius," *Revue d'histoire littéraire de la France* (1911), 112.

[53] *Lettres écrites de la montagne* (1764), O.C. III, 890.

[54] *Projet de constitution pour la Corse* (1765), O.C. III, 939.

[252]

men only to the extent that they all have something and no one has too much." [55]

Thus the economic problem becomes a major political problem. It is impossible to separate political power from economic power, and those having excessive economic power will always try to acquire excessive political power.

There is also the issue of the abuse of men used as tools and deprived of liberty and decency: "Man is a being too noble to be simply used as an instrument of others, and one cannot at all employ him for what is convenient to others without consulting him also for what is convenient to himself; for men are not made for jobs, but jobs are made for men, and to distribute things suitably, one must not so much seek the employment to which man is most adapted, but rather that which is most adapted to each man, so as to make him good and happy as much as possible." [56]

In a variant of this passage of capital importance, Rousseau expresses even more vigorously this antiefficiency position. In words which once more stress his man-centered ideal he writes: "It would be better to have society ill-regulated, and all citizens happy and honest, rather than to have a well-regulated society and all citizens miserable and bad. This order which is so much bruited about, is often only apparent and in effect we destroy it when we sacrifice the reality of things as one does in most countries." [57]

If the present system then goes against fundamental aspirations of man, and ties him rather to a set of rules which in the end deny him both freedom and happiness, what can be done about it? In Rousseau's mind there is no tendency to wait for doomsday, even though that will inevitably come, given a resigned acceptance of the present. For Rousseau it is possible to

[55] *Contrat social* (1762), O.C. III, 367.
[56] *Nouvelle Héloïse*, O.C. II, 536.   [57] *Ibid.*, 1657.

look for ways of improving the present. They seem to be the achievement of a better balance between what is private and what is public, and between city and country; a better use of man; and a decision to fix limits to the power, the wealth, and the economic development of the community.

He has not forgotten Bodin. The public domain should be as large as possible to give a sense of community to the country which possesses it. In drafting his project of a constitution for Corsica, he recognizes the gap between the ideal and the possible. Abstractly, "far from wishing the state to be poor, he would like on the contrary that it should own everything," and while not wanting to destroy entirely private property, because this is impossible, he would want "to confine it within the most narrow limits, to give it a measure, a rule, a check, to contain it, to direct it, to subjugate it, and to keep it always subordinated to the public good. In one word I want that state property be as great and as strong and that of the citizen as small and as weak as possible." [58] In practice, all this is not easy to bring about, but Rousseau knows there is in Corsica a great deal of excellent uncultivated land and that a plan of both private and public development of these lands could be undertaken. In Poland the same is true. It is tempting from a purely economic point of view to suggest that all royal lands be sold: "But the moral and political object of such a project is so little to my taste, that if the starosties were to be sold, I would like to see them bought back to establish a fund for wages and benefits for those who will serve their country or will have well deserved of her." [59]

The example of Switzerland in distributing industrial activity evenly through the country is one that Rousseau finds most beneficial in political terms. Switzerland is almost one large city with the population more or less evenly distributed, and it is

[58] *Projet*, O.C. III, 931.   [59] *Considérations*, O.C. III, 1009.

possible to find "manufacturing establishments in precipices and factories over mountain streams." This curious mixture of nature and art possesses for Rousseau "I do not know what of animation, of living, which breathes liberty and well-being." [60]

By greater reliance on man than on money Rousseau means the abolition, if possible, of wage labor and the transfer of the responsibility for doing what has to be done on the shoulders of the community. This is the equivalent of a system of *corvées* in a free society, an attempt to develop the common wealth by common work. The practice should extend from military service to public works, and thus do away with mercenaries of all kinds. [61]

But most important of all is Rousseau's effort to express the idea that, to achieve what he calls "prosperity," limits must be placed on the accumulation of wealth, on economic development and progress, and on the national power of states. Throughout his project of a constitution for Corsica, the idea is most clearly expressed, because Rousseau had the easiest case for the demonstration of his views. It was not difficult to say that a small, isolated, undeveloped island should limit its ambitions, fix modest goals, and try to maintain the peace by keeping to itself. And in the ideal republic of Clarens of the *Nouvelle Héloïse*, the idea had already been put forth of the superiority of a system of life which did not seek its fulfillment in a constant increase in the production of goods. Peace comes from the knowledge that in the future man will have what he has today. This ideal can be best realized by the application of man's labor to the land. "Here the fruit of past labor supports the present abundance, and the fruit of present labor announces the abundance to come; one enjoys at the same time what one spends and what one reaps and the different times are united to strengthen the security of the pres-

[60] Letter to the Maréchal de Luxembourg, 20 January 1763, C.G. IX, 7–8.
[61] *Projet*, O.C. III, 932; *Considérations*, O.C. III, 1006.

ent." [62] And even for larger states as complicated as Poland, the advice is the same: "Here is the spirit I would like to see dominant in your economic system: do not cast your eyes abroad, do not worry about commerce, but multiply as much as possible home commodities and consumers." [63] In the advice to achieve self-sufficiency and to fall back upon one's own resources, Rousseau saw the way to limit conflicts and national ambitions, and to slow down the preoccupation with economic growth, the source of competition among sovereign states. If Rousseau kept giving this kind of advice, it was not only because he believed it was good, but because he was convinced there existed in practice a clear choice of policies and that it was therefore the duty of citizens to concern themselves about the choices to be made. Men were not the helpless victims of an inexorable economic fate. The fate became inexorable only if men did nothing about it. The choices were there, and decisions could be made depending on the expectations of the community. Rousseau saw his duty as that of making clear the consequences of different choices. Nowhere is his position made more starkly clear than in his considerations on Poland, where the crisis facing the country makes the problem of choice one for today.

Poland can cultivate arts and sciences, trade and industries, a standing army, a money economy and luxury. As the strength of the country increases, it would be counted among the great powers of Europe, tied by treaties and alliances in such a way that it would not escape a single war in Europe. At the same time the Polish people would become ambitious and greedy and its social structure would develop along the extremities of poverty and opulence without any middle ground.

"But if by chance you would rather create a free and peaceful

[62] *Nouvelle Héloïse, O.C.* II, 551.
[63] *Considérations, O.C.* III, 1008–9.

nation . . . then one must choose an altogether different method. . . . Apply your people to agriculture and the arts necessary to life, make money contemptible and if possible useless. Seek out and find, to achieve great things, more powerful and more certain springs of action. I agree, that in following this road, you will not fill newspapers with the echo of your festivals . . . that the philosophers will not sing your praises, . . . that in Europe one will talk little of you . . . but you will live in veritable abundance, in justice and in freedom." [64]

Rousseau felt the two roads were irreconcilable; that a choice had to be made between an economy trying always to move forward, and based only on the motivation of personal utility, and a system appealing to what Rousseau calls the deeper springs of human action, namely the satisfaction of a job well done in the interest of the community. He was certain that on that choice depended the happiness and peace of the generations to come.[65]

[64] *Ibid.*, 1003–4.

[65] At this point John Stuart Mill might be quoted:

"While we repudiated with the greatest energy that tyranny of society over the individual which most Socialistic systems are supposed to involve, we yet looked forward to a time when society will no longer be divided into the idle and the industrious; when the rule that they who do not work shall not eat, will be applied not to paupers only, but impartially to all; when the division of the produce of labour, instead of depending, as in so great a degree it now does, on the accident of birth, will be made by concert on an acknowledged principle of justice; and when it will no longer either be, or be thought to be, impossible for human beings to exert themselves strenuously in procuring benefits which are not to be exclusively their own, but to be shared with the society they belong to. The social problem of the future we considered to be, how to unite the greatest individual liberty of action, with a common ownership in the raw material of the globe, and an equal participation of all in the benefits of combined labour. We had not the presumption to suppose that we could already foresee, by what precise form of institutions these objects could

The same awful dilemmas present themselves before Rousseau's mind when, shifting from economic issues, he considers the total social picture. The same tools and concepts are applied to the analysis of the problems of classes, the relationship of groups, and the requirements of a community anxious to come close to the ideals of democracy and equality of the *Social Contract*. The difficulties of social life can be seen everywhere—in the manner, for instance, in which popular festivals are organized. There one can measure the gap which separates the sick from the healthy societies. Drawing upon his faithful memory of the past, Rousseau compares different types of popular feasts. There is the sight of herds of men, humiliated by poverty, fighting brutally among themselves to seize hungrily bits of

most effectually be attained, or at how near or how distant a period they would become practicable. We saw clearly that to render any such social transformation either possible or desirable, an equivalent change of character must take place both in the uncultivated herd who now compose the labouring masses, and in the immense majority of their employers. Both these classes must learn by practice to labour and combine for generous, or at all events for public and social purposes, and not, as hitherto, solely for narrowly interested ones. But the capacity to do this has always existed in mankind, and is not, nor is ever likely to be extinct. Education, habit, and the cultivation of the sentiments, will make a common man dig or weave for his country, as readily as fight for his country. True enough, it is only by slow degrees, and a system of culture prolonged through successive generations, that men in general can be brought up to this point. But the hindrance is not in the essential constitution of human nature. Interest in the common good is at present so weak a motive in the generality, not because it can never be otherwise, but because the mind is not accustomed to dwell on it as it dwells from morning till night on things which tend only to personal advantage. When called into activity, as only self-interest now is, by the daily course of life, and spurred from behind by the love of distinction and the fear of shame, it is capable of producing, even in common men, the most strenuous exertions as well as the most heroic sacrifices. The deep-rooted selfishness which forms the general character of the existing state of society, is so deeply rooted, only

gingerbread thrown at them and soon trampled underfoot and covered with mud.[66] And there is the nobility, austerity, and essential equality of the fall festivals at Clarens where all the people—masters, workers, servants—eat at the same table at the end of a day of common work.[67]

Which of the two ways is more likely to produce that directness of relationships, that convergence of beliefs and solidarity of purpose which alone can produce a large central class capable of rescuing society from the dangers of the extremes? Geneva has often had a middle class, wise and good and restrained. As Rousseau describes it in the *Letters from the Mountain*, the Genevan bourgeoisie has been moderate in advancing its rights and always "it has been a middle order between the rich and the poor, between the leaders of the state and the populace. This order, made up of men roughly equal in fortune, in condition, in intelligence, is neither powerful enough to have ambitions, nor low enough to have nothing to lose. Their great interest, their

---

because the whole course of existing institutions tends to foster it; modern institutions in some respects more than ancient, since the occasions on which the individual is called on to do anything for the public without receiving its pay, are far less frequent in modern life, than in the smaller commonwealths of antiquity. These considerations did not make us overlook the folly of premature attempts to dispense with the inducements of private interest in social affairs, while no substitute for them has been or can be provided: but we regarded all existing institutions and social arrangements as being (in a phrase I once heard from Austin) "merely provisional," and we welcomed with the greatest pleasure and interest all socialistic experiments by select individuals (such as the Co-operative Societies), which, whether they succeeded or failed, could not but operate as a most useful education of those who took part in them, by cultivating their capacity of acting upon motives pointing directly to the general good, or making them aware of the defects which render them and others incapable of doing so." (John Stuart Mill, *Autobiography*, ch. vii.)

[66] *Rêveries*, O.C. I, 1092–3.   [67] *Nouvelle Héloïse*, O.C. II, 607–8.

common interest is to see the laws observed, the magistrate respected, the constitution upheld and the state at peace." [68]

But here again, precise choices have to be made and institutions and policies changed to bring about such a large and "mediocre" middle class: social mobility is one essential condition. The reform of the economic system is bound to create the conditions necessary for such mobility. Rousseau maintains that men are made unhappy not so much by the life they lead as by the fact that they are unable to change it: "The poor are unhappy because they are always poor, kings are unhappy because they are always kings. The middle orders, from which one gets out more easily, offer pleasures both above and below oneself . . . that is, it seems to me, the principal reason why it is generally at the middle level that one finds the happiest men with the best judgment." [69]

On the Inevitability of Change and Revolution

The problem of political freedom is not solved by mere economic change, social mobility, and the strengthening of the middle class. A large "mediocre" class may sink into passivity and equate restraint with resigned acceptance of tyranny. Again Geneva furnishes Rousseau with what he considers a typical example of the danger of complacency. On the one hand, he sees hard-working and law-abiding citizens "all taken up by their business and trade," inclined to be publicly prudent because of their commerce and patrimony, fearful of irritating their rulers: "They are driven by the strongest of reasons to sacrifice every-

---

[68] *Lettres écrites de la montagne*, O.C. III, 853, 889. J.-D. Candaux repeatedly (*ibid.*, 1702–3, 1720) praises Rousseau for the accuracy and keenness of his historical comments and of his analysis of what had to be done by the Genevan bourgeoisie.

[69] *Nouvelle Héloïse*, O.C. II, 608.

thing to peace because it is only in peace that they can prosper; and in this condition each deceived by his private interest likes more to be protected than free." [70]

On the other hand, a ruling group armed with all public power and depository of all authority, is sole interpreter of the laws which it uses to defend itself and to attack its enemies. "It is in the name of the law that it can transgress it with impunity. It can attack the constitution, seeming to defend it. . . . It can undertake easily anything it wants; it does not grant to anybody the right of stopping them or of being informed." [71]

Given this balance of power within the community, the end is clear: it is the establishment, step by step, of tyranny. This process can be carried out in a subtle way: "The true road of tyranny is not that of attacking directly the public good: this would rally everybody to its defense; it rather consists of attacking successively all its defenders and of frightening anybody who might still dare to come to its aid." The road to tyranny is made much easier, indeed tyranny is established automatically, if you succeed in persuading "everybody that the public interest is the concern of nobody." [72]

Rousseau finds no merit in the argument that some abuse of power can be justified to prevent the abuse of freedom or that there is any parallel between the two. For there is instead a fundamental difference between them: the abuse of freedom "is never more than a crisis and cannot become a permanent condition. While the abuse of power, leading not to a disadvantage of the powerful but of the weak, is by its nature without measure, without check, without limits. It must end with the destruction of the person alone who suffers from it." [73]

The first great problem of political freedom is, then, that of inducing the members of the community to accept full responsi-

[70] *Lettres écrites de la montagne*, O.C. III, 888.   [71] *Ibid.*, 889.
[72] *Ibid.*, 893.   [73] *Ibid.*, 891.

bility for it. But here at once another difficulty arises, that of the understanding the citizens have of the freedom they are supposed to stand for. The root of the trouble is in dealing with merchants and artisans and bourgeois, always busy with their private interests, their work, their trade, their profits; they are people "for whom liberty itself is just a means to acquire without obstacle and to own in safety." [74]

This is a limited concept of freedom which rests primarily on the notion of an acquisitive society, which is defined by the right to property, and whose limits coincide with those of the acquisitive process undertaken by each citizen. For Rousseau freedom means of course something different. It conveys struggle and possibility. He calls it a strong food, difficult to tolerate, the opposite of that of the peaceful enjoyment of earthly goods which he has just criticized. Freedom thrives in the midst of austerity conquered at heavy price and maintained with a severity harsher than the yoke of tyrants. Freedom cannot be defended by an occasional revolution: "I am amused at those enslaved people who, rioting on the word of revolutionists, dare to talk of freedom without knowing what it means, and, their hearts filled with all the vices of slaves, imagine that to be free, it is enough to revolt." [75]

It is, then, impossible, for Rousseau, to acquire freedom suddenly or automatically as a gift. A revolution will not bring freedom if one has merely waited for it, or if its outbreak is believed to be the inevitable outcome of a set of circumstances over which the community has no control. Such a sudden change or such a revolution can of course take place, but what will happen then will be a mere transfer of power from one group to the other while the corrupt citizenry will remain corrupt. What is necessary for the achievement of freedom by an

[74] *Ibid.*, 881.   [75] *Considérations*, O.C. III, 974.

enslaved community is clearly a combination of education and will: the capacity on the part of the individual to see what is necessary and then the expression of a will capable of sustaining the new belief in freedom. The revolution of chance, led by a small elite or caused by economic laws, does not lead to the creation of the free democratic community Rousseau has in mind. His revolution of freedom is the most difficult of all.

Indeed, from Rousseau's analysis, the strongest conclusion is that of the permanent difficulties of freedom and of the complexities of its meanings. Freedom is not the freedom of doing what one pleases. This much has always been clear. It is also the freedom of *not* doing what one does *not* want to do [76] or what one should not do. The position of Rousseau here is a difficult one, for he is caught between the two urges of wanting the citizen to exert himself to the utmost for the sake of the public interest, and of wanting at the same time to protect the sphere of privacy and of personal solitude and contemplation which was so essential to Rousseau's own happiness. In the end perhaps the choice is made, for Rousseau often repeats his belief in the incompatibility of freedom with rest and leisure, with an inactive life or with the avoidance of personal responsibility. He had already stressed in the *Discourse on Inequality* the need to choose between a stormy freedom and a peaceful enslavement.[77] He addresses the same warnings to the Genevans: "Those who cannot stand work will be slaves." [78] And to Poland he once more suggests that the peace of despotism and the sweetness of liberty cannot go together. There is a fundamental contradiction here: "Rest and liberties seem to me incompatible. One must choose." [79]

[76] *Rêveries*, O.C. I, 1059.
[77] *Discours sur l'origine de l'inégalité*, O.C. III, 181.
[78] *Lettres écrites de la montagne*, O.C. III, 881.
[79] *Considérations*, O.C. III, 954–5.

There is then a choice open to men; the oft-repeated invitation to do one's duty must mean in Rousseau's judgment that it is possible to do it, and also that it will bear fruit. When it comes down to the question of men and history, Rousseau's final answer seems to be that even though in the past man has for the most part failed to write his own history, by allowing the crooks and the tyrants to do it for him, he can do so in the future if only he wants it.

The difficulties of liberty are the difficulties of the political condition; that is, the result of the tensions and contrasts between the standards of the ideal state on the one hand, and the real and the possible on the other. Rousseau does not advocate return to the original state of nature, and he does not believe that the realization of the ideal state is possible. There is no utopia tomorrow, only perhaps the beginning of a change that will bring man closer to it. Even though the state of nature is no more than a vision of how man alone might have been in the beginning, and the ideal state is no more than a hope of how man in society might live in the end, they both remain essential guides to our thinking and our conduct.

When dealing with man in organized society, Rousseau is anxious to make the norms that inspire his ideal social contract clear. Nowhere does he succeed better than in the "short and faithful" account he gives of them in the *Letters from the Mountain*. The state must be the result of a free agreement among men, giving rise to certain obligations: "What surer foundation can obligation have among men than the free commitment of the person who obliges himself?" The contractual agreement envisaged by Rousseau has several "peculiarities." It is absolute and without reserve, and yet it cannot, by definition, produce injustice against its participants. It links them all firmly together, but without subjecting them to anyone, for only certain specific general expressions of their will are binding on them.

[264]

Since their general will alone rules, they are as free as before. It is in this general will that an indivisible sovereign power is vested. This abstract collective being can speak only through law which is "a public and solemn declaration of the general will on an object of common interest." Government is no more than an intermediate body between the individual citizen and the sovereign, with the precise task of administering the laws in particular instances. The best government, but the worst sovereignty, is the aristocratic kind. The reason is clear: in governing itself the community must use its own best skills to manage its affairs at any particular moment; in establishing a sovereign power, however, the community must allow all to participate in deciding the long-range direction of its affairs.[80]

The purpose of this exercise in abstraction is to establish a method with which to handle the practical problems of politics. Rousseau does again for man in society what he has done for man alone. He wishes to fix a point of reference by which everything will be judged and all decisions taken.

The first standard had been that of man alone in the original state of nature. This was the condition from which men traveled the road of civilization and progress to achieve their present corrupt state. The problem at this point becomes that of the recovery of some of the earlier traits of human nature, of some of the transparence and immediacy in human life which advanced men have lost.

The loss has been caused in part at least by institutions. Hence the need of identifying the ideal condition of man in society. This is the second standard, the social contract. Against it the present disarray can be measured. Using the contract as a

---

[80] *Lettres écrites de la montagne,* O.C. III, 806–9. This summary shows, by the way, the great importance Rousseau attributed to the ideas of the social contract, in spite of his occasional strictures against the book entitled the *Social Contract.*

guide, it may be possible to reach decisions on how to remedy the disarray.

This is what Rousseau is doing in the *Letters from the Mountain*. The sixth letter states the principles. The seventh narrates the downfall. The eighth outlines the possibility of recovery.

The passage from the theoretical to the concrete is achieved by translating ideal principles into constitutional principles, and the link to Geneva is achieved when Rousseau says that the Genevan constitution was the model for his political institutions.[81] The downfall is the abandonment of the constitution; the recovery must be the attempt to go back to it. This is Rousseau's realism. When he is facing a concrete political problem, as in Geneva, the remedies are to be concrete, limited in their scope, relevant to the situation which is being discussed. They ought to be a persuasive demonstration of the way in which a community can make a recovery from a deep crisis and avoid a revolution by asserting once more its control over its political life. If possible, what is done must be done within the broad historical values and purposes that the community had set for itself in its constitutional beginnings. Certain changes are therefore necessary while others must be avoided.

What does Rousseau want, confronted by the problems of a small and ancient community such as Geneva? He wishes first of all to reassert the expression of the general will, for in such a small community this is possible. Hence the General Councils of citizens should meet as in the past. They should also be given

[81] *Ibid.*, 809. In his comments on this passage, J.-D. Candaux ably sums up the debate on the Genevan origins of the *Social Contract*. The conclusion with which one must strongly agree is that, on the basis of all evidence, "if the book and philosophical sources of the *Social Contract* have little relationship to Geneva, as Professor Derathé has so well demonstrated, the inspiration of the book, or at least of many of its chapters, is Genevan in its very essence" (*O.C.* III, 1664–5).

back a substantive right of remonstrance against the Small Council. This right has to do with the way in which laws are applied and the right of the community to defend the application of laws according to its own understanding is vital. In any dispute concerning this issue, it is the government and not the people who must justify itself. To grant here a negative right to the government—that is, a right to refuse to consider the people's grievances—means tyranny.

On the other hand, the community must be guarded against the sudden and repeated enactment of new laws. They are not necessary and they can alter too rapidly the spirit of the constitution. New laws must be the solemn and infrequent expression of the general will: hence it is legitimate to secure for them the scrutiny of that "aristocratic" government which presides over the management of political affairs. The Small Council should therefore have a negative right on new laws, and any attempt to limit it should be resisted.[82]

Thus Rousseau is analyzing current events and reaching decisions with the illumination given him by his ideal community and the sense of reality provided by his study of history. He gains both perspective and purpose, and is able to engage in politics; that is, in the rough game of making choices and determining the specific content of what has to be done here and now, without vague moralizing, without having to proclaim any certainties for tomorrow, but speaking within the modest and at the same time harsh limits provided by the specific circumstances of the historical situation.

Rousseau's remarkable play of ideas and facts, of philosophy and history, in order to produce what he believes to be the political conclusions applicable to the concrete situation he is examining, is nowhere more evident than in the *Considerations on the*

[82] *Ibid.*, 846–50.

Government of Poland—that "first novel of national energy," as Jean Fabre describes it.[83] The *Social Contract* is never forgotten; it is constantly there supplying the inspiration of the true from which to proceed to deal with the limited and often shabby possibilities of the real.[84] To Mirabeau Rousseau had written that the evidence of the true "can never be found in political and natural laws, except if they are considered by abstraction. In a particular government made up of so many elements, this evidence necessarily disappears, for the science of government is nothing but a science of combinations, applications and exceptions, according to times, places, circumstances." [85]

This was nowhere more true than in a Poland, on the eve of a final crisis, suffering from a most complicated history and divided within itself by an extraordinary variety of peoples and institutions. Here the need of trying to cast the light of fundamental principles upon a dark reality was greater than ever, while the restricting influence of reality upon theory was

[83] Introduction, *O.C.* III, ccxliii.

[84] The very perceptive comments of Jean Fabre, the editor of the *Considerations,* must be reported: "The reading of the *Considerations* reveals a Rousseau in full possession of his genius and of his thoughts. It also testifies to the perfect (or perhaps excessive) coherence of his thought. Referring ceaselessly to the *Social Contract,* which he literally appears to know by heart, Rousseau offers the most shattering denial both of what he says of the weakening of his memory or of his growing indifference to his own thought, and to those of his critics who, with great levity, have thought it possible to denounce in Rousseau an inevitable divorce between theory and practice, if not the disavowal of principles which in a frenzy of pure right he had formulated in such radical fashion. To those critics and to all those who pretend to make of politics a science or a reasoned practice, he shows how his treaty of political right must be understood and, consequently, utilized. . . . A touchstone with the purpose of revealing, by approximation, the validity of all political institutions, the *Social Contract* takes on its normative virtue only if used by a nation which knows it is, or wants to be, legitimately instituted" (*ibid.,* ccxli).

[85] Letter to Mirabeau, 26 July 1767, *C.G.* XVII, 156.

stronger than ever. Nevertheless, Rousseau is capable of dealing with one of the most ticklish problems, that of peasant serfdom, in a way that combines a prudent realism with the defense of fundamental moral principles. His plan is one that does not call for the immediate liberation of the serfs, but his gradualism is not founded on an empty hope that somehow voluntarily the serfs will be treated better by enlightened masters. It is based on a call for action at the local level, by the recognition of the rights belonging equally to all human beings, provided they are capable of assimilating the strong food of liberty. The rights and privileges of freedom will come to all those who will have distinguished themselves through their own efforts, through culture and good habits and the fulfillment of their duties. The appeal is not to the masters to be gentle, but to the serfs to be better. Not revolt, but education is the tool.[86]

Thus "having gradually brought things to the point at which a large scale reform is feasible without revolution, it would be possible to give them back their natural right of participating in the administration of their country." [87] Gradualism does not concern principles and fundamental rights, but only their application. Gradualism is introduced because Poland is such a large country that a complicated chain of political structures must reach from the village to the center. The restoration of the general will cannot take place, as in Geneva, by a simple reinstatement of the rights of the people. It must proceed from the ground up through a long and cautious re-entry of all members into the processes of the body politic.

In the end, there will come into existence a country "whose vigor and forces will be at least ten times greater than today, and this with the inestimable advantage of having avoided all strong and sudden change and the danger of revolution." [88]

[86] *Considérations,* O.C. III, 1026.   [87] *Ibid.,* 1027.
[88] *Ibid.,* 1028.

Again and again Rousseau comes back to the expectation or the fear of revolution. At times revolutions appear inevitable, at other times they are to be avoided at all costs. He has little confidence that, in the future, institutions which the eighteenth century considers intangible, or which it would like to make intangible, will last. There is an inherent frailty in what man has done and nothing appears to Rousseau more reckless than to try to build permanently on what is so clearly transient. What can conceivably become permanent has still to be dug out from deep layers of accumulated habits and artificial behavior.

If, as he had written in *Emile,* the century is moving toward great revolutionary upheavals, then he can say confidently to Mirabeau: "Please, what will take place, what will happen to your sacred rights of property, in the midst of great dangers and of extraordinary calamities, when your available values will no longer be adequate and when the tyrant will say: Salus populi suprema lex esto?"[89]

All of Rousseau's work was intended to show that civilization was "in a state of crisis," and that inevitably Europe was approaching "the century of revolutions."[90] The reasons appeared to him to be obvious. Political systems were not only corrupt, they were also obsolete. The great monarchies of Europe could not possibly last much longer. They had reached a peak of glory, "and every state that sparkles is beginning to decline." There are, Rousseau hints at this point in *Emile,* "added particular reasons" to support his belief.[91] In his essay on Poland he again reminds us that these "magnificently" organized nations, these "beautiful" governments, are all threatened by impending death.[92] How can it be otherwise?

In the *Dialogues* Rousseau gives us his final overview of Europe. Again culture bears the initial brunt of the attack as the

[89] Letter to Mirabeau, *op. cit.,* 156.   [90] *Emile,* 224–5.   [91] *Ibid.*
[92] *Considérations,* O.C. III, 954.

purveyor of a comfortable philosophy for the happy and the wealthy, which is bound to be rejected tomorrow by the "multitude." What we witness for the moment, however, is the fruit of youth without discipline, its duties forgotten and exhibiting no love of country. Kings rule without laws because they have been taught by their teachers to recognize no other guide than their own interest. Europe is overrun by soldiers and comedians, corrupt books and famine. How easy it is to prophesy the inevitability of change in contemplating this state of affairs. How easy to say that a day will come when Europe will view "with the same horror both professors and disciples, and all those cruel doctrines which delivering man entirely to his senses and limiting everything to the enjoyment of this short life, make the century in which they rule as contemptible as it is unhappy." [93]

The meaning of inevitability is becoming clear. First of all there is the inevitability of change. It is idle to believe that any human institution can last forever: "All that men have made, men can destroy; the only unchanging traits are those impressed by nature." [94] In the second place, change will inevitably affect those social arrangements which Rousseau holds responsible for the crisis. Since nature has not created princes, the wealthy, great lords, the revolution will affect them first and the rich will become poor. The real test will then be the manner in which those who are overthrown from their pedestal of pride and power will be able to continue to live as men in spite of their destiny.

But, further, the new social arrangements that will follow the revolution are impossible to forecast, beyond the fact that "the great man becomes small, the rich man becomes poor, and the king becomes a subject." [95] It is also impossible to anticipate the actual occurrence of the revolution, for existing institutions can be tolerated even if bad, just in order to avoid anarchy and brigandage: there is therefore no way of avoiding being caught in the midst of a revolution.

[93] *Dialogues*, O.C. I, 971–2.   [94] *Emile*, 224–5.   [95] *Ibid.*

Does change, for all its inevitability, offer any alternatives? There would appear to be two. The basic premise is that today all social life and political institutions are based on force; that no social tie exists except force,[96] because a society resting on utility and private property leads all its members of necessity to rely, either explicitly or implicitly, on force. The state as well is an agency using repressive force to keep individual transactions, all relying at least on latent force, from breaking out into open warfare. This is a state of affairs which Rousseau condemns in the strongest possible terms, "because the conflict of men and of laws which creates within the state a perpetual condition of civil war is the worst of all political states." [97] Rousseau feels we must leave this intolerable condition. What he would like to see is a form of goverment placing the law above men and inspired by the principles of "the most austere democracy." If this is not possible, then there is nothing left except the most arbitrary possible despotism. The notion of a "legal" despotism is a fiction and a contradiction in terms. When mankind will no longer be able to tolerate the civil war which ravages it, then it will have to choose between Rousseauian democracy on one hand, or "the most perfect hobbism" on the other. Compared to the chaos and the danger of the present, perfect hobbism appears preferable to Rousseau. But he cannot stand the intolerable dilemma or the thought of who the fearful despot might be: "I wish it were possible that God be the despot." [98]

[96] *Dialogues*, O.C. I, 971.   [97] Letter to Mirabeau, *op. cit.*, 157.
[98] *Ibid.* The interpretations of this famous letter differ. Cf. Judith N. Shklar, "Rousseau's Images of Authority," *American Political Science Review*, LVIII (1964), 921–2; M. Launay, "Les Problèmes politiques dans la correspondance de Rousseau," in the volume published under the auspices of the Comité National pour la Commémoration de J.-J. Rousseau, *Jean-Jacques Rousseau et son oeuvre* (Paris, 1964), 275; and Pierre Burgelin, *La Philosophie de l'existence de J.-J. Rousseau* (Paris, 1952), 530.

There is then in truth only one way out of man's predicament, and man will be able to follow it only if, having understood the seriousness of the crisis to which historical development has brought him, he will undertake to work deliberately for an "austere democracy."

Rousseau has given us throughout his work a tragic, and dialectical, vision of history proceeding by stages, at each of which man, by chance or by choice, ends up by involving himself in ever more contradictory situations. Rousseau's progress produces a series of antagonistic developments, advancing man ever nearer to a final crisis.

History is the stage on which man's fate is unfolding. To this history we must refer in order to understand what goes on. Institutions, far from being the carriers of certain universal and permanent ideas, are often but devices used to entrap man and force him to do what dominant interests want him to do. Rousseau sometimes takes what a marxist could with some justification call a "class" position: he sees himself "alienated," outside of the ruling group, and with him the vast majority of the downtrodden poor are helpless and in no position to influence the course of history until a final confrontation will take place. This condition is the result of the role played by private property in human affairs and of a steadily increasing social inequality. Alienation can exist in a preindustrial society not only, as in Marx, because of the inability of the wage earner to control the goods he produces, but also because of man's deprivation of meaningful social activities and the insuperable barrier between being and appearing.[99]

Progress is indeed a double-edged affair for Rousseau. It real-

[99] Some of the writers who are developing these themes in a marxist direction are Guy Besse, "Marx, Engels et le XVIIIe siècle français," *Studies on Voltaire,* XXIV (1963), 168; and J. L. Lecercle, in his edition of the *Discourse on Inequality* (Paris, 1954), 39, 41–2, 115, 143.

izes the potential for perfectibility which is inherent in man alone and yet increases man's unhappiness. The movement away from the original state of nature is unavoidable owing to a combination of factors, some of them natural, some of them divine, some of them human. But the acquired skills of associated man brought with them gross inequalities, far greater than any existing in the beginning of history. Convenience, education, and rights were acquired at the expense of the original qualities of simplicity, goodness, and compassion, which together added up to natural virtue. Thus the course of history becomes one in which there is a steady hardening of divisions, of group conflicts from which there is no escape. Hence the impending sense of doom and final crisis which overhangs Rousseau's civilized world.

Much of the blame for this is to be laid at the door of private property. Private property is what has caused inequality, increased man's greed, led to despotism, and caused man to invent the tools through which wealth and power can be greatly extended beyond the capacity of any one man to work and accumulate. *In the end,* Rousseau writes, wealth is the ultimate explanation of human inequality. He is convinced that economic factors have played a central role in the historical development of mankind along a narrow and fixed path ever since recognition of private property was forced on mankind. Perhaps not much more than this "dialectical" interpretation of history based on the "ultimately" central importance of economic factors, and following certain "necessary" lines, is needed to convince a marxist of the "correct" place of Rousseau.

Rousseau offers added strength to the marxist argument by saying that there will be a closing of the historical cycle (or is it a spiral?). When man has reached the lowest point of his degradation and a complete loss of freedom, when society reflects a maximum of inequality and despotism, Rousseau imagines that, through a violent upheaval, everything can be redeemed. Violence is justified because the oppressors have no longer any title to their power, and violence can be met with violence. The loss of man's natural freedom can be transformed into a gain of man's social freedom. The original natural virtue of man can be reborn as moral and civic virtue in the ideal state. Thus Rousseau envisages a future condition of man which, in its apocalyptical renewal and in the downfall of private property and all the institutions built around it, carries a promise of liberation from the shackles which have so far prevented man from fulfilling himself.[100]

Marx and Engels both saw something of the revolutionary implications of Rousseau's thought and felt that here was a philosopher standing outside the traditional classifications. Marx was aware of Rousseau's detachment from the life of his times and of his inability to come to any understanding with the institutions or fashions that surrounded him. Here was a man that rejected contemporary reality. As Marx wrote in 1865: "Rousseau was always opposed to any compromise, even for the sake of form, with established powers."

But it was Engels who, as often happened, took upon himself in the *Anti-Dühring* the task of trying to get closer to what he thought to be Rousseau's hegelian heart.

Engels is first of all impressed by the dialectical power of Rousseau's analysis. Any action provokes a reaction, any advance a retreat. It is this which separates Rousseau from the unthinking propounders of unilinear human progress. History is not the history of freedom, but that of poverty and slavery through the introduction of private property. Thus the end of history will be ultimate inequality and oppression, brought about by the increasing use of the power of instruments of the masters of the economic system. As Engels writes: "These chiefs become neces-

[100] *Discours sur l'origine de l'inégalité*, O.C. III, 190–2.

sarily the people's oppressors and deepen their tyranny to the point at which inequality, pushed to its maximum, becomes transformed into its opposite, that is becomes a source of equality. Before the despot, all are equal, that is equal to zero." With this familiar terminology, Engels is making his own Rousseau's conclusion in the *Discourse on Inequality,* that in the final crisis of society one reaches a point at which the cycle of human affairs goes back to the starting point: "Here all private persons become once more equal, because they are nothing and because they have no other law than the will of the master."

The resolution of the crisis can only be a violent one. Rousseau's prophecy, Engels feels, is therefore not much different from the marxian one of the inevitability of a violent upheaval, once the necessary conditions of equality in total alienation are reached. And, again with Marx, revolution brings about a sudden change in which, as Engels writes, "inequality becomes at once equality, but not this old natural equality of primitive man without speech, but the higher equality of the social contract. The oppressors have to suffer oppression. This is the negation of the negation."

Here is Rousseau made to lend theoretical support to the *Capital.* Engels marvels at Rousseau's extraordinary anticipation of Marx: "We do not only find in Rousseau a train of thought which could be mistaken for that followed by Marx in the *Capital,* but even in the specific details we find a whole series of dialectical modes of expression used by Marx: historical processes which, by their very nature, are antagonistic and incorporate contradictory elements; transformation of an extreme into its opposite, and finally at the heart of the entire system, the negation of the negation. If Rousseau in 1754 could not yet speak Hegel's jargon he is, nevertheless, and 13 years before the birth of Hegel, deeply affected by the Hegelian 'disease,' the dialectics of contradiction." [101]

[101] Engels, *Anti-Dühring* (Paris, 1950), 170, 171.

This is an attempted appropriation of Rousseau more sweeping than any undertaken by recent marxists. A simplified reading of his work might show that Rousseau had written a history of mankind which in many key points anticipated Marx's own history. Man had progressed through time from innocence and happiness to complete alienation as a result of certain economic factors. The task was that of doing away with that alienation. Marx could even say this analysis was based on a specially attractive sort of dialectics, because progress produced results that were the opposite of those intended, and because it had as its terms of reference economic factors. In the end, these factors were the most important. The culprits were clearly identified as the owners of wealth and of whatever means of production existed in the eighteenth century. A class, separated by an unbridgeable gulf from the overwhelming majority of the poor, was singled out for bitter criticism, and Rousseau criticized most of his fellow writers and philosophers as paid lackeys of the existing order. Finally, Rousseau had considered the present state of affairs as intolerable and as leading to a crisis which he had, at one time, described as a total one, with the inherent possibility of the establishment of a higher order of communal life.

But we are now near the point at which the marxists can no longer keep hold of Rousseau and claim him as their own. Because in the analysis of how the crisis can be overcome, of how the deeply embedded injustices of human life can be set aside, the differences between Marx's "scientific" socialism and Rousseau's socialism become clear. The basic difference is to be found in the role attributed to politics by each doctrine, and in the specific degree of "inevitability" to be attached to the process of change. Marx downgraded politics because he upgraded the scope of the inevitable. Once total certainty on the inevitabilities of the future was accepted, then the political endeavors of man were without significant influence on the course of history.

Rousseau is anxious to upgrade politics, and because of that to believe that man might recover to some extent control over his own life. Everything depends on politics, Rousseau tells us, and we must find a way of creating a community in which men, assisted by new institutions and acting upon the principles of a new civic virtue, can manage their life better than in the past. Once this has been grasped, there is nothing inevitable about the future. What has happened so far has not happened because man was the victim of unseen economic forces which have automatically produced certain social and political consequences.

Man can, standing within history and within any given political framework, attempt to change the course of things, working and planning to that end. At worst, he can fail. He will then simply dream about a better ordering of communal life. The difference between Marx and Rousseau on this crucial matter can also be seen by looking at the way they consider the structure of the society of the future. Marx is not interested in it because his energy is concentrated on saying why the new society is inevitable. Rousseau is very much concerned with it because he is not at all convinced that its advent is inevitable, and rather thinks that men must work hard in order to achieve whatever lies within their limited powers. The revolution cannot be exploited by an elite which has found the mysteries of human history. It must be the result of the sacrificial work of the entire community of citizens, who, acting from within and having prepared themselves for the new day, have understood the meaning of their tasks. Thus, in the end, a train of thought which had dialectical vigor, placed immense reliance on economic factors, and preached a total dissatisfaction with the present, leads in its summing up, in its call for action and its forecast of the future, to a strong statement of man's responsibility and freedom of choice.

Index of Names, Works, and Subjects